TALES ᴬˢ TOOLS

The Power of Story
in the Classroom

TALES AS TOOLS

The Power of Story in the Classroom

THE NATIONAL
STORYTELLING ASSOCIATION

THE NATIONAL STORYTELLING PRESS
Jonesborough, Tennessee

Published by the
National Storytelling Press
of the National Storytelling Association
P.O. Box 309 ■ Jonesborough, Tenn. 37659 ■ 800-525-4514

and

Riverbank Press
801 94th Ave. North ■ St. Petersburg, Fla. 33702
a division of PAGES Inc.

Printed in the United States

99 98 97 96 95   5 4 3 2 1

Project Director: Sheila Dailey
Publishing Coordinator: Nell Tsacrios
Editor: Mary C. Weaver
Art Director: Jane L. Hillhouse
Cover Designer: Riverbank Press
Cover Photographer: Tom Raymond, Fresh Air Photographics
Illustrators: Mitzi Cartee and Eric Layne (selected illustrations)

Grateful acknowledgment is made to the following for permission to reprint copyrighted material.

The material that appears in chapter 1, pages 4 through 6, is reprinted by permission of Gregory Denman:
Sit Tight and I'll Swing You a Tail (Heinemann, a division of Reed Elsevier Inc., Portsmouth, New
Hampshire, 1991). Copyright 1991 by Gregory Denman.

The material that appears in chapter 5, pages 71 through 73, is reprinted from *When Stories Come to
School: Telling, Writing, and Performing Stories in the Early Childhood Classroom* by Patsy Cooper by
permission of Teachers & Writers Collaborative, 5 Union Square West, New York, N.Y. 10003. Copyright
1993 by Patsy Cooper.

Library of Congress Cataloging-in-Publication Data
National Storytelling Association (Jonesborough, Tenn.)
    Tales as tools: the power of story in the classroom/National
Storytelling Association [project direction by Sheila Dailey].
      p. cm.
    Includes bibliographical references.
    ISBN 1-879991-15-2
    1. Storytelling—United States.   I. Dailey, Sheila, 1947– .
II. Title.
LB1042.N35   1994
372.64'2—dc20
                                                   94-3753
                                                   CIP

PREFACE

When we first planned to do this book, we envisioned it as a "complete guide" to using storytelling in the classroom. We knew that educators were using stories in many innovative ways and that they had much to say about both practice and theory. But as project director Sheila Dailey combed the literature, networked with teachers and storytellers, and invited them to contribute articles, as the copy started flowing in, we realized we couldn't possibly cover all the intriguing ways narrative is used in schools today.

Instead we've tried to highlight major areas where storytelling is making a difference: in the teaching of reading, writing, history, science, and other subjects; in multicultural education and the creation of classroom communities; in improving students' emotional health; in enhancing children's grasp of our social and environmental responsibilities.

We hope that this book helps you see the limitless possibilities for using stories to make the classroom a more exciting and creative place for you and your students. Stories truly are tools—the familiar implements of a teaching method as ancient as speech yet utterly modern. Now we invite you to use those tools, to begin your own exploration of the narrative art, and to create your own set of instructions as you shape and are shaped by stories.

The National Storytelling Association
(NSA) is a nonprofit organization dedicated
to promoting the practice and application of storytelling.
Founded in 1975, NSA now counts as members
some 7,000 teachers, librarians, storytellers, therapists,
ministers, and others who have made storytelling
and story-listening part of their
work and life.

INTRODUCTION

"No, it'll not do just to read the old tales out of a book. You've got to tell 'em to make 'em go right."

—Tom Hunt, quoted by Richard Chase, *Grandfather Tales* (Houghton Mifflin, 1990)

Years ago I was an out-of-work language and reading teacher making ends meet by teaching art. The job required me to travel to seven schools, with 3,000 students in all. It was an extremely demanding job, one that called for frequent repetition of the same subject matter in different classrooms.

One bleak March afternoon I walked into my sixth classroom of the day, feeling especially weary. That week I'd been teaching an art concept by reading aloud a picture book—a Russian folk tale—then having the students do an extension activity. I had read that picture book so often and in so many places that I knew it by heart and dreaded reading the story again.

On an impulse I simply put the book down and told the tale instead. The effect on the students was startling. A look of deep, hushed attention came to their faces, and when the story was done, their interest in the art activity was higher than usual.

That was the day I began using narrative in many forms to teach art concepts. Doing so made my grueling job easier to bear—even fun— and by year's end the art curriculum was a favorite of both students and teachers. At the time I wouldn't have called what I did storytelling; I was merely trying to get through a difficult year the best way I could.

It was several years later, when I heard my first storyteller and began telling stories on my own, that I made the connection between storytelling and what I had done as an art teacher. I realized that all of it was storytelling—anecdotes, read-aloud stories, word pictures, biographies of artists. From there I went on to explore more deeply the exciting possibilities for using storytelling in the classroom.

Being part of producing this book for the National Storytelling Association and Riverbank Press has been a great privilege. I've had the opportunity to talk with and read about educators throughout the United States and Canada who are using storytelling in novel, creative ways. I've discovered storytelling in country schools and homeless shelters, and I've spoken to educators using narrative to teach everything from listening skills and environmental awareness to Civil War history and the concept of exponential numbers—and all of it is storytelling.

When stories come to school, everybody wins. The teacher gains a valid and useful approach to teaching; students find an avenue for learning that nourishes their imaginative and intellectual life. Administrators see educational priorities being met in innovative ways, and parents observe their children growing in confidence and enjoying school. I invite you to discover for yourself what the contributors to this book already know: storytelling is a wonderful way to teach.

Sheila Dailey
Mount Pleasant, Michigan

CONTENTS

1

THE TEACHER AS STORYTELLER

THE SAGE'S GIFT

Long ago in the city of Baghdad there lived a caliph who ruled over his subjects to the best of his abilities, yet the kingdom did not flourish. Worse still, the caliph had no heir to the throne to replace him when he died.

Then one year his wife conceived and bore him a son. To celebrate, he ordered a great feast to be held and invited all the notable and worthy people of the land.

On the day of the feast all the guests arrived at the palace, bringing gifts for the child. Each party passed before the throne and placed its gift at the caliph's feet. There were bejeweled toys, rich tapestries, and golden cups. Each gift was more beautiful than the last. Everyone brought a gift—except the young sage Meheled Abi. He stood before the throne with nothing.

The caliph, thinking he was being insulted, demanded, "Why come you empty-handed?"

The young sage opened his hands toward the caliph and said, "The other guests bring visible wealth, but my gift is an invisible wealth. It is this: Each day when the child is old enough to hear, I will come to the palace and tell him stories. And this I promise you, great caliph—when the child is grown, he will be both wise and compassionate."

Meheled Abi did as he had promised. Each day he came to the palace and told the boy stories. He told stories of wise men and fools, of the rich and the poor, of adventures and folly. The boy grew up hearing stories, and when he had grown to manhood, the old caliph died, and the young man took his place.

Just as Meheled Abi had promised, the new caliph was both wise and compassionate—more so than any ruler before him. His kingdom prospered under his hand, and he was beloved by his subjects. At the end of his life, when he lay dying, he asked that these words be inscribed in large letters on his tomb: IF I AM WISE, IT IS BECAUSE OF THE SEED SOWN BY THE TALES.

—Retold by Sheila Dailey

THE TEACHER AS STORYTELLER

In nearly every culture, the storyteller also plays the role of teacher. That role is rooted in the almost instinctive understanding that real learning takes place when both intellect and emotions are brought into play. We remember those things we care deeply about, and we understand those things we can see clearly.

Storytelling has the power to teach us to care deeply and to think clearly. In those cultures that prize storytelling, oral stories play a central role in passing on values, skills, and information. Hearing a story is regarded as an activity from which the listener can learn something and is, in fact, expected to learn something.

In recent years storytelling in the classroom has enjoyed a resurgence of interest. Some educators promote its use in order to interest children in literature, whereas others see its broader applications as a vehicle for communicating concepts, a way of providing perspective on topics that would otherwise be inaccessible to the student, a means of depicting the rich potential of the human mind, or a springboard for students' own creative endeavors.

Storytelling's ability to influence learning has also been noted by those outside the classroom. The government report *What Works: Research About Teaching and Learning* (U.S. Department of Education, 1986) cites storytelling as an important motivator: "Storytelling can ignite the imaginations of children, giving them a taste for where books can take them. The excitement of storytelling can make reading and learning fun and can instill in children a sense of wonder about life and learning."

In the articles that follow, you will hear from educators how the spoken tale stirs the imagination and clarifies thinking and how both teacher and students are changed once stories enter the classroom. In two personal narratives—one published in 1991 and one in 1910—two teachers discuss how discovering and using the art of storytelling dramatically changed their students' educational outcomes.

You'll also read a Q-and-A interview with an award-winning educator who uses storytelling to focus the entire day's activities, practical suggestions for starting to use stories, and tips on incorporating storytelling into the curriculum.

DARING TO TELL:
THE MAKING OF A STORYTELLER

BY GREGORY DENMAN

Teacher Gregory Denman describes his early storytelling experiences and success despite his then-minimal story-telling skills. His insights into the impact of told—not read—stories on his students' intellectual and emotional development suggest that stories need not be great works of art to delight and inspire. Indeed, the stories' most significant effects may not be visible for years to come.

My own beginnings as a storyteller can be traced back to a rather unpretentious corner of a third-grade classroom in Manitou Springs, Colorado. I was two or three years into my teaching career and had begun to hear of this thing called storytelling. Stories, picture books, and poems had always been a lively part of my classroom. My third-graders had frequently been read the story of Alexander and his very bad day, had heard many times over everything Maurice Sendak has written, had listened to the entire cycle of Roald Dahl books, had enjoyed repeated readings of the Bill Peet word masterpieces, and had cried through the touching moments of Robert Peck's *A Day No Pigs Would Die* (Knopf, 1972) and Wilson Rawls's *Summer of the Monkeys* (Doubleday, 1976) and *Where the Red Fern Grows* (Doubleday, 1961).

We had also written and illustrated picture books, adapted children's stories for readers' theater performances, and started a literary journal. In telling stories, I was simply a teacher, not an actor.

I did, however, have a couple of encouraging models. My undergraduate language-arts professor had been a master storyteller with picture books, and a friend of mine was starting to acquire a reputation as a local storyteller. It was not long before my wife had to weather repeated practice sessions of one story or another. Finally one day, without much fanfare, I gathered my third-graders for story time. "How 'bout I tell you a story today, kids? I've got some notes here in case I forget a part." That was the shaky premiere of my telling of Rudyard Kipling's "The Elephant's Child."

It still astonishes me how far one can go with little knowledge and less talent. They liked it! So did the second-graders the next day—and other groups of young people eight years later when I started my career as a professional storyteller and language-arts consultant.

I will always remember the delight of discovering the difference between reading a story and telling one. When I read a story out loud, I am tied to the print, locked to the page. But when I tell a story, my version can be as free as my unburdened hands and eyes. When my memory fails me, my imagination charges in to take over. In those early days, as my fondness for telling grew, so did my repertoire. Although I continued to read to my class, told stories became a frequent special addition to our story time.

Whether students hear a story from a storyteller, a teacher, or simply a teacher who reads aloud, they gain immensely from listening to a wide variety of stories. Listening to stories encourages the growth of children's natural love of language and verbal expression. It serves as a vital link in the acquisition of language, for both reading and writing.

My research and experience bear witness to the fact that from their earliest years, children listen and listen intently. During the preschool and primary-school years, children's imaginations and their ability to visualize are unhampered by a rigid sense of reality. They are free to delight in the mere sound of words and the way sounds blend together as they roll off the storyteller's or reader's tongue. They are also free to surrender themselves to the rhythm of words and sentences. Holding in mind the rhythm of a poem or tune or story helps children focus their thoughts, which theorists maintain is the foundation for a well-developed imaginative and intellectual life in adulthood.

Bill Martin Jr., the author and editor of the Sounds of Language reading series, stresses that each of us has a "linguistic storehouse" in which we deposit stories, poems, sentences, and words. Their patterns, which enter through the ear, remain available to our reading, writing, and speaking throughout our lives. Martin maintains that even children with a seemingly meager vocabulary can latch onto the structure or patterns of language they hear. Suddenly children find their vocabulary becoming stronger.

Hearing a variety of good stories can also serve to expand children's reading interests. When they get into a reading rut—continually seeking out the same story or story type—a storytelling teacher can give them examples of other kinds of written materials and gradually lead them into reading in other fields and subjects. The teacher's enthusiasm gives the reluctant child the impression that stories and reading are worth the effort.

Research in reading has highlighted the gap between children's read-

FEAR OF TRYING

Many teachers, although enthusiastic about the idea of their students telling stories, are reticent to try it themselves.

I wanted to teach my third-graders to tell stories, but I was terrified because I realized I'd have to tell a story myself. It reminded me of a time when I took one of my classes roller-skating even though I'd never skated in my life. A lot of my kids hadn't either, so I decided I'd have to try it. My ineptitude on the rink put me in touch with the feelings of frustration that kids encounter all the time as they try to learn new things. I have been a better teacher ever since. When I worked alongside my kids at telling my first story, it made me very aware of the difficulties they were confronting. I managed to work through my fear along with them, and I was astonished to see how fantastic some of my kids were. We had a great time!

—Marty Kaminsky

From Children Tell Stories: A Teaching Guide *by Martha Hamilton and Mitch Weiss. Published by Richard C. Owen. Copyright 1990 by Martha Hamilton and Mitch Weiss. Reprinted by permission.*

ing and their capacity to understand and enjoy literature at a higher level. Independent reading ability often lags behind listening comprehension by many years. But stories require no ability grouping. A 4- or 6-year-old can fully experience a story he or she may not yet be able to read. If the action is clear and the plot consistent with the listener's idea of what a story is, the storyteller can use mature, complex language.

Children delight in hearing unusual words and sentences. My third-graders have for years repeated Kipling's alliterative gem from my first storytelling attempt: "Go to the banks of the great grey-green, greasy Limpopo River." The words children hear while listening to a good story are easier for them to recognize and learn in print afterward. Their speaking vocabulary increases, and their ears become trained to the music of language. Their feeling for the beauty and power of words grows.

Hearing stories during the course of children's school life can strengthen their creative impulses, particularly in the area of writing. Through stories children become aware of how figurative language is used; by role-playing as writers they can try out this literary language. Enjoying a well-told story involves more than merely liking it. To enjoy a story is to be stimulated by its words and brought to new insights and linguistic perceptions.

Finally, storytelling and reading aloud expand and enhance the young child's exposure to literature. Through stories, students claim a bit of their literary heritage, for all children—regardless of their economic status—are born into a world of stories, a world filled with pleasure or the possibility of pleasures yet to be experienced. Whatever their tone or theme, stories reach out to listeners, reassuring them, reducing their alienation, and bringing a sense of belonging.

Beginning readers are not yet capable of truly reading literature. They are far too busy decoding words and sounds. But when they listen to a story, they can feel the warmth of the storyteller's or reader's affection for the material. Hearing the rhythm of the words, children can experience a sense of the ways in which literature brings us into closer contact with the rest of humanity. It is this same response that will bring these children back to literature as readers later in life. What the eyes cannot yet decipher, the ears and heart can absorb. As James Stephens said so well, "What the heart knows today the head will understand tomorrow."

Reprinted by permission of Gregory Denman: Sit Tight, and I'll Swing You a Tail *(Heinemann, a division of Reed Elsevier Inc., Portsmouth, New Hampshire, 1991).*

The Teacher as Storyteller

Like Gregory Denman, Richard Wyche happened on storytelling by accident and soon discovered its value to motivate students and nourish their spirit. Wyche's modest beginnings in a Southern country school led him to a lifetime of stories. He later organized the National Story League, the oldest and one of the largest storytelling organizations in the United States.

Storytelling in a Country School

By Richard Thomas Wyche

Once upon a time the writer undertook to teach in a little school in a far-off seacoast town in the South. I had never studied pedagogy and knew nothing of teaching except that which I had seen in university lecture rooms. The teacher who preceded me "heard" lessons, and the children "said" lessons. That seemed an easy proposition, for the questions were in the book, and the children could memorize and say the answers.

But I soon discovered that the children found no interest in the fact that one word was a verb and another a noun. They memorized the rules and repeated the lessons, but they were not at all interested in the subject. They were bored by this mechanical process, and so was the teacher. Something had to be done.

One day I told the class the story of Hiawatha's fishing from Henry Wadsworth Longfellow's epic poem "The Song of Hiawatha." Every child listened with rapt attention. I had found something that they were interested in. I requested the children to write the story out for their lessons the next day. The majority of them did so and read the story as they had understood it and written it down. One little fellow said, "I ain't got no pencil," which meant that he didn't write it. "Tell it then," I said. He told it in such a vivid and realistic way that the class applauded. I had found something that the child liked. The second day I told the story of Hiawatha's fasting, then Hiawatha's friends, and so on, two stories a week, until we had told the whole story of Hiawatha.

But you ask, What did that have to do with grammar? From the story we got the nouns and verbs we studied and the sentences that the advanced classes analyzed and studied. (The whole school heard the story, as it was an ungraded school with classes ranging from primary to high school.)

What else did we do with the story? When the children told the story orally or on paper, it was creative work and better for expression than memorizing "Mary Had a Little Lamb." The child received a mental picture. He heard the story, and retelling it in his own words, he created afresh the picture, thereby becoming a creator and an artist himself. In reciting "Mary Had a Little Lamb," he was dealing with words. In telling the story, he was dealing with mental images.

One day I saw the children playing out on the campus, and when I made inquiries, they said, "We are playing Hiawatha and Mondamin and Old Nokomis." They were dramatizing the story. It was taking effect. Had I been a trained teacher, I would have let them do it in class as a part of their work. Twice a week we got the words for our spelling lesson from the story. The children were so much interested in Hiawatha that they wanted to make pictures of Hiawatha. Then I let them illustrate the story, writing in their composition books the story and illustrating it. As we studied geography, the upper Mississippi Valley and the Lake Regions all took on new meaning because Hiawatha had once lived, toiled, and suffered there.

But what had I done for those children most of all? I had fed their souls—given them a masterpiece of literature. Starting with the childhood of Hiawatha, we had followed him and admired him. We had roamed through that fairyland of dark green forest, heard the whispering pines, seen Hiawatha when he caught the King of Fishes, slew the Pearl-Feather, prayed and fasted for his people, punished Pau-Puk-Keewis, wooed and won Minnehaha, and when his task was done, sailed away into the fiery sunset.

That something inexpressibly sweet and beautiful that I felt in the vision hour and longed to impart to the children and heretofore had not been able to, I had at last found incarnate in a hero, while the music, meter, and imagery of poetry had awakened the children's sense of the beautiful and revealed a new world to them. New life had come into the school.

Two months had passed. I had made an experiment, and it had succeeded. Grammar, language, composition, spelling, drawing, storytelling had been taught by that method. Formal language had become linked to literature and thereby to life.

From Some Great Stories and How to Tell Them *by Richard Thomas Wyche. Published by Newson & Company. Copyright 1910 by Richard Thomas Wyche.*

MAKING TIME FOR STORIES

BY MARGARET READ MACDONALD

Today's busy teachers often feel that learning stories to tell is too time-consuming, and they hesitate to add yet another task to their job. In fact, though, it can be simple and enjoyable to add storytelling to the curriculum—it can even become the curriculum. Margaret Read MacDonald and Gwenda Led-Better suggest easy ways to incorporate storytelling into the day.

It amazes me when teachers insist they have no time to fit storytelling into their curriculum. Most stories take less than 10 minutes to tell. And stories can fit easily into many areas of the curriculum. Use nature tales to enhance science. Select tales from the cultures in your social-studies units. Use singing tales in music class. Match math-puzzle tales to the math curriculum. And use any tale to enhance language arts.

Storytelling teaches listening. It models fine use of oral language. It models plot, sequencing, characterization, the many literary devices you wish to convey. There is no better educational tool to teach language-arts skills.

And yet teachers say, "If we get through our workbook, maybe we'll have time for a story." Teachers, the workbook will be forgotten by tomorrow, but the sound, the feel, the sense, the heart of that story may stay with children as long as they live. Make space in the classroom for true quality time today. Share a story.

The folk tale has so much to teach us. It brings us the voice of the past and the voices of distant peoples. The tale speaks with human wisdom; it bounces into the lives of our children, carrying the joy of another age, another people. Or it slides into our hearts, bearing their sorrows, their wonderings. It should be received as tales have always been, as a simple gift dropped from one mouth to another.

Let the children retell the tales orally, spoken again as they were in the past. Let the students play with the stories, acting them out, drawing them, dancing them, singing them. Use the folk tale as a springboard into the worlds of cultures distant and past. Talk of the story, and assess the humaneness of its actions. Wonder about its motives, its mysteries, its madness. Does the tale speak the truth?

Use tales also to lead students into the glorious worlds of literature and book illustration. Share beautifully illustrated editions of your tale; share literary pieces that draw on themes related to your story.

Many books have been written for the teacher suggesting story as a device for teaching structure, plot, characterization, and a plethora of other concepts. Story is suggested as a springboard for writing exercises. The end toward which many educators move is the piece of student writing. The child hears a folk tale told or read, dissects it via a chart, and finally writes a retelling or creates a new story, copying that tale's form. If you must dissect the tale to meet your curriculum's guidelines, please commit this brutality only after all the students have had a good time playing with their birthright—the untrammeled folk tale.

From The Storyteller's Start-Up Book: Finding, Learning, Performing, and Using Folktales *by Margaret Read MacDonald. Copyright 1993 by Margaret Read MacDonald. Reprinted by permission of the publisher, August House Inc., Little Rock, Arkansas.*

CREATING SIMPLE STORIES

An orphan boy sat on a great stone, mending an arrow. And the stone spoke: "Shall I tell you stories?" The boy said, "What are stories?" The stone answered, "All the things that happened in the world before this." From that stone came all the stories that the people of the Seneca nation tell to one another.
—A Seneca Indian tale

Norris Spencer is a storyteller who teaches sixth grade in Virginia Beach, Virginia. "I can say something as simple as 'My grandfather . . .'" she writes, "and the whole room gets quiet, every head swivels, and I see kids relax into wanting to hear a story, no matter how simple." Spencer often incorporates stories into the daily lesson plan. "I work up a lesson in social studies and then tell it as a story. The children are quite attentive. The other day I told a true story as my introduction to a health lesson. The supervisor was in the classroom. She said my introduction was a great way to get the children's attention and provide motivation."

Spencer observes that her students are better writers because they hear stories in the classroom. "Most of them," she says, "seem to be hungry for the spoken word or maybe the intimacy." Storytelling does create intimacy, and that's just the right atmosphere for passing on wisdom and for improving language and communication skills. Here are some suggestions for fledgling classroom tellers:

- Tell those "my grandfather . . ." stories. What could be better than to share your own special story? The spontaneity and life found in the true story are needed in any tale.

- Make use of professional storytellers. Most storytellers are happy to give workshops. They can suggest stories and showcase some of the world's finest for you.

- After choosing a tale, learn its "bones," its essence, and tell it "in small"—almost like a joke. Sneak it into a conversation, or tell it in the teacher's lounge. The story will flesh out and mature with retelling.

"Sometimes," Spencer writes, "I tell a story just for the fun of it." Once you have a story, use it; for storytelling, like art, is its own excuse for being.
—Gwenda LedBetter

From The National Storytelling Journal, *summer 1984. Reprinted by permission.*

The Teacher as Storyteller

Award-winning author and kindergarten teacher Vivian Gussin Paley intimately understands the value of story and play in young children's lives. In this interview with education journalist Marge Cunningham she describes her classroom, her story-playing technique, and its ability to integrate all the day's activities and themes.

THE MORAL OF THE STORY

By Marge Cunningham

Since storytelling began, our communities' elders have used the art for social and moral instruction. Vivian Gussin Paley's recent book, *You Can't Say You Can't Play* (Harvard University Press, 1992), describes her use of stories to introduce moral principles into a society of the very young: her kindergarten class. With the help of an ongoing story, which features the magical bird Magpie, a defender of the lonely and the outsider, Paley tackles the painful problem of children's rejecting other children. She ordains the rule "You can't say 'You can't play'" after months of intense debate among students from kindergarten through fifth grade. The book details her struggle to make the rule a reality and includes the ever-evolving story that helped her

and the children work out their differences and difficulties.

Paley, an elementary-school teacher for more than three decades, has taught kindergarten for 22 years at the University of Chicago Laboratory Schools. She began teaching, she says, because "I couldn't think of anything else to do. Finally, a good dozen years into the job, I began to think, *Maybe I can really become a teacher*. Fortunately with teaching, every year you get a new chance." For the past 16 years her teaching has incorporated a story-playing technique that focuses all activities on the children's stories and fantasies.

We wanted to touch base with Paley to learn more about her philosophy of storytelling in the classroom and the ways she uses stories to illustrate moral principles. Here's what she had to say.

Marge Cunningham: You've written that story is the child's preferred frame of reference and that storytelling plays a significant role in your classroom. How did you develop your teaching style?
Vivian Gussin Paley: I changed my style of teaching from a standard curriculum-oriented approach because I wasn't interested enough in what I was doing. It had become routine. I wasn't learning anything about myself or the children. But as I focused more on children and their stories, their play, their ways of learning about themselves, other children, the world, teaching became more exciting. I plunged into a trial-and-error pattern in which I still am. How's this working? How am I doing? How much are we learning about one another? How much more articulate are we becoming in our need to explain ourselves to ourselves, to one another?

What do you learn from your students?
The main thing I've learned is the value of fantasy. Unfortunately I don't remember my childhood fan-

tasies. I grew up with a far less imaginative life than I could have had. Through years of observing and teaching young children, listening to their play, their stories, my imaginative life has been reawakened. Children have taught me that it is through imagination that connections are made—to people, to disciplines, to all kinds of subject matter.

They taught me that natural continuity in life comes through storytelling. They enabled me to re-create myself in the classroom as storyteller because they are by nature storytellers.

In your classroom, storytelling is woven through the entire curriculum. How do you accomplish that?
Take the stories of this week. One was about Lincoln, because we're getting ready to put up Lincoln pictures and to think about his birthday and his life. So the story was in the story, which I believe is the way we think. We conceive of everything as a story within the story.

We are beginning to put words in envelopes, following [educator and novelist] Sylvia Ashton-Warner's notion of a key vocabulary. Each child gets an envelope. We call them good-word envelopes. If there's a word you would like to know and perhaps learn to read, you ask the teacher. The word goes on a card, which is placed in your envelope. You bring the words out from time to time, see if you can read them, fool around with them. A new character in the Magpie stories I tell is an orphan girl from India named Kavitha. She has just come to live with Schoolmistress, a childhood friend of Kavitha's mother, who has recently died. And her father is long gone. Schoolmistress says, "Kavitha, have you learned how to read yet?" and Kavitha says, "Well, I didn't go to school—we didn't have a school in our fishing village—but my mother gave me a good-

word envelope, and when I wanted to know a word, she wrote it down for me." Now, you see, I am about to introduce the concept of good-word envelopes. We find out from a new character in the story something we are about to do.

Next week Beatrix [a Magpie character known for her jealousy] will get into some kind of a snit because Schoolmistress is having a Valentine party, and she hasn't been invited. I'm not sure what I'll have her do. Steal all the valentines, or—I'm not sure. But it doesn't matter what. You give the children the gift of seeing things on many levels.

Teaching math in terms of fantasy and story is something teachers can probably do quite easily. If you look in the library, there are so many number books involving fantasy characters, animals, songs. "One little piggy" is the most ancient means of teaching, and we start those mathematical games and ditties when children are at the very youngest age. We incorporate them into stories, folk tales, songs, and poems.

This is what education is all about, is it not, and where do we get it from? Story. It is story that enables us to see things on many levels. It is the original scientific thinking. Cause and effect. Many approaches. Many prisms through which you view a single event.

What we don't realize is that this continues all through school on more mature levels. You can see that the Magpie stories are far more mature than "This little piggy went to market," but it's essentially the same thing. In high school and college the storytelling factor, the narrative factor, looms above all of our lives and is the way we make connections. The story within the story.

This is not thought about enough by teachers—at all levels. I believe that it is with the story that you build the emotional connections between teachers and students.

The characters in You Can't Say You Can't Play *are well developed and maintain continuity, I notice.*

Yes. That is essential for the believability of the characters. I think that Beatrix represents the most believable Magpie-story character to the children because jealousy is their most deeply felt emotion.

I brought in the new character, Kavitha, shortly after a new child entered our classroom at midyear in order to gain a venue with which we could describe the problems of a new child, even in a class that has a big sign that says YOU CAN'T SAY YOU CAN'T PLAY. Kavitha is very shy, and she came from a place where there were almost no other children. It's a good beginning because the sense of loneliness, even when you come from a place with many children, is important. How many poets have dwelt upon this theme—that man is essentially alone? It's very real for young children, especially leaving home and entering school. Kavitha sees the sign, and Schoolmistress explains it. One chapter has Kavitha saying to Schoolmistress, "It isn't that no one is telling me I can't play, it's that I'm afraid to approach other children." So there needs to be another sign. Something that says LOOK AROUND, AND SEE WHO'S NOT PLAYING. So we discussed what other signs Kavitha should put up. It's the endless vision of life being acted out in a classroom. It involves everything.

You can always get a new character and a new story, a new conflict and a new resolution. There is no other thing a teacher can use in this way.

You instituted the rule "You can't say 'You can't play'" in midyear after introducing the concept, *debating it, discussing it with students in higher grades, bringing the discussion back to your group, arguing its merits. Do you have any other rules you intend to implement?*

This is the second year in which we began the year with the rule. The way the rule evolved was very important to me. In the book I describe this wonderful process we went through of inventing the rule, worrying about it, arguing about it, debating it, questioning it. Then I felt sad because we wouldn't have to do that anymore. Now it was the rule. Now all of the learning aspects of rising to a higher level together would be diminished because we would start the year with the rule.

I couldn't have been more wrong. Each year the rule has to be reinvented, almost in the same way, because each year the children reinvent everything. They are just leaving babyhood and becoming schoolchildren who can look around and see what's going on and recognize their own feelings in other people. That's something they can't do when they're younger.

With storytelling we have another situation, which is not debated. From the beginning, starting a year ago, the rule was "You don't pick actors." We go around the circle, and everyone has an equal chance to be in everyone's story. This is never debated, which says to me that it makes sense right from the beginning. It is eminently fair, and the stories are better because of it. Never have I had such good storytelling. Once the elements of jealousy and fear and rejection are out of storytelling, we have story for its own sake, without concern about creating special roles for friends.

Do the children affect the direction of the stories?

Oh, all the time but very subtly. For instance, something can happen among several children, and a parallel incident will find its way into a soon-to-be-told Magpie story—some curious or sad event, a controversy, a celebration. I often create patterns, parallels, that mirror what's going on in the children's lives. It's easy to do.

Through your storytelling you make the children aware of trying to include the child who is not playing. Do you have a rule for that situation?

No. One of the reasons stories of this type are so valuable as a teaching tool is that I can walk up to a child sitting alone and say, using a literary allusion of my own creation, "Sally, you remind me of how Kavitha felt. Do you wish we had a sign that said COME AND PLAY WITH ME?" The literary allusion has always given us this opportunity.

The other day someone came up to me with a sign I couldn't read because it was in his own invented spelling. He read it to me. It said IF THERE'S ONLY ONE PERSON IN THE SPACESHIP, YOU HAVE TO HAVE TWO MORE. I looked around and saw that someone had made a spaceship all for himself. Carl got the idea that, yes, you can make your own rule, and you can put it on a sign, and maybe it will have some effect. The reverberations never stop.

Have you considered writing a book to help teachers be storytellers?

That's the number-one question I'm asked. Most teachers I talk to feel inhibited about exposing their fantasies. Personally, I don't think you can teach storytelling, but I do feel that the more stories you read to children, the more of their stories you listen to and act out, the more reflection you have upon your own childhood stories and dramas, the more ready you are to begin the habit of storytelling. Once you begin, nothing can stop you. But it has to be your own voice. It can't be someone else's.

This is where a lot of teachers sell themselves and their classrooms short. The children appreciate the smallest kind of story, a memory of your own sixth-birthday party, a memory of some story someone told you. As you begin to develop your narrative voice, the response from the children is what will encourage you. It is not the same as standing up in front of a group of teachers and telling a story. The teacher will find a positive response and an absence of criticism from the children. They are so delighted to find a teacher in a narrative mode. That in itself will bring forth the stories.

What changes have you seen in children over the years?

Despite the fact that they have more years in school before kindergarten; more educated parents, generally; more advantages of travel; more information imparted; and certain skills from television, videotapes, and computers, I sense that children today enter kindergarten less sure of themselves. They are more fearful of giving wrong answers, of not living up to some kind of standard. If ever children needed the old-fashioned kindergarten of blocks and doll-corner and painting and music and stories, stories, stories, they need it now. A good many kindergartens are switching to the full-day format, which I find essential because we sometimes have 12 children in one day wanting to tell their stories and have them acted out.

As long as we have stories and plays and drama and music and art, no one ever gets tired of school or worries about giving a wrong answer. They can't give a wrong answer—not when story is the basic curriculum.

From Storytelling Magazine, *spring 1993. Reprinted by permission.*

TELLINGWARE: A HEADFUL OF STORIES

News replaces narrative, broadcasters jam the tongue's frequency, and the chronicler loses the thread. As we master the technologies of memory, we forget how to ask what needs to be remembered. We have gathered a vast data-hoard, yet we've never had fewer stories to pass on to our young. "When the legends are lost," the Anishnawbek storyteller Gilbert Oskaboose once told me, "the people die." Lacking stories, we stop wondering what happens next and cease acting as if there could be a next for it to happen in.

Meanwhile, storytellers are making their way back from exile. The storyteller returns to the late 20th century, bringing news of a world we've never stopped longing for, even as we let it drift away from us. This is a world where voice, memory, and story make a powerful frame for everyday life, where, as they say at the end of Armenian wonder tales, "Three apples fell from heaven—one for the teller, one for the listener, and one for those who heard." These apples conjure up certain values. They remind us that the living voice is the proper medium for stories, that long-held customs of listening sustain the teller's art, that teller and listener conspire to let a story spark across the gap into that hearing that is also remembering.

When anthropologist Julie Cruikshank asked the great Yukon elder Angela Sidney what her stories meant to her, she replied, "I've tried to live my life right, just like a story." She had spent her long life listening to the stories of her people: stories about how Crow made the world, how the Yukon mountains and rivers were named; stories about the local families, stretching back for generations; stories from the days when Europeans came to the land. These narratives gave Sidney a language for expressing and reflecting on the moral, spiritual,

and practical qualities of everyday life.

Her African counterpart would agree with this view. "The story is our escort," says a village orator in Nigerian novelist Chinua Achebe's *Anthills of the Savannah* (Anchor Press, 1988); "without it we are blind. Does a blind man own his escort? No, neither do we the story. Rather it is the story that owns and directs us."

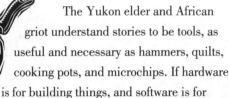

The Yukon elder and African griot understand stories to be tools, as useful and necessary as hammers, quilts, cooking pots, and microchips. If hardware is for building things, and software is for manipulating data, then "tellingware" is a tool for making imaginative connections between everyday experience and the higher truths and thought-ways by which a culture lives. The headful of stories you gather over a lifetime lets you refold the time and space of your history into meaningful, tellable patterns. The tellingware you share with other members of your family, classroom, community is a narrative force field in which a collective identity can be recharged, a common effort reanimated.

Canadian educator Jerry Diakiw, writing about the importance of building intercultural bridges in our increasingly fragmented world, notes, "The stories being shared . . . bind any group of people together into a cohesive society and allow them to communicate with one another and to work together with a common purpose." Unless its citizens create a shared body of narratives, a tellingware that includes a nation's diverse voices, the people of that land will have little power to imagine a common future for themselves.

—Dan Yashinsky

From Storytelling Magazine, *summer 1993. Reprinted by permission.*

Tips for Using a Simple Tale

By Flora Joy

Storytelling need not be complex to benefit students. Flora Joy, a professor of reading and storytelling at East Tennessee State University, describes easy ways to tell a story and make learning fun.

Storytelling can be used to enhance all language and communication skills as well as many other kinds of skills taught in the curriculum. It also builds positive attitudes toward the learning environment.

Let's look at how this can be accomplished by considering the uses of an old folk tale, "The Turnip," found in many anthologies. The story's simple plot involves an old man's attempt to pull an enormous turnip out of the ground. Unable to do so, he sought help from his wife. Still unable to pull it out, the two continued to seek help from farm and household animals until a tiny mouse made the difference.

When I introduce this story to a group of children, I have them gather on the floor in front of me. I then ask how many of them know what turnips are, how they grow, what they taste like, and so on.

I then place felt letters that spell the words *The Turnip* on a flannel board or floor and announce that I am going to tell them a story about an enormous turnip. The story includes lines that are repeated again and again, and I encourage my listeners to join in if they wish. Then I tell the story—thus giving the students an opportunity to hear the natural, rhythmic, repetitive, melodic flow of the language.

As listeners begin repeating the lines, they do so in a natural, expressive style. Thus the expressive communication skills of delivery (for example, enunciation, phrasing, fluency) are reinforced and practiced. In addition, students verbalize appropriate sentence structure, appropriate grammatical language subtleties, and so on.

Next I provide a copy of the story with prepared flannel-board characters. I place this story in a "story box" and encourage the students to tell the story to a classmate or alone in the classroom mirror carrel. Those who do so are now involved with all word-recognition and comprehension skills. An example is the comprehension subskill of sequence. Students must arrange the characters in the order in which they appeared in the story, then arrange the story structure in like manner.

After several students have retold the story, I engage all in a "word-fun session." This fun may be anything appropriate to the development of language skills. With this story, I ask questions such as "What words other than *enormous* could we use to describe the turnip?" Students then list synonyms for *big*. "Here are the letters I used earlier for the title of this story. Who can place them in the right order?"

I then request volunteers to reenact the story. These students plan how they will tell the story—thus becoming involved in plot analysis and coordinated physical movement (especially for the fall at the end). We later extend the activity into a playground "turnip tug-of-war."

If time permits, I take a real turnip to class (preferably one with greenery still attached). The students then examine the turnip, building skills in concept identification, noting details, and discovering scientific facts. We discuss how turnips grow and the relative difficulty (or lack thereof) of pulling them out of the ground. I pose the question "How large would a turnip need to be to require this many tuggers?" This helps students learn to make comparisons and to develop the higher-level comprehension skills involved in distinguishing between fact and opinion. I end the session by giving them a taste of the raw turnip.

From The National Storytelling Journal, *winter 1984. Reprinted by permission.*

THE ENORMOUS TURNIP

Once upon a time Grandfather found a turnip seed. He went to his garden, dug a hole, and put the seed in. As he covered the seed with dark earth, he sang, "Grow sweet, grow strong, grow big."

That turnip surely did grow. It grew and grew and grew until it was enormous. When the turnip was as big as it could get, Grandfather decided to pull it up and make turnip soup. Well, he pulled and he pulled and he pulled, but he couldn't get it out.

He called Grandmother to help. Grandmother pulled on Grandfather. Grandfather pulled on the turnip. He pulled and he pulled and he pulled, but he couldn't get it out.

So Grandmother called her grandson. The grandson pulled on Grandmother. Grandmother pulled on Grandfather. Grandfather pulled on the turnip. He pulled and he pulled and he pulled, but he couldn't get it out.

So the grandson called the dog to help. The dog pulled on the grandson. The grandson pulled on Grandmother. Grandmother pulled on Grandfather. Grandfather pulled on the turnip. He pulled and he pulled and he pulled, but he couldn't get it out.

So the dog called the cat to help. The cat pulled on the dog. The dog pulled on the grandson. The grandson pulled on Grandmother. Grandmother pulled on Grandfather. Grandfather pulled on the turnip. He pulled and he pulled and he pulled, but he couldn't get it out.

So the cat called the mouse to help. The mouse pulled on the cat. The cat pulled on the dog. The dog pulled on the grandson. The grandson pulled on Grandmother. Grandmother pulled on Grandfather. Grandfather pulled on the turnip. He pulled and he pulled and he pulled, and—*kerplop*—up came the turnip.

And Grandfather said, "At last we can have turnip soup."

—Retold by Sheila Dailey

2

STORIES IN THE CURRICULUM

STORIES IN THE CURRICULUM

Every teacher has a plan for teaching—a combination of agendas set by the school board, administrators, and the teacher herself. At its best a curriculum helps move students through various skill and developmental levels and by year's end produces measurable improvement. Yet the range of abilities among students is astounding. Children may stall for weeks and then make sudden leaps in understanding or never make the leap at all. The teacher's job is to attempt to meet all students' needs and guide them through the curriculum.

How is this to be done? Can storytelling really make a difference in the process? The authors whose work is included in this chapter think so. For them, stories are as important a teaching tool as any other. Indeed, for some, storytelling is the most important tool.

No matter what an individual's teaching style, storytelling can be used effectively in the classroom. Most teaching styles fall somewhere on a continuum between two modes: the interpretive and the transmissive. In the interpretive style, the teacher wants students to develop their own interpretation of knowledge—wants to be "the guide on the side" as one educator put it. In the transmissive style, the teacher's job is to pass on knowledge—to serve as "the sage on the stage."

Storytelling can bring new possibilities to teachers who prefer either mode. Because those who tend toward the interpretive mode value individual insight, the story form is ideal: students cannot hear a story without developing a point of view. And listening to stories strengthens students' grasp of language while introducing new patterns, word choices, and images, stretching children's imaginative powers.

For teachers who prefer the transmissive style, which often involves recall of facts or abstract concepts, stories are also ideal because they put facts and concepts in context, making them relevant to a larger body of knowledge. Students not only grasp the information but also recall it more readily because they've learned it in relation to something else.

The following articles give some general ideas and guidelines on how to make storytelling an integral part of the curriculum. Successive chapters explore specific themes, issues, and content areas pertinent to the typical classroom.

Teacher Mark Wagler centers his whole curriculum around stories. A former freelance storyteller, Wagler became a teacher because he believes so passionately in storytelling's power to teach not only the typical curricular subjects but also higher-order skills such as creativity, analysis, and self-discipline.

JAILBREAK! STORYTELLING IN ROOM 103

By Mark Wagler

Most talking and writing about storytelling in the classroom is an effort to add storytelling into existing pedagogy. We hear about units on folk tales and mythology, applications of storytelling in the language arts and social studies, methods for using narrative images to teach certain abstractly defined skills and concepts. Here, turning things upside down, I'll describe a paradigm in which stories and storytelling are the center of the curriculum, a narrative ground from which all curricular ideas emerge.

Story, in its largest connotations, is the center of the curriculum in room 103 at Randall School in Madison, Wisconsin. We write stories in our journals, read these stories or perform them orally, dramatize story problems in math, collect and tell stories to develop cultural understanding, and observe the events of nature.

We can view curriculum as subjects and skills, sciences and the three R's. A richer view, shaping our emerging educational paradigm, sees curriculum as process, classrooms as communities of inquiry, and students as characters in stories about learning and teaching.

Reading has been the queen of the elementary-school curriculum. Although oral language is extensively used throughout the curriculum, it receives little attention. Nearly all attention is given to written discourse from first grade on. A more effective strategy works with the oral–written relationship. It acknowledges that deficiencies in oral language lead to deficiencies in written language, that oral is by far the more common classroom language, and that most adults use oral language more often than written language.

When oral language is readmitted into the classroom as a full partner, a new set of processes becomes important. Now a teacher can teach oral-language proficiency, use the transitions between oral and written discourse, and make room for what Walter Ong calls "secondary orality," the use of oral discourse in electronic media. Meanwhile, the classroom becomes a livelier place since its primary language is again honored.

A similar readjustment is required to make room for narrative. Although narrative is allowed to serve as an important mode of discourse, it is described almost entirely with the analytical world-view of expository discourse. Hence it is reduced to such concepts as plot, point of view, characterization, "story grammar," and folk-tale types and motifs— all worthy ideas but not the ways narrative works within itself. Because expository discourse needs to name and classify everything, it tends not to see those realities it has not yet named. Oral narrative in primary grades is called "show-and-tell," in intermediate grades is placed in units with names such as "tall tales" and "myths," and at the university is largely relegated to ethnography and communications theory. None of these ideas allow that narrative discourse comes first developmentally, is predominant in both oral and written discourse during most of the school years, and holds its own in courtrooms, examination rooms, boardrooms, and most other places where adult professionals work.

Placing oral storytelling at the heart of the curriculum does not banish written exposition but instead makes it easier for all students to achieve some mastery of it. Teaching with narrative processes allows us to place images before ideas,  hear the fragments of personal stories that are as pervasive as air, harmonize disparate subjects into integrated learning, accept children's experience as the key to learning instead of a distraction from the concepts they are supposed to learn, and use narrative not only to study "literature" but also to explore every category of experience.

Narrative teaching is structured differently from analytic teaching, with its desks and schedules, textbooks and tests. According to an Armenian proverb, "If plants had goals, they would not have flowers." Our children, likewise, do not flower in schools that force experience into abstract categories. The old paradigm breaks curriculum into abstract ideas; the new integrates learning into living, changing structures.

Children experience, remember, and communicate their lives as stories. The world itself is a story, a process of atomic and cosmic events, a story of geological eons and biological evolution. Our human history is similarly structured in time, a story of people solving or failing to solve problems. To learn means to place ourselves in this large story.

Narrative teaching does not ignore the skills a child needs to learn, but sees the education of every student as a unique story. A classroom structured around narrative, with all its diverse activities, feels a lot like a healthy family, with regular rituals, important relationships, responsible adults, a rich environment, and lots of surprises. A rigid classroom is like a rigid family. In such dysfunctional environments some children obey and others rebel, but all are afraid, angry, and wounded.

Attention is learning

We learn what we attend to. Our perceptions are processed within our brains into patterns that make sense of experience.

Given choice, safety, support, and a rich environment, a child learns endlessly. Only children with severe handicaps, for example, fail to understand and speak their native language. Attending to language, we learn eloquence. Attending to numbers, we learn the patterns in which they are arranged. Attending to new information, we understand it. Attending to problems, we solve them. Attending to emotional and physical pain, we are healed.

Our emotions focus attention. Take a student who knows he is dumb in math, convinced by past tests and failures that he is inadequate to learn his multiplication tables. He now learns little except how to act appropriately dumb. But if he learns that feeling inadequate is not the same as acting inadequately and meanwhile discovers the extraordinary beauty and capacity of his natural mind, a few hours of firm attention will lead to mastery of his "times."

A teacher's first task is to provide a safe classroom in which a child is protected from abuse and supported in understanding feelings. Now attention can be refocused on experience. The stories a teacher tells grab a child's attention. The aesthetic shape of the telling is pleasing to listen to, and the problem holds interest until it is resolved.

Even more important are the stories students tell: when they are trained to speak effectively, students can more easily attend to one another.

A teacher's every action can focus and clarify attention. The most difficult task is to be constantly aware of our own perceptions, images, emotions, and energy. When I regularly observe my students, I know them—and I know how to teach them.

Imagery

The perceptions a child receives through sensory attention are stored and worked with as images. A child who has difficulty with imagery has trouble listening, speaking, reading, writing, memorizing facts, solving math and personal problems, understanding scientific and cultural processes, creating, discovering, and attending to complexity. A teacher can use endless strategies to assist children in developing skills in imagery, but none is as effective as telling vivid stories.

Storytelling is par excellence the art of combining language and imagery, of arranging images in time, of presenting exactly those images that present and resolve a problem.

Skill in imagery does not automatically transfer to mastery of academic skills, but it is the most important ingredient. A child with poor language imagery is always a poor reader, but a child who understands and creates elaborate images with oral language needs only to learn a relatively simple coding system to become a master reader. A child with poor imagery always has trouble solving mathematical problems, whereas a child who readily images patterns of numbers and shapes has only to memorize some math facts to become a whiz.

One way to develop imagery is by attending to repetition. In oral storytelling, everything is repeated. Every word, phrase, image, gesture, intonation, character, scene, and problem in a telling of *The Odyssey*, for instance, echoes another element of the story. Repetition need not be the exact duplication of "Who's that walking over my bridge?" It also moves by similarities and opposites—anything to which a listener responds, "I've heard something like that before."

I use repetition to teach every content and skill in my curriculum. It is the water cycle, oxygen–carbon-dioxide cycle, tides, the circulatory system, energy pyramids, nuclear fission, and the sequence of doing scientific experiments. It is present in farming, family routines, festivals, music-making, political terms, economic cycles, and every other facet of human culture. It's the regularly repeated steps of borrowing, doing long division, solving equations, and formulating geometric proofs. Recognizing repetition, a student can read complex language. Using repetition, she can talk with eloquent phrases and build written sentences with architectural precision.

Dialogue

Talking and writing become powerful when the creator of such discourse feels he or she is in dialogue with an audience. The story itself comes alive when the characters begin speaking to one another. Students read more fluently when they create images for the characters talking in a story, when they see the postures and gestures and hear the intonations from which meaningful talk emerges. In our daily journal-writing, I always see a quantum leap in fluency and clarity when students begin to use lots of dialogue.

Dialogue, by extension, also means the interconnectedness of everything. It includes an awareness of cultural and ecological cooperation and competition, food chains, chemical bonding, markets, teacher–student relationships, transportation, even "I and Thou." An active use of dialogue is the use of computers, video letters, and pen pals to establish sister schools and other learning networks.

Improvisation

A storyteller improvises, using traditional language and images to shape a story for one particular moment. The characters in the story, likewise, improvise solutions to their problems, often failing several times before passing a test.

Pedagogues have unfortunately taught problem-solving as an analytic process in which we list solutions, weigh their merits, and rationally choose the most likely. Oral language, culture, nature, and children operate more concretely. Evolution does not proceed by abstractly listing possible responses to an environment but by physically trying out every option that appears. Whereas a writer weighs the merits of alternate phrasings and edits out unwanted language, a storyteller keeps talking and works with everything that came before. There are no "mistakes" in oral language or in nature or in narrative teaching, only new challenges that emerge even while we respond to current problems.

Teaching is a performing art, best learned through experiences with storytelling. Only with improvisation can a teacher respond to the extraordinary diversity in a classroom. And only with improvisation can we help our students become learners who are able to solve their real problems. When children work through a fight, attempt to sound out a word, create an experiment, or explore a story problem in math, they scan all available patterns. Only the child who fears making a mistake loses the ability to learn.

Diversity

Each story is full of diverse elements. Every time we tell it for another audience, we vary it, and every teller performs with a different style. Print narrows that diversity to a single mass-produced performance. Textbooks are scripts for a similarly narrow curriculum. Narrative teaching is to analytical teaching as a prairie or even a diversified Amish farm is to single-crop farming. A monoculture appears to have short-term economic advantages, but it begins to bring about long-term devastation.

Though everything is connected and repeated, each natural and cultural event is unique. Whatever idea or image I present during a story, a number of students offer to tell stories about their personal variations on the theme. They are not satisfied with a bald idea but ask to hear and tell many incarnations of it.

The old paradigm prefers to find generalizations explaining the universe; the new delights in the diversity that bends abstractions closer to the truth. The health of a culture or an ecosystem is exactly revealed in the amount of diversity present.

Although we talk about cultural differences and the importance of diversity in our Lake Wingra watershed, much more important in our classroom is student choice. When students choose what they read, write, research, and experiment with and whom they interview and correspond with, they not only pay more attention to their work but also bring extraordinary diversity into the classroom.

Boundaries

Although abstract boundaries are exposed in narrative teaching as static approximations of reality, the world of stories presents many limits that shift with time. Cinderella is bound to the hearth until magic appears; a hero returns to change the world order; and even the gods change their minds. Our stories, both personal and traditional, begin at the moment when the old boundaries are about to change.

Limits also shift in natural and human ecologies. A map of Native Americans in Wisconsin looks different in every era; a language shaped with precise patterns of sounds and meanings has regional dialects; laws are repealed; a stable population becomes threatened; the reproductive system changes at puberty and menopause; and stars, after billions of years of regularity, become old and die.

My classroom rules emerge from circumstances, giving shape to our interactions. But many times a day students test the boundaries, bringing up a new situation to see how it applies, adjusting the boundaries. Regular small changes can be accommodated. The stories my students later tell their children will use the regular classroom events as a beginning context to highlight the moments when large changes occurred. And every day we tell stories about how boundaries are adjusted, violated, or maintained.

Body

Stories, like classrooms, are full of moving and talking bodies. In storytelling, much more than half of the story is communicated with eyes, faces, gestures, and voice inflections. Words are experienced as coming out of the body with our breath, and all learning is experienced as a change in the body. There are no disembodied ideas in stories since even ghosts use voices.

In my classroom, I know how students are learning mostly by observing their bodies. I see shoulders moving back, eyes coming up, muscles relaxing, pencils moving, voices becoming stronger, students moving together and apart, and hands arranging experiments. No objective test can tell me as much about student learning.

As a storyteller, I teach my students how to use their eyes, hands, voices, brains, breath, and senses so that learning is experienced as a physical activity. Similarly, I teach them how to observe the bodies of rocks, cells, microscopic animals, classroom plants, machines, dancers, talkers, writers, enemies, and teachers. Learning, internally, is personal body awareness; externally it is awareness of the body of the universe.

Ideas

Ideas grow from image patterns. As senses, images, and patterns accumulate, children begin forming abstracted statements. Expository language develops from narrative, where it has been embedded in the dialogue of characters. In Plato's *Dialogues* we see this process succinctly: Socrates builds abstraction through conversation and from concrete experience.

If we teach from this developmental perspective, remembering Jean Piaget, we help our students master both narrative and expository discourse. We also give them transitional tools for working with ideas. Repetition, for example, arranges ideas as well as images. The scientific method is a scintillating example of both improvisation (constantly trying out new approaches to nature) and of the process whereby ideas emerge from images.

This précis on narrative teaching relies primarily on abstraction. When I label these images, they are no longer the lively processes I had in mind. The ideas I use allow me, as a writer, to summarize processes it would take me many chapters to write as narratives or days to tell as a storyteller. Consider these ideas program notes for a storytelling performance in which I would communicate much more fully. By observing your every reaction to what I say, I would discover our common ground for exploring these questions.

Jailbreak!

Every Friday at the end of the school day, after reminders have been given for homework and students have begun putting their chairs on the tables, I yell "Jailbreak!" at the top of my voice. They reply, "*Jailbreak!*" as they surge toward the door. Like every other myth, this one emerged gradually.

However many stories I tell, regardless of how dramatic my teaching, the most popular ritual in my classroom is "free time," when à la Summerhill students can choose any activity except running around. Typically they knit, play chess, read, play piano and violin, write stories, play in the sandbox, draw, create and perform plays, spend time with the animals, and gossip.

They complain, of course, because much of our time is spent doing the things I choose. "It seems like a jail at times," I agree. "All 25 of us have to stay in this one room, with far less space, equipment, and supplies than most of us have at home with our much smaller families. You ask to go to the bathroom; you line up for art when I say it's time; you eat when I give the signal." For the moment they believe I am a converted jailer, ready to set them free.

"But," I continue, "if I don't teach you the skills I am required to teach, you would simply get another teacher. So I am in this jail with you; I am not the jailer but a grownup who is helping organize a jailbreak. If we want to be free, we'll have to learn how to be free in this room together."

TEACHING STORIES '94

Much that was vision in 1991, when the previous text was written, becomes visible in 1994. When I returned to the classroom seven years ago, after nine years as a full-time freelance storyteller, I decided to recast our entire curriculum into narrative contexts. The narrative processes, in evolving together, have created a complex, integrated curriculum, with braided rituals, skills, and projects. Realizing how difficult it is to create a narrative curriculum in an isolated classroom, I have given much of my effort the past few years to helping create an extended network of teachers and classrooms—to building a culture in which narrative teaching can flourish.

Prairie time

Visitors sometimes look into our room, see the sandbox, couches and tables, piano and lab, and plants and animals everywhere and comment, "It looks less structured than other classrooms." I often tell this metaphor:

Traditional classrooms are like corn fields. The farmer plows the whole field at one time. One type of corn is planted, with a standard distance between the rows and between seeds within the rows. Every row receives the same amount of fertilizer. Each plant should look about the same and will be harvested at the same time. A very simple structure.

My classroom is more like a prairie. The grasses, insects, mice, and hawks co-evolve. Each species is dependent on countless others and also on soil and climate. A prairie is difficult to establish, but in place it endures— a very complex structure.

Several years ago, after reviewing corn fields, prairies, and learning, I said, "Today we will have 'prairie time.'" Stories about learning abounded. As students worked on individual projects, they created many anecdotes to report to the class: their intentions, struggles, and successes. Group discussions became vital as individual stories became vivid.

Learning networks

Removing textbooks, worksheets, and carefully planned units only leaves a hole in the curriculum. In a narrative-based curriculum, content and skills are learned in context and in process. Phone calls, field trips, local media, folklore projects, and assigned home observations bring nature and culture into the curriculum in a language-rich environment. A web of community connections replaces standardized curriculum.

Stories both create and emerge out of community. For the past three years we have been a combination classroom. About half the students each year are new fourth-graders, the other half fifth-graders returning for their second year. By overlapping and extending our community, students become our primary learning network, the veterans modeling the processes we use.

Information, energy, ideas, and stories must come from many sources. Parents walk in our door every day and tutor students, take kids on video shoots and nature walks, arrange speakers, type student articles for publication, and coordinate our efforts at telecommunications. Parent-teacher conferences, parent-planned family social events, and a parent-coordinated classroom newsletter support our family network. At Randall we create various multicultural events, including a powwow, a semester-long residency celebrating African-American music, and a Hmong dance residency. These schoolwide contexts occasion many stories in room 103: civil-rights history, Native American mythology, Asian folk tales, and family stories that reflect our wonderful diversity.

A major research institution, the University of Wisconsin, is next door. We have a student teacher most semesters, visitors, and student and faculty volunteers. We visit science labs, drama labs, museums, and conferences. Students regularly call professors with their questions. My kids are interviewed for graduate students' projects and help evaluate instructional media. Sometimes they are asked to speak at teacher-training programs.

That's only the short list. Add in friends, the PTO, curriculum specialists for the Madison Metropolitan School District, Edgewood College, government agencies, computer links, and former student teachers—and you'll understand why our main text is the telephone book!

Guest speakers tell the class many stories: the origin of the Lake Wingra basin, the history of the Ku Klux Klan in Madison, a trip to Cuba, a Br'er Rabbit story from Sierra Leone, an escape from a World War II concentration camp, family stories in Iran, portions of "The Ramayana," Swedish children's books, a marriage in Tunisia, and a recitation of "The Cremation of Sam McGee."

I Wonder

For five years I explored the idea that kids can do science much as grownups do: asking original questions, setting up experiments and controlled observations, collecting and analyzing data, and presenting the results to classmates. An extremely difficult idea to bring to life because 25 students often needed help at the same time.

Three years ago I asked for help from some of our networks. During lab time there were usually five teachers, parents, and university volunteers working with students. With such support for their problem-solving, students were able to sustain more extended research. They observed squirrels and beans, tested storm-sewer water, researched ESP, explored buoyancy, studied the effects of exercise on pulse, and compared soils. We expanded the network still further by sending a letter to about 300 classrooms, telling them of another idea—that student scientists, like grownups, need to publish.

The first year it was published, *I Wonder: The Journal for Elementary School Scientists* had 16 articles, full of charts and tables, and 1,200 copies were distributed. Last year 64 articles, 2,000 copies, and our first daylong conference, where students gave oral reports on their research. This year 95 articles and an agreement by teachers to ask conference presenters to tell the stories of their research (we noticed students listen better to improvised stories than to written speeches).

Each observation or experiment is many times a story—imagined, in process, reported. Teachers in our project use narratives at every stage to structure student inquiry. Returning students explain the *I Wonder* process with accounts of previous research. Teachers iterate lab procedures by telling truncated anecdotes, some from experience, others created to fit the teaching moment. In regular lab meetings students tell their progress—finding and setting up materials, unexpected problems, current observations, breakthroughs.

It Figures!

Story appears almost everywhere in our math curriculum. At the simplest level are the story fragments teachers tell to focus attention, describe a process, or illustrate an application. At the beginning of the year I expect my students to master their multiplication tables. I challenge them with the story of my most memorable intellectual discovery as a 4-year-old: the day I learned to multiply 8 times 8.

Last fall, attempting to illustrate the kinds of problems we would tackle in the algebra group, I told this story: "Several hundred years ago a smart kid got in trouble in his classroom because he had finished all his work. To keep him busy, the teacher gave him a hard problem: 'Add all the numbers from 1 to 100.' Within several minutes Karl Friedrich Gauss gave an astonished teacher the correct answer. This kid became one of the greatest mathematicians of all time. How did he do it?" On the board I wrote "$1 + 2 + 3 \ldots + 100 = ?$"

Within several minutes Wenpei, just arrived from China, wrote the correct answer on the board. My students were hooked on mathematical stories.

Life develops, theorists of complexity suggest, at the edge of order and chaos. Likewise learning. The mathematics curriculum, crystallized for years in the order of flawless computations, is now being nudged by the National Council of Teachers of Mathematics toward some of the chaos of problem-solving. To help students tell the story of what's on their mind when they work with hard problems, we created *It Figures! The Journal for Elementary School Mathematicians*. Students have written about infinity, graphing quadratic equations, symmetry, non-Euclidean geometry, trigonometry, statistics, fractions, tessellations, and fractals. They have also tried to figure out how many cubic feet of water are in Lake Wingra and how many globes would fit into a hollow earth. The articles are mostly narratives.

Raji wrote last year, "When you just do things you know how to do out of the textbook, math is very boring. But when you work on things you do not know how to do and you learn new things, it is tons of fun."

Kid-to-Kid

Let's recast social studies for a 10-year-old by observing what a culturally sophisticated adult does: she observes human patterns, tells stories about her own people, talks respectfully with strangers, and solves problems cooperatively. A single project in room 103 helps our students practice the same activities: creating a documentary video of our community, exchanging it with classrooms around the world, and studying the videos we receive in return.

Kid-to-Kid took more than two years to make. The kids did a survey to help us decide what to include, formed teams, did background research, scheduled interviews, arranged rides with their parents, used a camcorder, indexed tapes, created rough scripts, and worked with me in the editing studio. In a hundred excursions, they interviewed Mayor Soglin, Donna Shalala, our state archaeologist, and the university hockey coach; they shot our farmers' market, a Hmong New Year celebration, the arboretum, and ethnic restaurants. The final videotape depicts neighborhood stories, historical photographs, wildlife species, and kids at play.

$$\sum_{a}^{m} \frac{x - y^2}{a}$$

Heads & Tales

A global shift to oral narrative as our educational paradigm is under way. Theoretical articles on narrative proliferate. Inquiry-based, community-based, and network-based learning projects, similar to those I describe in my classroom, emerge like mushrooms. How will our principals know our intuitions are on track? What structures will support this emergent culture?

Heads & Tales: An Inquiry Into Storytelling in Education is at once a conference coming to Madison this year and a grass-roots network taking shape among educators in and out of classrooms. We are scheduling in-depth lab sessions where storyteller–educators can observe one another at work, theoretical presentations about research and curriculum design, and lots of stories about what changes and what is passed on when we teach and learn with storytelling. We are also facilitating exchanges between participants before and after the event—through newsletters, videos, conference calls, caucuses, whatever ad hoc cooperation supports local practice. We expect everyone in the network to maintain, change, and own it.

Because Heads & Tales has already revitalized our storytelling community in Madison, we hope other localities take their turn in hosting the conference. It has prompted us to create an adult storytelling series, to meet more scholars working with narrative at the University of Wisconsin, and to collaborate closely with the Madison Metropolitan School District. Delighting in our communications with presenters coming from Bangladesh, Hungary, Michigan, Norway, New York, Texas, Virginia, and Zimbabwe, we imagine their presence in our classrooms means school will never be the same.

When we escape from the jail of linear curriculum, with our heads reconnected to our tales, we see the world with new ears.

Mark Wagler of Madison, Wisconsin, is a teacher, a father, a gardener, and an urban Amishman; a storyteller and a folklorist with projects from California to Connecticut; a Woodrow Wilson Fellow, graduate studies, Universität Bern and the University of Chicago; the founder of I Wonder: The Journal for Elementary School Scientists *and* It Figures! The Journal for Elementary School Mathematicians; *the first president of the Northlands Storytelling Network; the co-chair of Heads & Tales; and the project director of "Training Teachers to Utilize the Connections Between Oral and Written Narrative" and "Storytelling in the Social Studies Curriculum."*

Promoting a
Good Response to Stories

Create a good listening atmosphere

Establish a ritual: light a candle, ring a bell, dim the lights. A regular "signal" for story time will come to mean the start of a special activity, commanding attention. Wait until everyone is settled and quiet before beginning. Allow a hushed, expectant silence to develop.

Let few interruptions disturb the flow of the story

- Don't stop to ask comprehension questions.
- If students interrupt to ask what a word means or raise a question, quickly define the word or answer the question and move on.
- Handle distracting student behavior nonverbally whenever possible.
- Ask aides or visitors to join the audience. This minimizes peripheral distractions and provides good listening models.

Encourage active involvement in the story

- Encourage students to create the story atmosphere. For instance, when the wind blows in the story, have the children whistle softly to create the sound.
- Encourage students to chime in with you ("Let's all say it together").
- Occasionally pause to allow students to finish predictable sentences: "Papa Bear said, 'Someone's been eating my porridge!' Mama Bear said . . . "

Concentrate fully on the story during the telling

Good teacher concentration promotes good student response to a story. Don't rush through the story. Take your time; do your best to bring the story to life.

Choose and tell excellent stories

The better the material, the better the response will be.   —Catharine Farrell

From Storytelling: A Guide for Teachers *by Catharine Farrell. Copyright 1987, 1993 by Catharine Farrell. Published by Scholastic Professional Books. Reprinted by permission of Scholastic Inc.*

Developing the Right Side of the Brain

By Vicky Crosson and Jay Stailey

In 1981 a Nobel Prize in physiology was awarded to a group of neurologists whose work concentrated on the roles of the left and right hemispheres of the brain. Their research noted that the left hemisphere controls cognitive functions. The right hemisphere, which controls creative processes, was also found to be the center for our understanding of right and wrong and the spiritual.

In years past our society has called on our schools to look after our children's cognitive (left brain) growth. The development of the creative right side of the brain has more often been addressed by the immediate family, the extended family, the church, and other structured and unstructured influences on children's lives.

During the past several decades, however, we as a nation have seen these influences diminish in their impact on children's lives. At the same time the schools have continued in their role as developers of the left side of the brain.

Storytelling can facilitate cognitive learning by placing information to be learned in a relevant framework. Storytelling can also help address higher-level thinking that facilitates the imaginative process upon which our values and beliefs are built. Specifically, storytelling addresses many of the essential elements for teaching English as identified by the National Council of Teachers of English in 1982. These essential elements, given below, were identified as contributing to the "knowledge, understanding, and skills of those who will make up the society of the future."

Storytelling enhances the study and enjoyment of literature, enabling students to
- recognize the importance of books as a mirror of human experience as reflected by motives, conflicts, and values
- identify with fictional characters as a means of relating to others
- become aware of important writers and familiar with great works
- develop effective ways of talking and writing about literature
- appreciate the rhythms and beauty of the language
- develop reading habits that carry over into adulthood.

Teachers often intuitively sense that storytelling has a place in the curriculum but may not have concrete reasons to support their belief. In this article Jay Stailey, an elementary-school principal, and school librarian Vicky Crosson look at why storytelling is important and suggest that it can nurture both the imaginative and the analytical sides of a student's brain.

Storytelling helps students in speaking, as they learn to
- clearly and expressively convey their ideas and concerns
- adapt words and strategies to fit varying situations and audiences
- participate productively and harmoniously in small and large groups
- present arguments in orderly and convincing ways
- interpret and assess various kinds of communication, including intonation, timing, gesture, and body language.

Hearing stories helps build listening skills that allow students to learn
- that full understanding depends on determining a speaker's purpose
- to attend to detail and relate it to the purpose of the communication
- to evaluate the messages and effects of mass communication.

Storytelling contributes to reading development as it helps students
- learn to approach reading as a search for meaning
- develop the skills to comprehend material in many formats
- learn to read accurately and make valid references
- learn to judge literature critically on the basis of personal response and literary quality.

Storytelling can build writing skills by helping students learn to
- write clearly and honestly
- generate ideas, find appropriate modes for expressing them, select and arrange ideas, and evaluate and revise their work
- adapt their form of expression to various audiences
- use techniques of writing intended to appeal to and persuade others
- develop their talents for creative and imaginative expression.

Finally, storytelling promotes creative thinking. The storytelling process can teach students that
- originality derives from the uniqueness of the individual's perception, not necessarily from innate talent
- inventiveness involves weaving new relationships
- creative thinking derives from their ability not only to look but also to see; not only to hear but also to listen; not only to imitate but also to innovate; not only to observe but also to experience the excitement of fresh perception.

From Spinning Stories: An Introduction to Storytelling Skills *by Vicky L. Crosson and Jay C. Stailey. Copyright 1988 by the Texas State Library. Reprinted by permission.*

MAKING STORIES THE
HEART OF THE CURRICULUM

BY JO PUTNAM PAQUETTE

Stories work! They are examples of whole language, and they enrich the curriculum. But can they be its focal point?

To answer this question, let's look at the phenomenon known as whole language. Whole language, as defined by Judith Newman and Susan Church, is a philosophy of learning and teaching based on the assumption that learning is social and involves

- risk-taking and experimentation
- relating new information to prior knowledge
- active involvement, requiring purpose and decision-making
- the use of language, mathematics, art, music, drama, and other communication systems as vehicles for exploration.

Whole-language philosophy bridges the entire school curriculum, not just those aspects traditionally considered language arts. Any areas of the curriculum can be linked, with story as the nucleus.

A well-told story can be the springboard for curriculum integration because one need not be limited to the confines of language arts. Activities from storytelling can span and thereby aid in integrating the entire curriculum.

Here is a plan for using storytelling as the heart of the curriculum, using the concepts of whole language:

- Learn to tell a story or use an audiotape or video of the story.
- Gather colleagues and brainstorm ideas, using the following chart. Brainstorm with students for ideas. Then, using knowledge of your students' capabilities and interests, plug feasible ideas into the chart.
- Tell the story to students (or use a tape). After two or more hearings, have students work in pairs and take turns telling the story to each other, each helping the other with forgotten parts. Guide students to "play through" all or part of the story, using the techniques of creative drama.
- Choose a curricular area on the chart, then an idea from that area. Design a lesson plan with your class's needs in mind. Implement your plan, evaluate it, and revise as necessary. Repeat in another area.

From the Yarnspinner, *May 1992. Reprinted by permission.*

Reading and literature teacher Jo Putnam Paquette of Harvard Junior High in Harvard, Illinois, suggests that the whole-language approach allows teachers to make stories the heart of the curriculum. Her concise guide can help teachers who may be new to storytelling get started.

Tales as Tools

33

WHOLE-LANGUAGE IDEAS AND ACTIVITIES

Language arts

Listening

- Do listening exercises featuring well-crafted language
- Visualize scenes from the story
- Listen for sensory images
- Identify a story's structure
- Retell a story to a partner
- Feature speakers on a given subject

Speaking

- Retell a story to a partner
- Discuss the story as a group
- Discuss the story, using student-crafted questions
- "Re-speak" the dialogue in cooperative learning groups
- Tell the story as a news report
- Tell a student-crafted story

Reading

- Use readers' theater technique for all or part of the story
- Read cultural variations of the story
- Read other tales of the same nature
- Read stories with similar motifs
- Read to research the story
- Read the story repeatedly as part of learning to tell

Writing

- Write a new ending for the story
- Write an original story with the same pattern
- Write the story in play format
- Write an original story with a similar motif
- Write a variation after posing "what if" questions
- Write lyrics for a song based on a story
- Keep a journal of feelings, ideas, profundities, parallels evoked as a result of story listening, reading, crafting
- Take notes on story-related research

Science

- Study the habitats of characters or animals in the story
- Study the ecology or ecosystem of the story locale

Social studies

- Research the country, people, and culture of the story's origin through history, geography, sociology, anthropology, psychology, and archaeology

Physical education

- Do stretching exercises
- Imitate the movements of human and animal characters in the story
- Choreograph and perform an interpretive dance of a scene from a story

Mathematics

- When telling an Anansi the spider story, for example, study a number system for eight or the symmetry of arachnids
- Use Anansi stories that involve concepts of quantities and comparisons

Fine arts

Visual arts

- Create a mural depicting scenes from a story—planning and rendering as a cooperative group project
- Draw a picture-story map
- Create and construct a variety of puppets
- Make a diorama
- Create scenery, props, and costumes for a play

Drama

- Act out a favorite scene from a play
- Conduct interviews with a sto-

ry's characters
- Act out a story written as a play or with puppets
- Act out a soliloquy

Music
- Write original music for lyrics based on a story
- Create your own simple musical instruments
- Rewrite the story as a musical play

High-level thinking
- Compare cultural variations or versions of a story
- Create different cause-and-effect situations to make a new tale

- Compare a story character's traits with your own, then reconstruct the tale as though you had exchanged places with a story character
- Reconstruct the story as though it were happening in today's world or a future, imaginary world

From the Yarnspinner, *May 1992. Reprinted by permission.*

3

STORYTELLING AND LANGUAGE DEVELOPMENT

STORYTELLING AND LANGUAGE DEVELOPMENT

Stories give children language experiences that enable them gradually to think about and comprehend their environment. How do stories and storytelling affect children's language development and mental capacity? The answer lies in the way children learn to speak and think. Language and thought are closely linked, though not identical. When language is internalized, it becomes thought; when thought is externalized, it becomes language. Through hearing, children develop a repertoire of abstract symbols (words) that correspond to their internal experience of things.

Without a rich language environment, children have fewer representations of experience to draw from and internalize. The result, child-development experts say, is that children "know" less. Because stories are structured experiences with a plot and a beginning, middle, and end, they are among the very best language experiences. Story structures become scaffolding for other experiences in life and in story.

This effect has several causes. First, stories are composed of words, usually spoken rhythmically, and have both primary meaning and secondary, or connotative, meaning. Even simple rhymes such as "Jack be nimble, Jack be quick, Jack jump over the candlestick" are rich with a sound and sense not found in everyday speaking and reading. Second, the story is a springboard for related forms of speaking, thinking, writing, reading. When children are language-rich, they bring more to an experience and as a result engage the subject more deeply and come away with more.

Hearing a wide range of stories from an early age in both the classroom and home confers a treasure upon a child. The early stories take root in a child's inner life and grow, giving it structure and meaning. The person blessed enough to have had a lifetime of hearing stories is like a well-watered tree: the roots go deep; the branches reach to the sky.

This chapter looks at ways to put down story-roots in children through further exploration of the relationship between storytelling and language development; makes suggestions for creative ways to use storytelling techniques to enhance language development; and presents some novel language-enhancement activities that use storytelling.

SEEING LANGUAGE SKILLS
AS A WHOLE

BY CATHARINE FARRELL

The teacher–storyteller draws from a venerable tradition, and ample scholarship shows that exposure to stories and storytelling enhances reading comprehension. As we approach the subject of storytelling in the classroom, however, we must see the four basic language arts—listening, speaking, reading, and writing—as essentially interrelated skills. They are simply different modes of communication.

Substantial research in education has indicated over and over that listening comprehension is the cognitive base for reading comprehension, that students who can speak well are more likely to write well, and that students who have a large listening vocabulary are more likely to sight-read with greater comprehension. The ways the language arts work together are frequently given lip service in academic literature, but few programs have developed actual language-arts activities in simple day-by-day lesson plans.

First, let's look at the four language arts: listening, speaking, reading, and writing.

Oral skills come first in the general order of things. Of course, we know this from watching infants acquire the ability to speak. And we know how important listening is as a first step when we attempt to learn a second or third language ourselves. Our listening ability is always greater at first than our speaking ability. Also, we can read our beginning German, for example, much better than we can write it. So it is with the average student.

Primary students (kindergarten through third grade) have a critical need to listen to language. The richer and more varied the language students hear, the greater their chance to generate language of their own based on those models. Then when they begin to decipher words in print, they bring that level of language comprehension to reading.

The writing process is simplified for us if we have experience in extemporaneous speaking, role-playing, creative dramatics, choral readings, retelling stories, improvisation, or round-robin storytelling. It's like priming the pump. We begin to write as though we were speaking—and we have a sense of an audience that is listening. Our writing has the immediacy of speaking, and it connects. It appears that the purpose of language is to enable us to connect.

Catharine Farrell believes that language development in the elementary and secondary classroom must involve all four aspects of communication: reading, writing, listening, and speaking. This excerpt from her guide for teachers demonstrates the intimate connection between them and the need for educators to teach them through storytelling.

Storytelling provides the model of immediate connection that stirs primary students in their first use of language, but storytelling then becomes a point of reference for enhancing language abilities through all phases of education.

THE DISTINCT USES OF LANGUAGE

We can easily see that language creates communication. Language is a commodity of daily life: it is an exchange of information and a practical necessity. But being literate means more than the ability to sign checks, order appliances, or read the labels on aspirin bottles.

Recent language studies in the English-speaking world have brought attention to the distinct uses of language. British educator and author James Britton has made a distinction between two fundamentally different ways we use language: as participants whose language is a tool of exchange and as spectators whose language helps us create and interpret experiences. The participant role includes all exchanges of objective information—just the facts. The spectator role includes all ways of interpreting and representing life experiences—from over-the-fence gossip and childhood stories to the most sophisticated literary art forms.

When we relate experiences and gossip, when we create poetry, drama, and story, when we daydream and fantasize, we use language as spectators. The way we structure and interpret the events of our world is determined by our sense of story. Our ability to interpret true life events and create new scenarios is based on our experiences, of course, and on our exposure to stories themselves.

Arthur Applebee, an American scholar who adapted James Britton's theories, studied the development of a sense of story throughout childhood (ages 2 to 17). He found that children became more sophisticated in their sense of story with age and that this ability gave them a way to structure the everyday world.

The basic components of a sense of story are
- narrative organization
- a protagonist
- character types
- an initial conflict or problem
- the rise and fall of the plot
- metaphor
- dialogue
- the solution of a problem
- a satisfying conclusion that ties up loose ends.

A child who has a well-developed sense of story will be able to predict outcomes once enough information has been established. There is no way to develop the various senses of story except through exposure to stories themselves.

A sense of story is an awareness that goes on developing throughout a lifetime. We might learn new stories, for example, Beijing Opera story plots, through travel or cultural exchange. Every culture has its own sense of story, but if we are familiar with a story type, we need only hear the first part of its framework to be able to predict the outcome. For instance, try to predict the outcome of this scenario:

It was a dark and stormy night in early spring. Clouds gathered in the dark gale of the windstorm, gathered on the rise of the mountain. And when the lightning struck, flashing brightly against the bank of clouds, one could see the silhouette of the ruined castle on the mountaintop, its single tower rising to the highest point in the land. On nights such as this, one could often see a figure on the ramparts of the castle, clutching a long cloak and wearing a deep hood. Drenched to the skin, it would restlessly walk back and forth, scanning the distance around the castle as if waiting for someone to come. This night, being in fine spirits and ready to try the fates, I mounted my black horse and began the harrowing ride up the old stony road to the castle gate to see what I could see.

What would you predict? And what story type is this? Perhaps a gothic tale or a romance—or is this a pure and simple ghost story? Depending on your experience with stories, you will predict one or two probable outcomes.

Now, having a sense of story can help us interpret our lives (and possibly enjoy them a bit more), but there also appear to be direct correlations between sense of story, reading comprehension, and writing ability. Garth H. Brown, who conducted an exploratory study to determine the extent of the correlations, found that students who were better able to retell a fairy tale in an oral interview also achieved higher levels of reading comprehension and writing language with story features. Brown's concluding remarks suggested that students be immersed in stories because listening to stories told or read aloud throughout elementary school seems crucial to reading and writing.

When we think of what we know about the four language arts—with listening the first step toward skill in all four—we must agree with Brown about the crucial role of storytelling and reading aloud in the primary grades. I wish to emphasize that students at this early stage should not simply listen to factual information and learn to follow simple directions. They should also listen to a higher level of language use, the language that interprets the world—that is, the language of literature.

LITERATURE-BASED LANGUAGE ARTS

Because the oral tradition of storytelling draws from the multicultural store of folk literature, it can provide a base for the study of all literature. Its plots, character types, and conflicts are the very stuff of classical literature. Telling stories rather than reading them aloud preserves the essence of primary communication of culture itself. Storytelling is, indeed, the first art form and one as natural to the human voice as song.

The ultimate effectiveness of storytelling in the classroom, however, is that it begins at the first step in the language-arts skill-building process—it's a listening activity. It uses language in the interpretive mode without any of the distractions that reading aloud from a book can bring. It is immediate and speaks directly to the listener with continuous eye contact, full body gestures, changing voices, facial expressions, descriptive language, and extemporaneous details that are created freshly each time the story is told.

The teacher–storyteller models the magic of language, the creative power of the human voice. Without a book in sight, students imagine all the events of the story for themselves and sometimes think that they are true or that they happened to the teacher. Students' identification with the story characters is stronger than when a tale is read aloud. During the telling, the story is more real than life.

To breathe life into a tale or a book for students is an unqualified invitation for them to retell the story, add new details, tell an original story, read, and write. Because there is no book, the students believe that telling a story is easy, as easy as talking. And because they believe that—well, then, it is! We have seen special-education students go home and retell a story perfectly, even a story with complicated sequencing. What has occurred is a subtle transfer of higher-language use and the beginning of an enduring love of that fascinating and instructive art we call literature.

POCKET TALES TO GO

Some of the youngest children in the Sacramento, California, school district are pocketing valuable prereading and social skills, thanks to an innovative storytelling method created just for them.

The pocket-story program was introduced in the 1987–88 school year and involved 150 inner-city students. Its creator was Mary Lynne McGrath, a library-prep specialist with a deep interest in storytelling as an art form and a teaching tool.

"I wanted to turn all my first-graders into storytellers," says McGrath. "At that age they don't read very well. But in America there exists a big body of folk literature that can be told. Storytelling gives children a way to share literature."

Every week McGrath reads and learns to tell a short story. Then she ushers in her classes of 6- and 7-year-olds and launches into the story, using character voices and repetitive refrains the students can chime in on.

After the telling McGrath gives each student a sheet of paper divided into eight squares. Each square contains two words that are key to the sequence of the story's action, and McGrath asks the children to draw in each square a picture that represents the words. Their assignment is to pocket the paper, take it home, and use it as a guide to help them remember the story and tell it to their families.

"Children love to draw," says McGrath, "and I wanted them to be able to tell a story." She developed the program when she figured out how to put the two elements together. Because small children often have trouble getting things home from school and remembering assignments, the "pocket" aspect of the program comes in handy.

Besides being fun for the students, the program helps them both educationally and socially, says McGrath. It teaches them the prereading skills of listening, imaging, and learning to understand a story's structure. By the time they begin to read, they're no longer novices—they know a story has a beginning, a middle, and an end.

But equally important is the sense of self-esteem the children gain from telling the stories to their families. "The little moment you have when you are a storyteller is precious," says McGrath.

"Your family really pays attention to you. Built into storytelling is the fact that it sets up social contact." As one student told McGrath, "I told the story to my grandma. She said she liked it and asked me to tell her all the stories I knew."

The pocket-story program has been a learning experience for McGrath too: she's discovered that children can pick up a story much more quickly than adults can. "They have fabulous memories," she says. "They can learn in five minutes what it takes me an hour to learn—and I'm a storyteller."

And she's finding out what kinds of stories work best. The children especially enjoy humorous stories and tales featuring animals. One of her favorite sources is Margaret Read MacDonald's *Twenty Tellable Tales* (H.W. Wilson, 1986) because its stories are short and easy to tell and come from many different cultures.

"A whole lot more storytelling should be done in schools," McGrath says, "but the subject doesn't get much attention in teacher training. Storytelling empowers children who can't read yet to go out and 'do' literature."

—Cynthia Moxley

From Storytelling Magazine, *summer 1989. Reprinted by permission.*

STORYTELLING PROPS TO ENHANCE SENSORY EXPERIENCE

By Elner C. Bellon

Elner Bellon under-stands children's need for sensory experiences to draw them into the world of words in a mean-ingful way. She makes excellent sug-gestions for activities to use with preschool and early elementary students. Many of these activities can easily be taught to older children, who in turn can perform them with young children, as "Story-telling Pairs Learn Together," the short piece that follows, indicates.

Today's children have spent much time watching television, and they are accustomed to the frantic noise and movement of Saturday-morning cartoons. Many of these children have not been read to, and storytelling is a new experience for them. At the beginning of a story-telling program it is often wise to use props such as puppets and story-telling devices to help children focus their attention and visualize the action. As the children become better listeners, many of the props can be put away, and the story can become a true part of the oral tradition. The activities discussed here focus on beginning experiences planned and used as incentives for speech and communications.

FLANNEL-BOARD STORIES

For many years teachers have used flannel boards to aid them in pre-senting stories to children. Most of the figures used have been simple outlines, in keeping with the belief that children were more active par-ticipants if allowed to fill in the details of the characters in their own minds. Learning theorists, however, have pointed out that children learn best through their senses. This is especially true of young children. They respond to the touch, taste, and sound of their world. It seems probable then that they might respond more readily to stories that incor-porate texture into the flannel-board figures.

Many children have not felt a sheep's wool or a horse's mane. The teacher might prepare figures that use wool for sheep or fake fur for bears and other animals. One good book that lends itself to this sensory technique is *Jeanne-Marie Counts Her Sheep* (Scribner's, 1951) by Françoise Seignobosc. Jeanne-Marie makes many plans for spending the money she will realize when the wool from Patapon's lambs is sold. The idea of shearing the sheep becomes much more concrete when the figures of the sheep and the lambs are cut from a fleece or from one of the realistic woolly materials available in fabric shops.

A variety of textures can be introduced when telling stories such as Roger Duvoisin's *Donkey-Donkey* (Grosset & Dunlap, 1940). The teacher can use fake fur to create the figures of the donkey, the horse, the pig, and the dog. Many such fabrics adhere to the board without flannel backing. As children discuss the animals, they learn the

Storytelling and Language Development

descriptive words associated with the various textures chosen for each animal.

Whenever possible, it is a good idea to construct the figures so that children will recognize them when they see the book's original illustrations. In this way children can be led to discover that the story they liked so well is written in pictures and words in a book on the library table. When this happens, they also discover that printing is just "written talk." They will "read" the pictures over and over, and their motivation to read words will grow and grow.

Some teachers prefer to use pictures from the story mounted on cardboard, passing them out to members of the group after presenting the flannel-board story. The children then help arrange the pictures in the right sequence and explain what is happening in each illustration. Paperback editions of books are a good source for such illustrations.

TRANSPARENCY STORIES

Young children love variety, so the teacher might tell some stories with transparencies too. In fact, some stories are easier to use with a large group when told in this manner. Beatrix Potter's *Peter Rabbit* (Warne, 1902), for instance, is just the right shape and size for use with one child, but it is a bit small for use with a group. When using transparencies during a storytelling session, the teacher should choose a few illustrations that highlight the main events of the story. If the teacher uses too many illustrations, the changes may stop the flow of the story's action. Many illustrations can be traced with a soft lead pencil or India ink and reproduced on transparency film. [Those with access to high-tech copiers can easily create transparencies from books or drawings.]

Cumulative stories are very effective when presented with transparencies. As each new character is introduced, the storyteller introduces a new transparency or adds an overlay to the transparency already being shown. Two stories suitable for this technique are Else Holmelund Minarik's *Little Bear* (Harper & Row, 1957) and Ramon Royal Ross's interpretation of "Paco" from *Storyteller* (Merrill, 1972). While telling *Little Bear*, the teller would leave the first transparency of Mother Bear on the projector and slide Little Bear off the stage each time he left the room for a new article of clothing. Overlays are helpful in telling "Paco." The hero in this story adds a new room to his house every time an animal decides to move in to stay. The teller might begin with the ground floor of Paco's house and add an overlay each time a room is added to the structure.

Teachers can easily do shadow stories on the stage of the overhead projector, cutting small figures from paper and adding them as the story is told. "Henny Penny" might be told in this way. The figure of the hen would appear first and be projected as a silhouette on the screen. Each new animal would be added as the plot progressed.

Many language possibilities exist for storytellers using these projected figures. The teacher might introduce the characters first and encourage the children to make predictions about the type of character each might be or the role each might play in the development of the story. This technique encourages children to use their imagination and language in order to make good predictions. Children who are willing to think about the kinds of characters in the story and predict what might happen have a purpose for listening and often gain more from the story.

Tomi Ungerer's story *The Mellops Go Spelunking* (Harper & Row, 1963) could be used for predictions. This story is illustrated in black and white because much of the action takes place in a cave. The underground scenes can be reproduced and cut out for projection. The teacher might use these for a discussion of caves and predictions about things that might happen in such a setting. If the teacher adds a cutout of the scene above ground during the rainstorm, children can speculate on the effect a heavy rain might have on the river flowing through the underground cave. Each character might be introduced, and a discussion of the type of person he or she might be would prepare the children for listening.

After the teacher has read the story, children might enjoy comparing their original ideas to the plot. Sometimes children like to speculate about other trips into the cave or invent new adventures for the Mellops. Each of these experiences offers opportunities for children to talk and provides an interesting topic for discussion.

PUPPETS

Children enjoy using puppets to react to stories or to dramatize parts of a book the teacher has read. The most creative experiences with puppets are the result of the child's ability to identify with the puppet. Children must become involved with the puppet if they are to portray it in new situations or create dialogue for it. Children often feel greater involvement with animal puppets. This is especially true if the puppet is constructed of fake fur and lined with soft cotton or nylon. Scratchy, unlined puppet bodies seem to constantly remind children that the puppet is not a part of them. This results in a lack of identification with the puppet character. Tom Tichenor has some excellent patterns for cloth puppets in his book *Tom Tichenor's Puppets* (Abingdon, 1971).

Once puppets are available, it is important that the teller prepare the children for their use. Each puppet should be presented and discussed. This is where characterization begins. The children can decide what kind of person or animal the puppet might be. They might be led to describe the way this type of character would talk and behave. Then the teacher might introduce another puppet character, and discussion might center around the way these two characters would react to each other. After the story has been told or read, children can check to see if they were correct in their assumptions.

Later the teacher might review the story with the children and ask two of them to use puppets to show what might have happened just after the story ended or just before it began. Other children might use new puppets to show what might have been going on off-stage during some portion of the story. Other children might show what might have happened if a new character had been included in the story. In this way children might show what Tikki Tikki Tembo's father did when he came home and discovered that his son had almost drowned in a well. Or they might react to Arlene Mosel's retelling of this story (*Tikki Tikki Tembo*, Holt, 1989) by dramatizing the scene at the well and including a sister for the two boys. Would a sister warn the boys of danger? Would she threaten to tattle? Would she offer help while Chang ran for the ladder? The possibilities are endless and require real thinking.

There are many other possibilities for the use of puppets. At the beginning of a session a favorite puppet may be used to introduce the story or to focus attention on the storyteller. The puppet acts as a narrator, providing background information and helping children understand the meanings of words they will hear in the story. At other times the students may create their own stories for the puppets to act out. These stories, with their exaggerated movements, often remind one of a Punch and Judy show. As children become more experienced in performing and evaluating the performance, their plays improve, and more planning goes into the production. All of this requires language.

These techniques for storytelling are designed to capitalize on opportunities for children to listen to words and to hear language spoken in a meaningful context. The techniques offer built-in opportunities for children to talk, think, and communicate with an understanding adult. The stories are the starting point for a literature-extension program that fosters language development.

Children's book author Gail Haley defended storytelling as a language-development activity in her Caldecott Medal acceptance speech. Her words seem to summarize the relationship so well: "Deprive a child of love, and he will reach for affection or clamor for attention at the expense of all other aspirations. Deprive him of fantasy, and he may try on his own to make up even for that deficit. But children who are not spoken to by live and responsive adults will not learn to speak properly. Children who are not answered will stop asking questions. They will become incurious. And children who are not told stories and who are not read to will have few reasons for wanting to learn to read."

From Storytelling for Teachers and School Library Media Specialists, *edited by Elner C. Bellon. Published by T.S. Denison. Copyright 1981 by Elner Bellon.*

STORYTELLING PAIRS LEARN TOGETHER

High-school students can learn better storytelling and story-writing skills by working with primary-grade students. So match each high-schooler with a primary-school child. For the first session, have each high-school student select, prepare, and tell a story to the young partner. Encourage the pair to discuss what they like about the story and what made the storytelling work. Why did the high-school student choose that story to tell?

In the next session, have each primary-school child dictate a story to the older partner. The high-school partner will then type the story and illustrate it for the younger child.

In the third session the pair will share the dictated story and the picture. The younger child will receive the project as a gift.

For the fourth session, have the high-school student examine what makes a story work. Each high-school student should then write an original story and reproduce it on pages that leave ample space for illustrations. During this session, older students will tell and read their stories. The primary children can illustrate the text later.

At the fifth and final session the pairs can share the added art. The primary children will tell the stories to their partners. Together they can discuss telling, writing, and illustrating stories. In these five sessions both individuals in each pair will have learned a lot.

The language-arts skills each student uses include reading, writing, listening, and speaking, along with a variety of problem-solving, artistic, and creative skills. All of the students involved will work not only on academic learning but also on interpersonal skills.

In family-living classes these experiences will provide skills useful immediately in babysitting as well as establish a model for the future, when these high-school students assume the responsibilities of parenthood.

To extend their relationship and their experiences, the students might plan to write a poem or song to go with one of the stories.

—Norma Livo and Sandra Rietz

From Storytelling Activities *by Norma J. Livo and Sandra A. Rietz. Published by Libraries Unlimited, P.O. Box 6633, Englewood, Colo. 80155. Copyright 1987. Reprinted by permission.*

Storytelling and Language Development

In this recent interview with Catharine Farrell, we hear her belief in the benefits of providing youngsters a language-rich environment.

SPEAKING CHILDREN'S LANGUAGE

Young children love to listen. Read them a bedtime story once, and they ask to hear it time and time again. Utter a new phrase that arouses their imagination, and they repeat it till they very nearly wear the edges off the words. Listening and repeating, listening and repeating—that's the natural rhythm children use to develop language skills.

Storytelling enhances that rhythm, says Catharine Farrell, a former teacher and children's librarian now living in Sacramento, California. "Language and thought development are one and the same," she says. "Language is a meaning-making facility. Children think in terms of fantasy and imagination. If you talk to them through storytelling, you're speaking their language."

Farrell doesn't suggest that storytelling should replace long-used skill drills such as word articulation and spelling aloud. But she says it adds a dynamic dimension to teaching language development. Stories grab children's imagination and rivet their attention. Second-graders won't often sit still while just repeating words. Before long, boredom and restlessness set in. But Farrell can hold a group of those youngsters wide-eyed and attentive simply by telling "The Gingerbread Man."

Telling a story also adds meaning to language— meaning that isn't found in the skill drills. Such stories as the tale of Peter Rabbit or the traditional Jack tales have stood the test of time because they hold meaning for a child's imagination. Through storytelling, language and content intertwine.

"Language can't be taught without content," Farrell says. "You can't have language without having something to say. If the communication is important, children will learn the language skills necessary to make the communication happen."

Educators don't need a large repertoire of stories to hold students' interest. Stories that repeat phrases and contain repetitious actions—for example, "The Three Little Pigs"—always captivate youngsters, says Farrell. She points out that five or six well-developed tales can carry a teacher through an entire year of storytelling. By changing the focus of a story each time it's told, a teacher can use the same tale to teach music, science, art, history, and a whole array of other subjects. Developing activities around each story can stretch the tale's uses even further. Farrell calls the process "building a cycle of storytelling."

For example, after telling a story once, tell it again another day. Before the second telling, suggest that the students listen carefully and picture a part of the story in their imagination. After the story the children can go to their easels and paint the part of the story they imagined. Tell the story again on another day, this time picking a fun, repetitive phrase for the kids to chime in on each time it appears in the story. Or encourage students to act out the story after it's told. Other ideas include making masks or finger puppets of story characters.

Those activities and more are described in *Storytelling in Our Multicultural World: An Early Language Development Program* (1994), a multimedia publication Farrell put together. The program is available through Zaner-Bloser Educational Publishers and is directed toward educators who want to use storytelling as a language-development tool for children ages 3 to 8. The program includes dozens of stories and activities that focus on themes such as family stories and animal tales, as well as teacher guides, audiotapes, and props to use when telling stories.

Farrell suggests that teachers can easily begin telling stories in the classroom by choosing one of their favorite traditional tales—one they remember and cherish from childhood. "It should be a story that also teaches them," she advises. "The story should be selected for the theme, for the curricular area the class is studying. For instance, if you're teaching about animals, use an animal fable. The key is to hook the students into something that interests them."

That's not difficult when working with the active imaginations of young children. Teachers will know when they hit upon a story that hooks the students, Farrell says, because the kids will ask to hear the tale again—and again and again and again.

—Suzanne Martin

4

STORYTELLING AND READING

STORYTELLING AND READING

"A literate person is not one who knows how to read, but one who reads

fluently, responsively, critically, and because he or she wants to."

—Glenna Sloan, *The Child as Critic* (Teachers College Press, 1991)

A natural bridge exists from the spoken to the written word. When they are encouraged to do so, children make the connection between the two at an early age. The young child sees that the word *cow* means the same as a picture of a cow—and that is the beginning of reading for oneself. Children's experiences from that point on, however, vary dramatically. The home whose environment includes magazines, books of many kinds, letters, notes, and so on is one that encourages reading at an early age and usually for pleasure. Children whose homes have little or no printed matter or whose parents do not read to them usually get the message that reading is not important.

As a result, when children are ready for school, they come as fluent speakers but may lag behind in reading readiness. The problem often compounds itself as years go by because the bridge between the spoken and the written word still has not been made. Reluctant readers have not been given enough incentive to read well.

Storytelling can provide that bridge for children at every age. Children recognize and respond to language-rich stories and readily become involved in extension activities such as creating their own stories, retelling stories, illustrating stories, and acting out stories because they have been led to care about the subject. Word recognition is higher too because once children hear a story, they can more quickly recognize the words in text. They already have an experience of the meaning since they "know" the word; they are merely rediscovering it in another form.

The articles that follow explore the concept of storytelling as a bridge from the spoken to the written word. Though each looks at hearing stories from a different angle, there can be no doubt that hearing stories is itself a powerful means of bringing children into full membership in the marvelous worlds found in books.

ECHOES OF STORIES PAST: STORYTELLING AS AN INTRODUCTION TO LITERATURE

BY HUGHES MOIR

My earliest story memory is of hearing "The Three Billy Goats Gruff." Now that I am a storyteller and teacher, it has become a powerful and pleasant recollection, though at the time it happened, I was confused, embarrassed, and probably a little angry.

I was a very young first-grader at Buckhorn School in Piru, California, the fall following the end of World War II. Mrs. Clark was the teacher for all 14 of us, grades one through eight. I was issued a well-worn Dick and Jane reader and math book, but paper and pencils were scarce. We had little in the way of playground equipment and certainly no movies, filmstrips, or other audiovisual materials. There was no library, though the bookmobile came weekly. We had no lunchroom and no bathrooms. There were two outhouses that we knew were hiding places for snakes and black-widow spiders, and we used them only in absolute emergencies. Times were simpler then, but we had benefits not found in all schools.

An important and certainly memorable advantage of our tiny school was that Mrs. Clark made sure we heard stories. I have no knowledge of her educational philosophy in those days before psycholinguistics, whole language, inferencing strategies, and metacognition. But stories were as regular and natural a part of the school day as recess and the flag salute. Though of necessity she individualized her lessons, we formed a single audience during the daily story time. The 14 of us would gather around Mrs. Clark—the older girls on chairs in the back row, all the boys on the floor—and enjoy this time together.

On the morning of this particular day I remember asking what story we were going to have. Mrs. Clark said if we were good, she would read us "The Three Billy Goats Gruff."

I could hardly wait! It had been my favorite story since she had told it to us some months earlier. I had remembered the story almost word for word. I was just as afraid of the troll as the goats were because he seemed so absolutely evil and so invincible. I rejoiced that the goats had outwitted the troll and, in the end, killed him off for good. And now she was going to read it to us from a new book with pretty pictures.

We must have been good that morning, because after lunch we gathered around Mrs. Clark and her copy of *The Three Billy Goats Gruff.*

From "The Three Billy Goats Gruff" to adulthood and back again, Hughes Moir shares the delights and perils of his early story experiences and the impact they had on his teaching of literature. He also looks at story's implications for creating reading experiences, explaining that it is not the story per se that is important but rather the connection made between storyteller and listeners.

When we were quiet and comfortable, she began, as she always did, by reading the first page—telling us the title, who wrote the words, and who drew the pictures. Then she turned the page and began, "Once upon a time there were three billy goats by the name of Gruff . . . ."

This was great. I could see the very goats I had remembered from the story before. When she turned the next page, I saw snowcapped mountains and lush meadows even more spectacular and green than I had imagined. On the next page was the bridge the goats had to cross, smaller than I thought it would be, but that didn't matter. It was really the troll I was looking forward to seeing. I'm sure I squirmed a lot.

When the youngest billy goat came to the bridge, the troll yelled out, "Who's that trip-trapping across my bridge?" I knew the fear on the face of the youngest billy goat.

And when Mrs. Clark turned the page, there was the troll . . .

Except it wasn't a troll. It was a small furry creature with a somewhat friendly face. This was not a troll. Trolls, everyone knew, were hairy, not furry. And they were huge because they lived under a bridge and had to be at least a hundred feet tall to reach up and grab billy goats! This couldn't be a troll.

Even more important, trolls were never friendly looking, especially since they had "a nose as long as a poker," pointed metal teeth, and fingernails that dripped blood. I remembered distinctly that Mrs. Clark had described the troll as having teeth "like daggers and fingernails to match."

I knew this was not a troll. So before she could finish the page, I spoke up. "That's not a troll," I said.

"Oh, yes it is," Mrs. Clark said with a smile. She probably winked to the older girls sitting behind me.

Poor Mrs. Clark. She had forgotten what she'd told us before, or maybe she'd gotten confused. So I pushed the point.

"Oh, no it isn't," I began, firmly, confidently.

At that point Mrs. Clark did a trick she'd learned from many years of teaching youngsters like me, a technique I never mastered as a teacher and one that I am certain is not taught in teacher-education programs: she stopped, withdrew her smile, fixed her eyes on mine, and said slowly, meaningfully, and finally, "Oh, yes it is."

She held my attention for what seemed a very long time before turning back to the book (with its faulty portrait of trolls). She resumed her friendly tone of voice and went on with the story.

I didn't hear another word of it. I knew she was wrong, and I couldn't understand why she didn't know it.

Life at Buckhorn School went on, and I was left to stew for the rest of the day until something else caught my attention. But to this day, each time I see a copy of the story or hear it told, I remember what happened on that afternoon a half-century ago and my first lesson in storytelling.

As a teacher and storyteller I draw on this memory for insight into why stories demand our attention and why we should continue this ancient art and entertainment.

The connection between what we think of as storytelling and what we call children's literature has too often been blurred by intellectual definitions and artificial taxonomies. Mrs. Clark infused in us the love of stories. We made no distinctions between storytelling and literature. Told or read, stories are a source of wonder, of joy and laughter, of awe or sadness, of momentary terror or lasting inspiration. All we knew—or cared about—was that wonderful or terrifying things happened to real or imaginary characters in settings that were far removed from the orange groves of Southern California. They were simply marvelous moments to be lived through, perhaps to be remembered and thought about for the rest of the day or week—perhaps a lifetime.

Stories have that power to transport the listener to a different and maybe better place and time—to escape, yes, but more important, to return renewed with a greater understanding of ourselves and our world. This is among the greatest gifts of stories. The story is a journey of the imagination from which we return with newfound wisdom and satisfaction. Like Gilgamesh and Ulysses, like Alice and Max, those who set out are instructed and guided by the journey in fact and in story.

It should not be surprising that the art of storytelling, whose universal existence has been challenged by the advent of printing and more recently by electronic communications media, endures. Despite a temporary waning in its popularity, storytelling now enjoys a renaissance of interest and wide support. Mrs. Clark would understand why.

STORYTELLING AND STORY-MAKING

The act of sharing stories defines literature as a social event. Storytelling is an intimate literary encounter that creates a sense of community among individuals who may otherwise feel isolated or disconnected from others. Classrooms are not always places of security or cohesiveness for all students. Storytelling unites the attention of those who come to share in the pleasure of the story, whose emotions and aspirations are touched in very different ways. A story can open unexpected doors or permit unanticipated guests to enter our lives.

Our experiences—what we have done, seen, and read—separate us.

At the same time, stories bring us together and give us a chance to explore how we differ from and resemble one another.

Unlike reading aloud to children, storytelling is a direct human encounter—from one person to another with no object or image to muddle the connection between teller and listener or to interfere with the individual's creative role in the story-making. As we listen, each of us is guided by the highly individualistic feelings, dreams, fears, and experiences that make us who we are—and who we can become—in creating the story for ourselves, in our own images. (Mrs. Clark, of course, was right about trolls. For many reasons it was silly and fruitless of me to argue.)

As an early encounter with literature, storytelling defines our role in story-making and teaches us our relationship with literature. The lesson of active story-making carries over when we read for ourselves. Experiencing literature, whether by listening to a story told or reading one on our own, is an act of making meaning, the result of what Louise Rosenblatt calls in her book *The Reader, the Text, the Poem* (Southern Illinois University Press, 1978) a "transaction" between the story ("the text") and the reader. The result of our reading or listening, the meaning we make (what Rosenblatt calls generically "the poem"), will necessarily differ from another's meaning because of what each of us brings to the listening or reading. It is a lesson learned well during storytelling and one that we teachers must anticipate and respect and build upon during other literary experiences.

STORYTELLING AS A MODEL

For many years I endured piano lessons at the behest of my long-suffering mother, whose insistence on daily practice was unswerving. In the end, like many others in a similar situation, I learned to read music and play middling well. Among my shortcomings as a musician, then and now, is that although I learned the language of music, I could never hear the music until I played it. I have since learned that only a few among us can see the notes on the paper and hear the music. It is probably a job requirement for conductors and composers.

Many of us respond to written stories in much the same way: we know the words and can "read" what is prompted by the written forms, but we cannot hear all the rhythms and melodies of the language of the story as it lies lifeless on the page. I think this is especially true for poetry, which begs for someone to perform it—to show us what it sounds like and therefore what it means, at least to the performer. Subtler meanings, images, jokes and puns, and other nuances of a story may elude us until it is performed by someone who has studied it and plumbed its range of meanings to the extent that he or she is capable. The storyteller's performance often brings much more of the story to life than we might otherwise experience.

Because storytelling is such an intimate and powerful encounter with literature, the storyteller holds the potential to teach the listener how literature works to create the rich and varied tapestry of emotions, images, and meanings that may lie within. Storytelling is the act of crafting a literary document in public and in the process making language patterns and literary structures visible in ways no other experience can. A story is built linearly through the use of conventional language patterns and plot structures, just as an architect specifies brick and mortar or steel girders and concrete to support a building. As we listen, we learn the grammar of a story and its structure and components.

Stories that have endured, especially fairy tales and other traditional literature, succeed precisely because of the structures and patterns that they follow and that audiences anticipate. The many variations of "The Gingerbread Man" all retain the repetition of phrase in this cumulative tale. The delight of Wanda Gág's repeated phrases in *Millions of Cats* (Coward-McCann, 1977), a literary tale, springs from the remembered pleasures of similar structures occurring in timeless stories told and retold over countless generations. The repetition of episode, phrase, or characterization is part of the literary foundations that are used and brought to life in the storyteller's performance of the story.

Those who have heard a traditional story both told and read aloud intuitively understand and appreciate the difference between the two. The story reader is guided by the images and expressions of another. The author who retells the story in print is merely the latest in a long line of storytellers reworking old literary territories. If the writer–reteller is successful, the written version carries the echoes of those nameless tellers whose creative energies helped to shape it.

But after all, the story is not the reader's, and the audience knows it. Because storytelling is always an act of re-creation, the teller's voice— his or her language, imagery, experiences, insights, emotions—remakes the story with each telling, interacting with the particular audience and giving each performance of the story the interpretation appropriate to the moment.

Recognizing familiar language structures and literary conventions is a fundamental literacy skill. Because certain motifs, patterns, archetypes, and other conventions are widespread among world writings, so much of what we read throughout our lives rests upon these fundamen-

tal literary building blocks. Although many authors achieve their greatest successes through the use of the unexpected original phrase, image, or other literary device, it is the listener's or reader's understanding of the conventional that gives the unconventional form the desired impact. Storytelling, particularly of traditional stories, introduces and reinforces basic features of the literary infrastructure in an easily recognized form.

TOLD STORIES AND OTHERS

Mrs. Clark's decision to read us the story she had told us earlier was not made on the spur of the moment. She understood, I am certain, the maxim that a good story is worth hearing more than once. And a great story can be appreciated in a variety of forms and styles by storytellers who use different media. Each version, Mrs. Clark might have said, reveals something new that was understated, omitted, or misunderstood in previous performances.

It is no secret that many teachers of young children often and intentionally tell stories that children later find written in picture storybooks. Such "discoveries" intensely motivate many children to read or retell a much-loved story on their own. Children find the same delight when they recognize a familiar story that was read to them or one they experienced through audiotapes, television, videos, or motion pictures.

One of the first stories I learned to tell younger audiences is that of how Edward Bear came to be called Winnie-the-Pooh (the first chapter of A. A. Milne's *Winnie-the-Pooh* [E.P. Dutton, 1926]). I enjoy the story of Pooh's search for honey because of the visual pun at the end as well as the drama of Pooh's hanging from a balloon and his airborne encounter with the "suspicious" bees. But for me the naming of Winnie-the-Pooh is the central issue that holds the story together and gives it its ultimate shape and meaning. Furthermore, it has always seemed a story that fit me well, and I've always taken delight in telling it.

Fortunately, the story is also a favorite of children who have heard me tell it. Sometimes as I'm telling the story, I'll see or hear children whisper to one another that they "know this one." Sometimes they'll tell me right out loud, which causes a ripple of nods from others who are in on the story. I take real pleasure from such recognition because now the story can be shared and enjoyed more intimately and on many different levels. When I have finished the story, the group's response is often a mixture of satisfaction and curiosity. Many have felt a measure of personal control over the story because they had known it beforehand. They are quick to tell where they heard or saw it before and how much they liked it. These same critics will also admit that they didn't know Winnie-the-Pooh was originally called Edward Bear and that blowing flies off his nose had somehow led to a new, albeit more familiar, name.

As kids often say after hearing the story, "It's the same but different." Then they go on to discuss the merits of my retelling and the version they had heard or seen before. I hear a great deal of literary criticism at such times as well as instant critiques of my storytelling skills.

The "same but different" concept remains with us throughout our literary lifetime as we constantly hear the refrains of earlier works echoing in a new story as we appreciate the fresh approach of the latest storyteller–writer. The possibility of rediscovering the familiar while exploring new literary pieces can lead to a lifetime affair with literature in all forms. The capacity to appreciate how one approach or version deviates from another—the same but different—helps to develop taste and judgment in future literary encounters.

CONCLUSION

When teacher–storytellers really get down to why they tell stories, most will admit that fundamentally they are driven by the pleasure they get from sharing stories with audiences of all ages and the pleasure they know people get from hearing them. Such pleasures are both immediate and far-reaching in influence on children's future literary experiences— what they learn about literature and their attitude toward opening their minds and hearts to stories.

We should never sheepishly or guiltily acknowledge the personal delight and satisfaction we get and give as storytellers. When we bring storytelling to young people in schools, we join an ancient, honorable, and respected tradition of cultural enlightenment through stories. Literature in all forms is a guide to the values and mores of the society that tells the stories, providing us a pathway to understanding our dreams and aspirations. Storytelling brings recognition and appreciation of those human qualities to all who will hear what lies within each story. And in the process, it brings us together.

I'm sure Mrs. Clark would have smiled and understood.

Hughes Moir of Nederland, Colorado, is a professional storyteller and a professor emeritus of the University of Toledo. He has been a featured teller at national and state professional conferences and festivals and has shared stories with school and family audiences across the country. Moir has written scores of articles on storytelling and children's literature and edited the book Collected Perspectives: Choosing and Using Books for the Classroom, *second edition (Christopher-Gordon, 1993).*

TELLING STORIES:
A KEY TO READING AND WRITING

BY R. CRAIG RONEY

More and more children are now reaching adulthood semiliterate, and 70 million adults in this country cannot read beyond the most basic level. Clearly, reading must be taught differently. Craig Roney, a professor, a parent, a storyteller, and a former teacher, discusses how storytelling can play a role in the process of improving the way children learn to read.

Compared with their success in learning to communicate orally, children's success rate in learning to read and write is dismal. Nearly all children are in control of oral language by age 5, yet many fail to learn to read and write after 12 years of formal education, a curious anomaly given that a child's capacity for mastering both oral and print discourse is basically the same. The implication for classroom instruction is obvious: success follows when students are encouraged to employ the same strategies they used in developing oral-language skills. Storytelling is a vital strategy in helping children master print as efficiently as they earlier mastered oral language.

When preschoolers learn to speak, they are in complete control of the process. They determine what, when, and how long to learn. Language acquisition is effortless and enjoyable because nobody places arbitrary conditions on the children, as is often the case in schools. Meaning is the single focus of the children's attention. Gradually, by trial and error, they determine "how to mean," that is, what formulations are most effective at getting across their meaning. The result is that they come to employ the basic language used by individuals around them, who serve as models of the mature formulations, provide feedback, and support children in their efforts to improve their language skills. They do so by conversing with them. In short, children learn to listen and speak by listening and speaking. Actual practice is performance. Language development is therefore holistic, undertaken as part of real events.

Although practice is nonstop, it is risk-free. Children are rarely penalized for experimenting, even when their utterances are only a rough approximation of mature language. From practice, children learn that listening and speaking are in themselves active and "experimental" processes in which they use their background knowledge to predict and create the oral text they hear or speak.

IMPLICATIONS FOR CLASSROOM INSTRUCTION

From this description it is possible to generate guidelines for improving classroom instruction in speaking, listening, reading, and writing:

- Oral language must serve as the basis for all reading and writing.
- Reading and writing must always be enjoyable.

- Activities must be valid, holistic, and realistic.
- The emphasis must be on real communication—not concocted, meaningless activities focusing on isolated language elements abstracted from context and completed solely as an academic exercise.
- Children must be given an opportunity to engage in many firsthand experiences and then encouraged to employ their knowledge when reading and writing.
- Teachers should serve as models of the behavior they expect students to emulate, by using all modes of communication with students.

Teachers must structure classroom activities so that they involve listening, speaking, reading, and writing in a meaningful context. In this way, students will be encouraged to practice reading and writing in the same way they developed oral-language expertise.

STORYTELLING PLANS

I have included outlines for two story sessions. In each case student enjoyment is enhanced when the teacher chooses stories that both teller and children enjoy.

Teaching objectives vary according to age. In preschool through first grade, children learn that stories reside in people's minds or in books. They learn to predict what will happen next and to read along when parts of stories are repeated. They also develop higher-level thinking skills as they discuss art in published books and illustrate their own "big books."

In second through fourth grades children develop a functional understanding of story structure and become acquainted with the notion that folk tales naturally change from one telling to another. The students retell and write stories while improving their ability to communicate and to work cooperatively with others.

Each outline gives the content and sequence of storytelling activities. The teacher tells or reads stories, which are followed by one of several related activities. In preschool through the first grade, children analyze illustrations and produce their own pictures for the class book. In second through fourth grades the groups write and edit their own stories. (See "The Civil War as Seen Through Story," chapter 8, for a storytelling plan geared to fifth- through 12th-grade students.)

Sometimes the original stories are changed to meet the demands of the lesson. For use with preschool through first-grade students, Diane Wolkstein's original story *The Visit* (Knopf, 1977) is altered to make the "big book" version more predictable. The revised text reads:

One morning a little ant left home. She stepped over a pebble, and on she went. She walked over a stone, step by step, and on she went. She walked over a rock, step by step by step, and on she went. She walked over a boulder, step by step by step by step. And there on the other side of the boulder, she met her friend.

"Hello," he said.

"Oh, hello," she said.

They hugged and kissed and talked for hours and hours. Then it was time for the little ant to go home.

"Goodbye," he said.

"Goodbye," she said.

Then the little ant walked back over the boulder, step by step by step by step, and on she went. She walked back over the rock, step by step by step, and on she went. She walked back over the stone, step by step, and on she went. She stepped back over the pebble and got home that night and went to sleep.

The class then makes a big book as a group. (To make a big book, the teacher uses railroad board [cut to 19 inches by 25 inches] for the covers, oak tag [cut to 18 inches by 24 inches] for the pages, and binder rings to hold the book together.) The text is recorded in the big book so that the print is large enough to be seen by the entire class. The teacher leaves sufficient space on each page for the children's illustrations.

For second through fourth grades, several published variants of the folk tale "The Enormous Turnip" can serve as models for the flannel-board version: *The Turnip* by Janina Domanska (Macmillan, 1969), *The Enormous Turnip* by Kathy Parkinson (Whitman, 1986), and *The Great Big Enormous Turnip* by Alexei Tolstoy (Watts, 1968). (See "The Enormous Turnip," page 17, for a simple version.)

TYING THEORY TO PRACTICE

Both lessons employ oral-language activity as a lead-in to print activities. Students listen to the

---

A PRESCHOOL THROUGH FIRST-GRADE STORY SESSION

1. Teacher tells "The Ant's Visit" and encourages children to participate in the telling by speaking the predictable parts of the story.

2. Teacher reads big-book version of "The Ant's Visit" and encourages children to read aloud the predictable parts.

3. Teacher reads *The Visit*.

4. The class discusses illustrations: Why is it easy to see the illustrations? What shapes were used to create the ants? How can you tell one ant from another? When the ant left and returned to her home, in what direction was she headed?

5. Extension activities

   a. Children reread big book, *The Visit*.

   b. Children illustrate the book in teams of two. Each team illustrates one page, front and back, after class discussion: What medium shall we use? What color should the ants be? How can we tell them apart? Which is bigger, the boulder or pebble? The boulder or stone? The boulder or rock? The rock or stone? In what direction shall the ant go when she leaves and then returns to her home?

teacher recite, tell, or read various works—some from folklore—to begin each lesson. In all cases the print activity flows naturally from the oral language: listening, speaking, reading, and writing become integrated experiences always involving whole, meaningful texts. Attention in each activity is on meaning. Because reading and writing are enjoyable experiences for all, motivating students to read and write is easy.

The rewards are multifaceted. Teachers serve as models for student behavior and augment the children's background experience, in particular their store of knowledge about narrative structure. Students use that background knowledge to predict and create text. Because the teacher provides a basic story framework, the pupils find prediction and creation relatively easy. For example, the vegetable–problem–solution story frame makes it easy for children to create a story. As a result, students are not usually reluctant to tell a story and are rarely heard to mutter, "What should I write about?"

STORYTELLING VERSUS READING ALOUD

Although storytelling is a versatile medium of instruction, teachers are sometimes reluctant to tell stories. They may be satisfied simply to read stories aloud to children because reading aloud is a proven teaching tool, particularly when literacy training is an issue. They also say that, without question, storytelling is a more difficult skill to develop than reading aloud. It involves more risk-taking by the storyteller, who may forget what to say or deliver a story in a stumbling, rambling, disjointed manner. With no text to fall back on, no book to hide behind, storytellers expose something of their innermost personalities through the stories they choose to tell and by means of their unique style of delivery. They therefore run the risk of rejection every time they perform.

With so much at stake, why tell stories rather than read aloud? The answer is simple: storytelling is a more powerful, creative art form. It also has its own rewards. True, storytelling is more risky than reading aloud, but the

---

A SECOND-THROUGH FOURTH-GRADE STORY SESSION

1. Teacher tells "The Great Big Enormous Turnip," using a flannel board.
2. Several children volunteer to retell the turnip story, using the flannel board. After each retelling the teacher encourages the class to identify similarities and differences between the retold versions, reinforcing the notion that variation is natural and normal.
3. Extension activities
   a. Pupils name some vegetables, then select one vegetable from board list. Brainstorm potential "problems" for that vegetable; list on the chalkboard. Recall the solution to the problem in the turnip story. Brainstorm potential solutions for one chalkboard problem; list them.
   b. Teacher directs pupils to write and illustrate vegetable stories in teams of two or three. Teacher tells them to choose a vegetable, a problem, and a solution before writing and illustrating. Teacher encourages and supports revision and editing.

perceived weakness can also be viewed as a strength. No book obstructs the line of communication between teller and audience, no illustrations impede the audience's ability to concoct images along with the teller, no text limits the teller's ability to alter and personalize the telling to accommodate the audience. The audience is therefore more actively engaged in creating the story than when listening to someone reading aloud. The teller and audience co-create the story from moment to moment in a more direct, personal, and creative way than can be expected in oral readings. The result is that storytelling is more powerful and satisfying for audience and teller alike. Greater risks by teachers result in greater gains by students.

Reprinted by permission of the publisher from Blatt, Gloria, Once Upon a Folktale *(New York: Teachers College Press, copyright 1993 by Teachers College, Columbia University. All rights reserved), chapter 1 (pages 13–18, 20 and 21).*

Paul Kaiser of the Lab School of Washington, D.C., sees storytelling as play and play as the medium through which children can learn most readily. His attempts to teach story structure to children with learning disabilities by using reading, writing, storytelling, and computers yielded dramatic results.

KIDS CRAFTING FAIRY TALES

Fairy tales are one of the oldest tools for teaching children, but Paul Kaiser of the Lab School of Washington, D.C., keeps finding innovative ways of making them new. Kaiser, the head of the school's writers' lab, combines computer technology and storytelling techniques to introduce 5- to 9-year-old learning-disabled students to the skills they'll need to begin writing.

Reading and writing are hard for his pupils—who have conditions such as attention-deficit disorder and dyslexia—because of their short attention span and the "exhausting work of decoding in reading or of coordinating handwriting and spelling in writing," says Kaiser. While trying to deal with these difficulties, students often lose track of a story's content.

To help his students learn how to follow stories, Kaiser began to tell fairy tales, whose clear narrative structures, repeated plot elements, and recognizable cues helped the students progress. Still,

many of the kids found the stories difficult to understand. He needed another method to demonstrate story structure. He found it in play.

"The best way to teach is to look at where children learn the most, and that's in play," he says. "The problem is that that process is private. I tried to make it usable and communicable."

To do so, he made simple clay figures and settings that he—or the students—could move and change while telling a story. These physical cues helped the children understand the concept of setting, visualize a story's structure, and remember its chain of events.

Using these figures, twigs, and cotton wool, Kaiser created a fairy glen, the setting for "The Man Who Had No Story to Tell." In the story a rod-cutter walks into a fairy glen in search of rods to cut but finds adventures that give him a tale to tell. While telling the story, Kaiser invited the students to join in on familiar phrases as they learned them and to recap the story's action at the end. He then asked the kids to enter the fairy glen themselves and return with a story of their own to tell. As the students told their stories, Kaiser had them explain specifically how they wanted the figures and props to be set up. This gave the children practice in using formal explanatory language.

The teacher then used technology to monitor the students' progress and to give their stories tangible form. The students dictated their stories to Kaiser, who would scan photographs of their tabletop miniatures into a computer and produce printed books. "An Angel in Hell," one of the resulting stories, is an inventive, perceptive, and funny fantasy about a girl and a sheriff who rescue an angel from a devil's clutches. An excerpt: "[The devil] didn't let them see anything he had promised. Instead, he had an ugly bed, coal, and heavy-metal music. There was

Tales as Tools

65

also squeaky violin music and fingernails on the chalkboard. This was hell, and they were prisoners!"

Once the children had experience with oral storytelling, Kaiser's next task was to get them started in writing. "I found that moving the kids into the world of pure text was difficult, so I looked for an intermediate step," he says. The Macintosh software program Hypercard filled the bill. The older students now use it to draw pictures and write poems and stories that can be scanned into the program and manipulated in various ways. The activity not only gives the children experience in the use of computers but also enables them to express their feelings and mental images in ways that previously would have been difficult or impossible. Says Kaiser, "These processes give you a window on the minds of these children, whose thoughts are quite different from other people's."   —David Rhoden

From Storytelling Magazine, *fall 1991. Reprinted by permission.*

5

STORYTELLING AND WRITING

TELLING TO WRITE • 69

STORYTELLING AND WRITING

Book jackets often tout popular writers such as Stephen King as "master storytellers," alluding to the fact that writers as well as oral storytellers can tell a spellbinding tale—that storytelling and writing have a natural kinship. Teachers have long recognized this relationship between the spoken and written word but may not know how to mesh the two because they lack storytelling experience or aren't sure how to inspire young writers.

Writing is but one component of the group of skills students must employ as they explore language. Ideally the language skills—reading, writing, listening, and speaking—all work together. Students may write about what they have read or speak about what they have heard, written, or read. Often, though, children gain facility in reading but lack confidence in writing. Writing becomes a terrible chore.

Perhaps part of the problem is that writing is often taught as an end in itself. For example, writing a book report is required for its own sake rather than as a means of sharing a book the student enjoyed. The problem is exacerbated when students know that their grammar, punctuation, and spelling will be checked. Under this approach, writing becomes mere exercise rather than a means of thinking, creating, exploring, or responding to experiences. Something is missing for the student: a living connection to the words themselves.

Storytelling provides the missing link, as the storytelling-related activities in this chapter demonstrate. When storytelling in all its myriad forms is added to the curriculum, writing becomes a means to a desirable end. The articles that follow explore ways of meshing stories and writing, using a variety of forms and contexts. The key point of each is that storytelling can contribute to the teaching of writing because it is, after all, spoken literature.

TELLING TO WRITE

BY SHEILA DAILEY

Too often when creative writing is taught, the composing process begins with writing itself. As they write, students usually feel that their writing must be perfect from the start. The teacher is then at loggerheads with students, who may be very verbal yet may not have developed the skill to recognize the relationship between spoken and written language.

Writing can begin differently: first, with a structured exploration into a certain type of literature (circle stories, for instance); second, with a series of story-related activities that pattern the form the literature takes; and third, with ventures into inventing and revising orally. Only then should students write and revise what they have orally composed.

Here is a step-by-step description of the process:

- Select one of the eight basic story types (see the box that follows), and get as many examples of the type as possible from the school library. Tell the stories, read them aloud, assign silent reading, or provide an area where students can listen to recordings of the stories. The idea is to saturate students with examples of the story type.

- Encourage discussion about the tales. Explore students' likes and dislikes. Ask what makes one story better than another.

- In another session, discuss two or three tales of one story type. Invite students to find similarities among the different versions of the story.

- On the blackboard write down the plot patterns that repeat in each story. I call these a tale's bare bones.

- Brainstorm a class version of the bare bones, based on a pattern that has emerged in the story type. Developing the story as a group gives you a means of modeling the process for the students. Keep the tone light, and give suggestions rather than directions.

- Divide students into groups of three, giving each group 10 minutes to brainstorm its own version of the story. Make sure students incorporate the main elements of the story, make creative alterations, and keep to the 10-minute limit. Additional time encourages digression.

- Appoint a teller from each small group who will share the new stories with the entire class. The students will be surprised at the stories' differences and similarities. Ask for comments and critiques.

- The next stage, oral revision, is critical. Help students understand

Teachers encourage creative writing in the classroom because the process of learning to write stories, poems, and descriptive passages teaches children to think clearly, develop their imagination, and express themselves well—vital ingredients for adult life.

Tales as Tools

the revision process by asking the small groups to identify two things they like about their own stories. Next, have them name two things they'd like to change. The goal is to teach children how to work with language and ideas until they reach a satisfactory result. Students may be helped by your modeling the process, using the class story.

- Once the stories take shape, encourage the children to write them down as a group or individually. Have students practice their tales aloud in small groups, and encourage them to make further oral revisions.
- Ask them to write the story idea in full narrative form. If the students have problems at this stage, consider discussing them individually or having them read their tales aloud to the entire group for feedback.
- During a separate session, have the children rewrite to correct grammar and spelling errors. Emphasize the importance of producing a polished product. Point out that writers often make minor changes in their stories at this point. If the students want to make major changes, have them go back to oral rehearsal of the story.
- Publish the stories in some form: Tell them to students in the school's lower grades. Read them over the school's public-address system. Or turn them into a class book.

Storyteller and former teacher Sheila Dailey, the author of Putting the World in a Nutshell: The Art of the Formula Tale *(H.W. Wilson, 1994), uses folk tales as the springboard for students' fictional writing and for storytelling.*

EIGHT STORY TYPES

- Circle story: A tale that follows a circular pattern, ending just as it began. The main character learns by the end that he or she is the best or the strongest after all.
- Chain story: A tale whose form is based on a series of interrelated events. Each is a consequence of the event that precedes it.
- Fable: A brief story designed to teach a moral, usually by using animal characters. Aesop's fables and Arnold Lobel's *Fables* (Harper & Row, 1980) are good examples.
- Ghost story: A tale about a supernatural apparition. Often the apparition returns because of some unmet need—revenge, lost love, to give warning, or to regain a misplaced object.
- Scary story: A tale that focuses on fears—such as finding crocodiles in the sewer or being pursued by a one-armed man.
- Tall tale: A story in which bravado and exaggeration are the main element (e.g., tales about Paul Bunyan or Pecos Bill).
- Pourquoi, or why, story: A tale that explains the origin of some characteristic (e.g., why cats have nine lives), event, or creature.
- Myth: A story, usually about gods or demigods, that explains a natural event, the creation of the world, or the existence of a race of people. Myths differ in scale from why stories. The latter tells the origin of traits; the former deals with the creation of worlds or cosmic events.

—Sheila Dailey

Storytelling and Writing

The ability to speak fluently is an important resource as children learn to read and write. Patsy Cooper, the author of When Stories Come to School *(Teachers & Writers Collaborative, 1993), explains her technique for making students stronger readers and writers through dictating their own stories.*

SEEKING MEANING IN THE WRITTEN WORD

By Patsy Cooper

As an experienced teacher, I know that learning the letters and sounds of the alphabet may enable a child to decode a sentence, but that learning probably doesn't help the child "read" it in the advanced sense of understanding it.

True understanding of the written word is the result of a search for meaning. In my experience, dictating stories provides children with the ultimate reason to seek meaning in the written word: to discover one's own story. At first the discovery may be accidental: "Teacher, look"—pointing—"That says my name. And there's Joey's name." Children past the age of 4 or 5 who dictate stories on a regular basis, however, carefully observe the teacher's writing, like small detectives in search of some great treasure: their story in words. At the same time, dictating stories provides young storytellers with many opportunities to learn such subskills of reading as the formation of letters in a consistent manner, the

progression of words from left to right and top to bottom, discrete word spaces, and all of the other information necessary for successful decoding.

Similarly, learning to print letters is not the same as writing in the sense of conveying an idea. To be a writer is to control the form and function of print to communicate with the reader. Writing is an even more complex task than reading because writers not only have to be able to read print but also to reproduce it from memory in order to say what they have to say, which can be an arduous physical and mental task for children under 8. Becoming a writer, like becoming a reader, depends mostly on an experienced adult's inviting a child into the process. In my experience, becoming a storyteller—in the sense of using a recognizable format—is the first step in becoming a writer. An invitation to dictate a story is a great way to begin this process for the child.

My understanding of young children's early literacy development improved enormously the year I started using award-winning kindergarten teacher and author Vivian Gussin Paley's dictation activities in my kindergarten classroom. Following Paley's lead, I also used a complementary activity: the dramatization of stories written by both adults and children. I've come to appreciate their value to young children's development as readers and writers as I've used them in my classroom and helped other teachers use them in theirs. In my work with teachers, however, I am careful to point out that my interpretation of Paley's ideas is largely that—an interpretation, based on many years' experience.

Dramatization of adult-authored stories
The dramatization of adult-authored stories is a well-known activity in early childhood education, but it is used in surprisingly few preschool classrooms and hardly any primary ones. Although it lays important groundwork for children's dictation and

dramatization of their own stories, it's well worth considering as an activity with its own rightful contribution to early literacy development and the overall life of the classroom.

The first step in dramatizing adult-authored stories is for the teacher or children to choose a story to act out. Then the teacher reads the story aloud at least once, usually at a group time. When the story is finished, the teacher assigns children to play the different parts. Most teachers prefer to have the children sit in a circle. The interior of the circle thus becomes the stage. If the story has a large number of characters, it is better to limit the cast to a manageable size. Next the teacher rereads the story while the performers take up their roles. Their job is to interpret the text as best they can, with some help from the teacher and the audience. ("How would the bad wolf sound if he were pretending to be Little Red Riding Hood's grandmother?") In this type of dramatization, there are no rehearsals. There are rarely props. The idea is not so much to perform as to play. Like all good play, the drama should be spontaneous and imaginative.

Stories that please the children can be dramatized over and over again. I once directed the dramatization of "Snow White and the Seven Dwarfs" at least 12 times in a single week, changing the cast each time in order to give everyone a chance at the different parts. Paley said that her kindergarten class dramatized "The Tinderbox" 17 times over the course of the year.

When faced with time constraints, one kindergarten teacher I know has three casts acting simultaneously in different corners of the room. The important thing is to satisfy the children's desire to experiment with trading roles. Of course, some stories don't appeal to the children as much as others,

and they don't ask for those to be repeated.

When selecting stories to dramatize, teachers should keep in mind that some stories lend themselves better to this type of dramatization than others, especially in the beginning. I found that "The Carrot Seed," for example, works wonderfully for all ages on a first try, whereas "The Ugly Duckling" is far too cumbersome. Also, a story with too much dialogue will not be successful without some modification of parts. Young children can hardly be expected to memorize their lines. The same goes for lengthy narrative descriptions, which the teacher may want to shorten in order to keep the action flowing.

The dramatization of adult-authored stories accomplishes three goals. First, it provides the children with a model of "book language" and story form. Second, it furthers the presence of stories in the classroom. Once young children have had the experience of dramatizing stories, they invariably think of dramatizing a new one, thus becoming players as well as listeners in the world of stories. Finally, it sets the tone for dramatization of the children's own stories.

Children's dictating their own stories

Dictation allows each child the opportunity to tell his or her story to the teacher. The stories can be original or borrowed (from friends, the media, or a book). The teacher should feel free to ask whatever questions are necessary to help the children express themselves. ("Matthew, do you mean to say the kids went to sleep in Alaska?" "No, no. They got on a plane and went home and then they went to sleep.") The teacher's role in taking dictation is complicated. Primarily she must strive to understand what the child intends to say in the story and write it down accordingly. To do so, she must balance the scales carefully between serving as scribe and facilitator.

My experience is that children generally take three to 12 minutes to dictate their stories, depending, of course, on their age and interest. I encourage teachers to ask children to tell their stories in a regular rotation. Dictation should also occur regularly, two or three times a week. Some teachers take stories every day. A reasonable goal is to give the youngest children at least one turn every two weeks and the older ones a turn every three or four weeks.

Classrooms with 20 to 25 children simply can't squeeze any more time out of the schedule. Although the wait may be a little long between stories for the other kids, they learn a great deal from listening to their classmates tell stories as well as from the opportunity to dramatize their classmates' stories. Most teachers find it practical to impose a one-page limit on the stories. This is a sensitive point with teachers and writers who fear that the artificial limit will inhibit the children's creativity. I've never observed this to be a problem. Younger children seem to run out of steam after 10 or more minutes of storytelling (some are done in less than two minutes). Older children, who often have much more to say than a page allows, are routinely offered the opportunity to close with "to be continued."

The one-page limit helps the teacher budget his or her time for other children to have a chance. After 20 or more minutes at the storytelling table, some teachers understandably begin to get anxious about returning to the group at large. A one-page limit may be a little artificial, but the trade-off is a classroom where all the children have the opportunity to tell stories.

Dramatizing children's stories

Child-authored dramatization follows the same format as adult-authored dramatization except that most teachers I work with prefer that the author, not the teacher, choose the classmates who will be in his or her cast. Paley has revised her views on this subject. Now, in the interest of fairness, she distributes the roles in her students' stories on the basis of who's next on the list. Paley describes the events that led up to this decision in her book *You Can't Say You Can't Play* (Harvard University Press, 1992). Fairness, of course, is a central interest of young children, and Paley's book has great implications for early childhood education. But many teachers I have talked to still vote in favor of the author's making the final decision. They seem to feel that choosing one's own cast represents the only area in which children have any real control in the classroom. I urge teachers to watch the selection process carefully. If some children are routinely excluded, some intervention may be needed, at least until the pattern is broken.

The dramatization of child-authored stories is not usually repeated, for the simple reason that it doesn't need to be. Experiencing each story once with the class seems to be enough.

As is the case in adult-authored dramatization, if the text includes dialogue, the actors repeat it after the teacher. The teacher might offer technical assistance. ("Show us what you look like when you eat breakfast.") The children in the audience might offer suggestions. ("Close your eyes when you're sleeping.") Faithfulness to the text—not a polished, uninterrupted performance—is the priority.

FOLK-TALE NEWS: A WRITING ACTIVITY FOR KIDS

Reporting the news about a folk-tale character such as Pecos Bill, Little Red Riding Hood, or the troll in "The Three Billy Goats Gruff" can give you a surprising view of the character.

Here's how you do it:

- Pick a story that you have read or that you know well—for instance, "The Three Little Pigs."
- Gather the facts, then organize your notes in the pyramid shown below.

- Write the story. Give all the important facts first. Avoid big words and long sentences. Keep the story short and lively.
- Now write a headline for your story.

—Nancy Polette

From Enjoying Fairy Tales *by Nancy Polette (Book Lures, 1991). Reprinted by permission.*

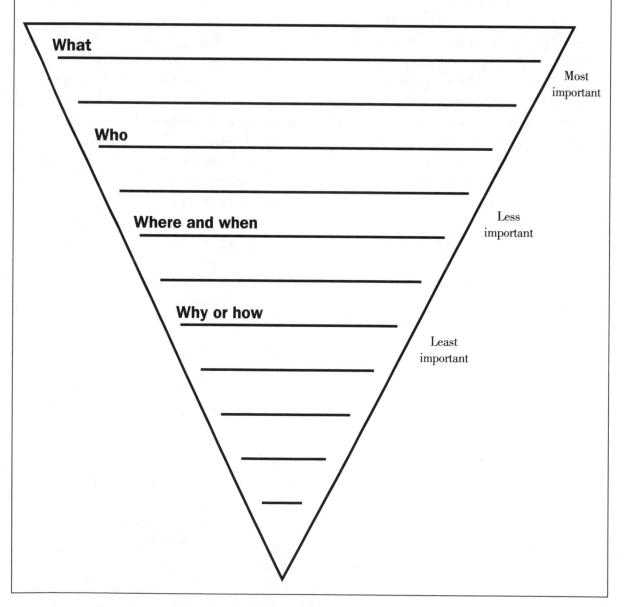

What

Most important

Who

Where and when

Less important

Why or how

Least important

TEACHING WRITING WITH FAMILY STORIES

BY SUSAN GUNDLACH

Recognizing the power and the importance of family history, I have for several years involved my eighth-grade writing classes in a project based on family lore. The assignment is called "family stories," and it requires each student to conduct at least one interview with a family member and then produce a one-page piece of writing—the family story. In addition to talking with parents, grandparents, and other relatives, the eighth-graders gather material for their stories by writing letters, researching their own memories, and sifting through family photo albums, documents, and other memorabilia.

When they have completed their research, they shift from audience to teller by shaping the information they have collected, putting it into written form, and making it their own. Thus, each student becomes a writer–storyteller of tales that illuminate for us the lives of people in past generations. Here, for example, is an excerpt from eighth-grader Eden Hall's account of her family farm:

> My great-grandparents bought the farm in Ludington, Michigan, in 1910. The land was very cheap because it had been lumbered off and was full of big stumps that took any money they had to uproot. Great-Grandmother grew tired of it because she loved fancy clothes, furniture, and jewelry, but there wasn't enough money for the stumps and the fine and fancy items. Dynamite was used to blow the stumps out of the ground, and teams of oxen or horses were used to haul them away. There is a story of a man who was dynamiting a stump and gave it an extra charge. Off it went, up into the sky and down right through the roof of a neighbor's house.

I have two goals for the family-stories assignment. First, as with all writing tasks, I want to help the students gain control over each step of the composing process—choosing a topic, gathering and organizing material, drafting, revising, and editing. The family-stories project is especially good for this purpose because it provides numerous subjects from which students may choose and virtually ensures the accessibility of large quantities of information.

The second goal, specific to this assignment, is to help students

A common complaint of students is that they have nothing to write about. Teachers Susan Gundlach and Syd Lieberman use students' personal and family histories to short-circuit that attitude and help youngsters generate ideas. In the process they learn more about themselves, their families, and one another.

establish links with their past. And I am always pleased to observe that the boundaries of their adolescent subculture are not closed to ideas that might at first seem unrelated to the immediate concerns of this age group. I find that 12- and 13-year-olds enjoy discovering and sharing the wide range of human experience that exists within their family heritage—examples of wisdom and foolishness, courage and cowardice, the determination to do what must be done. The family narratives unearthed and recorded become a source not only of entertainment but also of insight and strength to the middle-schoolers as they reflect upon those bits and pieces of family lore that help make up their own history.

To get the project off the ground, I sometimes begin by emphasizing the content of family folklore. To show that everyone possesses such material, I ask the students to reminisce about their own experiences and tell their stories to the class. Some questions we use to bring those memories to the surface are What do you remember about your first day of school? What is a memorable experience you've had with your grandparents? What was your most frightening, successful, or embarrassing moment? What are some early childhood scenes you can clearly remember? Once we start exchanging narratives, we never have enough time to hear all the stories that emerge.

Another way I have introduced this project is to invite a professional storyteller to visit our class. This approach calls attention to the forms as well as the content of storytelling. One such artist captivates the middle-schoolers with tales about her grandmother's life on the plains of Nebraska, illustrating her stories with artifacts from those times and old photos of the characters.

After three or four days of getting into the storytelling mood, the students are ready to make plans for their family-stories project. They start by jotting down in their notebooks the names of relatives they could interview and listing topics they would like to learn about ("how we got our farm," "life during the Depression," "my grandfather's emigration from Poland," "my mother's school days"). Then I ask them to select their first-choice interviewee, preferably someone who is readily available and likely to be a good conversationalist.

As we work on designing the interviews, I have the students read some family stories written by previous classes, and I direct them to a variety of appealing resources that are useful for this phase of the project: the Foxfire books (Doubleday); *A Celebration of American Family Folklore* (Pantheon, 1982) by Steven Zeitlin, Amy Kotkin, and Holly Cutting Baker; and David Weitzman's *The Brown Paper School Presents My Backyard History Book* (Little, Brown, 1975). These books not only contain instructions on how to plan and conduct successful interviews but also provide examples of completed interview-essays.

The following sequence of questions is fairly typical of those produced by the eighth-graders. This boy was interested in his mother's early school experiences.

- When and where did you attend school?
- Where was the school?
- What did the grounds and the outside of the building look like?
- How did you react to the school and its setting at the time?
- Which lower grade do you remember most clearly?
- Who was your teacher, and what did she or he look like?
- Describe the teacher's personality, including habits or mannerisms.
- What kind of child were you at that time (shy, outgoing, etc.)?
- Describe the classroom and any schoolmates you remember.
- What attitudes and values about school did your parents and the school itself pass along to you?
- What was your happiest (most discouraging, most frightening, most satisfying) experience in that grade ? Who was involved? Where did it take place? What issue did it center on? How did you feel?

Another student's questions about his father's war experiences elicited this story:

This incident took place after the war with Japan had ended, which was in August 1945. My father was in the U.S. Navy at the time. The destroyer that he was serving on, the U.S.S. *Hurst*, was ordered to the Marshall Islands in the South Pacific. It was a known fact that Japanese soldiers were hiding in caves there. My father's ship and two other destroyers, along with a group of Marines, were ordered to search the caves for these Japanese soldiers, who were called stragglers. They captured about 70 Japanese soldiers and placed them in a stockade, which had a huge 25-foot-high fence around it.

On a Saturday afternoon my father was serving as a guard at the stockade. The temperature that day was over 100 degrees. While my father was drinking ice water within sight of the Japanese, suddenly something was thrown over the fence to him. He picked it up and discovered it was a rock, and wrapped around it was a cloth that had been painted with the American flag on one side and the Japanese flag on the other. My father felt that this was a gesture of friendship and was not meant to harm him in any way. So he got some ice water and gave it to all the Japanese prisoners. They said thank you.

Although each student will want to take an individual approach to interviewing, I offer certain suggestions and admonitions that usually apply to everyone. About preparation and equipment, I advise the students to

- Make an appointment with the interviewee, even if it's Mom, and brief her about the nature of the assignment and the types of questions to expect. She will see that the interviewer is serious about doing a good job, and she'll have time to think ahead about stories and other information she wishes to tell.
- Be well prepared. Students should write out questions on notebook paper and leave space to write the responses.
- Take notes, even if they use a tape recorder. Otherwise they may forget the sequence and content of the interview. I forewarn students that transcribing tapes is a long and tedious process.

On the topics of conducting the discussion and responding to the person being interviewed, I recommend that students

- Remember to ask for background information on the person who will be featured. Specific details about where and when Great-Grandmother was born, her physical appearance, and her strongest personality traits can add a lot to the story.
- Use follow-up questions when necessary so that they can get anecdotes, not just opinions. For example, in response to the statement "life was very hard during the Depression," the student might ask, "Can you tell me about one of your most difficult experiences during that time?"
- Be flexible. Although they have a list of questions, they shouldn't cut Grandpa off in mid-sentence because he's talking about a point that's not on the list. Students shouldn't overlook good material simply because they didn't plan for it.

If family members are unavailable or unwilling to be interviewed, I have the student use himself or herself as the subject and do the project exactly as the rest of the class does. This can work out well, for it allows us to juxtapose stories from the students' generation with the accounts of parents and grandparents.

Once the planning is finished and the interviews completed, we enter the stages of organizing, drafting, and revising. We continue to do much of the work in class so that students can consult with me or one another if they have questions. For example, on the day rough drafts are due, students meet in small groups to read their papers aloud. As each member reads, the others listen carefully to determine whether the overall organization of the draft is clear. In each story we look for a vivid setting, a plot with no gaps or confusion in sequence, and characters with distinct personalities. I collect the essays, add comments and questions, and then return the papers to the students.

Publishing the final drafts is a must, for what is a story without an audience? The group's compositions can be shared in many ways: during a family-story festival within the class, with other classes, with a gathering of parents and grandparents; in a booklet; on a bulletin-board display of stories, photos, maps, and other illustrative materials. One class conducted a school assembly at which they showed slides while they read. Some of the pictures documented stages of the project, and some depicted family members in the stories.

Many of the students' stories center on incidents from the lives of immigrant grandparents or great-grandparents. One student re-created this moment:

When my ancestors came to America, my great-grandfather, Mr. Reuben, had an unusual experience. He was 15 or 16 then and had given up his life in Lithuania and come to America on a boat. He knew no English, had no job, and knew no one. So when he arrived, he immediately sought work. A man who knew his language played a joke on him and told him to say these words when asking for a job: "How about a date, hot stuff?"

Mr. Reuben said he was forever indebted to the man and set out to find a job. He went around, knocking on strangers' doors, uttering the magical sentence. At one doorway his question brought a loud shriek. Then a big, husky man came out and chased him for miles and miles to a strange town . . .

Because the family-stories project usually generates much interest and enthusiasm, grading the students' work often seems anticlimactic. But it's a job that must be done. I base my evaluation on three criteria: the student's attitude and effort throughout the process, the form and content of the final draft, and the complexity of a given project—the last consideration meant to encourage more ambitious attempts, not to penalize students who fulfill the minimum requirements of one interview and one story.

How can this project's success be determined? One measure, obviously, is the quality of the stories, and given the time and energy the students devote to the assignment, the quality is usually very good. So if the students produce engaging, well-written pieces, my first goal—helping them manage the writing process—has been reached.

Attainment of the second goal is more difficult to assess. Have the eighth-graders gained some insight into their roots, established some continuity between previous generations and their own, and developed a sense of the importance of making those connections? I look for evidence that the students have been part of those special moments when memories come to life. And I think there are at least three ways during the course of the project in which they can do so: as listeners during the interviews, as writers of the stories they collect, and as tellers.

The students' observations and reflections show that many have indeed been able to participate in storytelling experiences that join the generations: "My grandmother enjoyed talking to me about our relatives. She seemed happy that someone was interested in her family." "I got a better understanding of my grandmother and great-aunt. It was sort of like reading an autobiography." "One of my greatest joys was when my great-grandfather called me from Japan, replying to my letter." Whether such moments last for only the duration of a long-distance phone call or in a form that will surface later, for retelling to new generations, I cannot presume to know. But that the moments have occurred means to me that my second goal for the project has been reached.

Projects such as this hold many implications for teaching. The compelling nature of narrative and the students' keen interest in family history suggest that adapted versions of the assignment might be used effectively in different ways throughout the curriculum. For example, in English classes, family stories fit nicely into lessons on writing, reading, speaking, and literature; in social studies, into units on immigration, ethnic heritage, and specific historical time periods. In the arts, family stories might be the basis for oral storytelling, dramatic productions, painting and drawing, or puppetry. And in science, students might do research through their families on advances in technology or changes in ecology. Whatever the subject, chances are that it can be enriched by the humanizing, personalizing touch of family stories.

From *The National Storytelling Journal*, fall 1986. Reprinted by permission.

BRAINSTORMING FOR SELF-DISCOVERY

By Syd Lieberman

Students in junior high and high school are in the identity business. Storytelling is a wonderful method for helping them discover who they are because it allows them to talk about a familiar subject: themselves.

But one problem you will face is getting them to understand that they actually have stories to tell. We've all heard the universal cry, "Nothing ever happens to me." Here are three ways to address this problem.

The first is to use the following topics in brainstorming sessions with students. The topics represent categories of stories, and the first nine are the chapter headings in a book called *A Celebration of American Family Folklore* (Pantheon, 1982) by Steven Zeitlin, Amy Kotkin, and Holly Cutting Baker. Zeitlin collected a number of oral histories and discovered that people like to tell stories about certain subjects, so the authors organized the book around them. The last nine categories are ones I have used successfully.

- Heroes. Concentrate on both small kindnesses and heroic deeds. These are usually touching tales.
- Rogues. Look for stories about really bad guys. I'm often shocked at the kinds of people and situations kids face.
- Mischief makers. I focus on funny pranks. Memories about siblings, Halloween, and junior high seem to be good sources.
- Survivors. I tell students that these stories can be about true survival or about surviving something like a boring evening with relatives.
- Innocence. I have often been surprised at how readily students will tell you about times when they were really naive.
- Migrations and trips. Students love to write about where they used to live or how it felt coming to a new city or country. Family vacations also produce great stories.
- Lost fortunes. "If my grandfather had not sold the land, today my family would own downtown Aspen . . . . "
- Family feuds. Be careful of this one. I stress the lighter battles between siblings.
- Names. Nicknames are fun, but many students also have stories about their first and last names.
- Firsts. You can pick an area to concentrate on (e.g., the first time on a roller coaster) or focus on any first.
- Mosts. The most embarrassing time, the scariest time, and so on.
- Life-cycle events. From birth to death, we mark our lives by such events. This is a good area to look at early on.
- Courtship. Many students will want to talk about their own relationships. I also get them to interview their parents and grandparents.
- Objects. We cherish special objects in our lives. The story's focus is usually how the student got the object.
- Mannerisms. Sometimes people behave in ways that define their personality. Quirky people make for good stories.
- Disgusting things. A student told me I should add this category, and the rest of the class agreed.
- Pets. I can't tell you the number of papers I've

received from sophisticated high-school students that deal with the death of a pet.

- Holiday tales. See life-cycle events.

A second way to prime the pump is to give students themes to write about. Garrison Keillor used the following themes for his tales about Lake Wobegon that were broadcast on American Public Radio, but you and your students can add others.

- We're only human
- Home is where the heart is
- Renewal, spiritual growth, insight
- Childhood
- Growing up
- Temptation
- Breaking the rules
- Love of family
- Tolerance for others
- Sacrifice
- Shyness

A third method I use is to have my students focus on the themes in their reading. For instance, when a class is reading William Golding's *Lord of the Flies* (Coward-McCann, 1962), I ask them whether they have ever experienced a "Jack" or a "Ralph" inside themselves. They can then tell the story of a time when they did something evil or stood up for a principle even if it made them unpopular. Such a book can help provoke their tales. If it does, you will have done more than help the students write a story. You will have enabled them to see the connection between literature and life.

Syd Lieberman of Evanston, Illinois, is an award-winning teacher and a nationally known storyteller. In 1986 the Foundation for Excellence in Teaching presented him with the Golden Apple Award for his work in the classroom. His audiotapes have garnered four awards from the American Library Association and two from Parents' Choice *magazine. Because of his writing ability, the town of Johnstown, Pennsylvania, and the Smithsonian Institution have commissioned Lieberman to create stories for them. He is the author of the children's book* The Wise Shoemaker of Studena *(Jewish Publication Society, 1994).*

6

STORYTELLING, SPEAKING, AND LISTENING

STORYTELLING, SPEAKING, AND LISTENING

> *"Three apples fell from heaven: One for the teller, one for the listener, and one for the one who heeds the tale."*
>
> —Armenian saying

In the Armenian tradition storytelling involves a listener, a speaker, and one—speaker or listener—who understands the tale deeply enough to act on its meaning. This is wisdom we can all benefit from. In the modern classroom many teachers feel students do not listen well, do not heed them.

Perhaps a partial solution to the problem lies in simple practice of the arts of listening and speaking by turns. Both listening and speaking involve several activities at the same time: language, thought, sensory awareness. Use of these faculties in a setting in which they are valued can yield amazing results with children who formerly showed poor speaking and listening skills.

Storytelling provides much-needed experience in speaking and listening. While a story is told, members of the audience are called to listen actively, imaginatively, and responsively—regardless of their age. One has only to be present during storytelling and to hear the powerful stillness to know that students truly attend to every word.

Most classroom listening does not require this high level of mental activity. When a lecture or demonstration is being given, students often listen with only half an ear because the information is communicated in abstractions; the whole mind is not engaged. When teachers incorporate a story or anecdote into instruction, however, both hemispheres of the brain are engaged. The results are usually better listening, higher comprehension of the material, and better recall.

Teaching students to tell stories is another approach to enhancing their speaking and listening skills. Much of this chapter deals with training students to become storytellers, as performers or simply as participants in stories the teacher tells.

Teaching Children to Tell Stories

By Martha Hamilton and Mitch Weiss

Children love listening to stories, and they gain many skills from doing so. When they learn to tell stories, the benefits are even greater. Learning to tell a story builds confidence and poise, improves expressive language skills, stimulates inventive thinking, builds listening skills, and develops an appreciation of other people, places, and cultures. Children experience personal growth through risk-taking. Best of all, when they bring books to life through storytelling, children gain a love of language and stories that is theirs for keeps.

One of the secrets to motivating children to tell stories is making storytelling look like so much fun that they want to try it. Show them videos of storytellers, invite storytellers to your school, and most important, try telling a story yourself. Stories need not be told perfectly in order to succeed, as children are a forgiving audience. Even student tellers recognize this. At the end of one of our storytelling residencies, one fifth-grader wrote: "I learned while telling my story in front of my class or other classes that they really didn't care how many mistakes I made. They just liked having me or anyone else tell them a story."

Children can actively participate in storytelling in many ways. One good way to get started is to have students retell stories they've heard you or another storyteller tell. When you see how much they enjoy retelling, you can move on to a unit in which students go to the library and choose their own stories to tell.

RETELLING STORIES

Children learn naturally by imitation, and retelling stories they've heard is a valuable and fun language activity for any age. As a teacher, you provide an important model, so be sure to put expression in your voice and on your face. If you're looking for a simple story that even very young children will enjoy retelling, try "The Dark Wood," a traditional folk tale:

In a dark, dark wood was a dark, dark house,
and in that dark, dark house was a dark, dark room,
and in that dark, dark room was a dark, dark closet,
and in that dark, dark closet was a dark, dark shelf,

Telling stories to students can be rewarding for the teacher. Helping children learn to tell their own tales can have even more positive results. Martha Hamilton and Mitch Weiss, also known as Beauty and the Beast Storytellers, know that teaching children to tell stories is tremendously empowering for youngsters—and also helps teachers accomplish their curricular goals.

and on that dark, dark shelf was a dark, dark box,
and in that dark, dark box was a—
Ghost!

Before telling, darken the room to create the right atmosphere. Tell the story very slowly, putting in every bit of spooky expression you can muster, especially in the repetition of the eerie words *dark, dark*. Use simple gestures and movements to act out the scene. Look around as if you are in the middle of a creepy, dark forest, then as if you suddenly see a house, and so on. As you get near the end, lean a little closer to the children. Pretend to open the box very slowly and then say *Ghost!* as if you are really startled.

After telling the story, review by asking What happened first? and What happened next? It's helpful to make a brief outline on the board. For nonreaders, do the outline in picture form.

Let students retell in small groups. They can tell the story in round-robin fashion or with one student serving as the narrator while others take speaking roles or even mime roles. You could also let them retell with a partner and then ask for volunteers to tell the story in front of the whole group.

CHOOSING THE STORY

If the children you're working with are old enough, the next step is to have them choose stories to tell (see the lists in chapter 13). Story choice is an important component of their success as storytellers. For some this may mean choosing a story no longer than three or four sentences. Other children may be drawn to stories that fill their emotional needs and reflect their ethnic heritage. The most important quality of the story is that it be one a student really loves and chooses independently. Try the following tips to guide your students' selections.

Select a pool of stories for younger children and those who have never told a story. Try to have at least 50 stories for a classroom of 25 students. Few children know their own capabilities. Some children can read far beyond the level of story they can tell orally, whereas some poor readers are excellent storytellers. Your gentle guidance will help. It is better for a child who has difficulty learning or who is shy to tell a five-sentence story and feel successful than to struggle with a longer, more complicated one and end up not telling it.

Students should consider the audience before choosing a story. Eighth-graders, for example, might want to choose stories to tell primary-school children, or they might feel more comfortable with spine-

Storytelling, Speaking, and Listening

tingling ghost stories for sixth-, seventh-, or eighth-graders.

Each student should tell a different story. The children will work intensely with the stories, hearing the same ones again and again as they listen to their classmates practice. Using a sign-up sheet helps avoid duplication of stories.

When you have extremely reluctant students, take them aside and help them pick a very short but very good story. For example, Arnold Lobel's "The Bad Kangaroo" from *Fables* (Harper & Row, 1980) is such a crowd-pleaser that other students will beg to hear it again and again. You can't force students to tell a story, but with some encouragement, they'll almost always come around eventually.

LEARNING THE STORY

Every storyteller has his or her own way of learning a story. The following suggestions can help students discover what works best for them.

Have students read their story over and over again. Some tellers find it helpful to tape the story and listen to it several times.

Have students make a pictorial outline of their story. Once they know the sequence, they won't fear getting lost as they tell the tale. The idea is to do a series of quick, simple drawings (stick figures are fine) that will help tellers remember events in the correct order. They can use the outline to tell the story the first few times.

Pictorial outlines help students make a story their own and tell it in their own words. Instruct students to use simple, powerful language that conveys a feeling in harmony with the story's style. Suggest that they consider the time and place of the story and avoid using language or expressions that would destroy the mood.

Some students find it difficult to do anything but memorize the story, but they run a greater risk of being tense or "blanking" in the middle of the story if they forget one word. Others who memorize do a marvelous job and can sound quite spontaneous. Memorizing is not necessarily wrong: it is a useful exercise in discipline. But most children learn much more if they tell a story in their own words, even if the telling is not as polished as it would be if they memorized the story.

Students might find it helpful to tell their story to a mirror. This lets them see themselves as their audience will see them. Have them try telling their story to an imaginary audience or to pets, stuffed animals, or plants. Next suggest that they try family or friends, a small group of classmates, then half the class, and finally the whole class.

TELLING THE STORY

There is no one right way to tell a story, but you can give your students guidelines and help them avoid certain pitfalls. Some suggestions and exercises follow.

Voice • The voice is a storyteller's most important tool, and it must be filled with expression. The storyteller must always be aware of the tone or mood being conveyed to the audience. Have students say, "I lost my homework" in a voice that is sad, happy, frustrated, furious, boasting, nervous, sleepy, rude, apologetic, and lazy.

The speed at which students speak should vary throughout the story. Have students repeat the sentence "The snow is falling, and school has been called off today" quickly to convey excitement, slowly to show disappointment, and at a moderate rate to simply state a fact.

Demonstrate the effect of pauses in storytelling by saying the following sentence: "There was a loud knock at the door, and when she opened it, there stood [pause] a strange old man with a long gray beard." Ask students what they were thinking or imagining during the pause and how the telling would have been different without it. Help students overcome the discomfort they may feel during pauses by having them count to three in their heads before speaking again.

The pitch of the teller's voice is an excellent tool not only for indicating different emotions but also for portraying different characters in a story. Have students say, "Someone's been eating my porridge" the way they think Papa Bear would say it. Then have them say, "Someone's been eating my porridge, and he ate it all up!" in Baby Bear's voice. Now have them think about the characters in their own stories. Is it appropriate to change the pitch of their voice for any of them?

Facial expression • Good facial expression is essential to a well-told story. Demonstrate this by telling part of a story that the children have heard you tell before—this time without using your voice. You can also show a few minutes of a videotaped storytelling performance with the sound turned off.

Gestures and movements • Whether to use gestures can be a tricky topic with beginning tellers. The best advice you can give students is to keep their telling simple and do what comes naturally. When they rehearse their stories, they should be able to justify and explain any gestures they use. If they cannot explain a gesture, they should eliminate it. The following exercises can help students loosen up, develop their imagination, and learn to use their body to communicate feelings.

Have students try "saying" these sentences without speaking: "Watch out!" "I'm so cold." "Come on in!" "I'm not sure of the answer." "I am so mad!" "Do you expect me to believe that?" "I'm so sorry."

Have students stand in a circle. Have the students walk in circular formation, and as they do, call out different situations that will change their walking pattern. For example: "Pretend to walk home from school, knowing that when you get there you will have to do all your chores . . . across the schoolyard after a foot of snow has fallen . . . barefoot through a very sticky, squishy swamp . . . through honey . . . with your right foot in a cast."

Beginnings and endings • At the beginning of a play the curtain opens, alerting the audience that something is about to happen. Storytellers must create the same kind of feeling by making eye contact with listeners and pausing for a moment.

Students should think in advance about how they will introduce their stories. Have them practice by introducing themselves. The introduction might include the title of the story, its country of origin, and its author's name. In general, the introduction should not be long.

Endings are equally important, and students must be taught how to respond to the audience when a story is finished—for instance, accepting applause gracefully.

COPING WITH STAGE FRIGHT

The nervous energy students feel during a performance is perfectly natural. Pre-performance anxiety can spur us to prepare well, get our energy going, and make us come across as vibrant and enthusiastic. As one fifth-grader wrote: "Speaking in front of a group is not all that scary as long as you know what you're talking about. You have to learn your story well, and that teaches you responsibility."

The more you talk about students' anxieties, the less discomfort they will feel about telling their stories. Share with students your own experiences of feeling nervous and let the children talk about when they've felt that way. Remind students that everyone has been given the same assignment. When someone gets up to tell a story, he or she faces a roomful of sympathetic listeners. This supportive atmosphere will go a long way in helping to dissipate stage fright.

Let your students know it's only natural to stumble over a word here and there. Tellers should correct the mistake if they think it's necessary and then go on—but they must never apologize to the audience. One fifth-grader was telling "The Lucky Man" from Maria Leach's *The Thing at the Foot of the Bed and Other Scary Tales* (World Publishing, 1959), in which a man shoots his nightshirt as it hangs on the clothesline, all the time thinking it is a ghost. The boy telling it said, "He shot it five times; no, it was 10 times." Then he laughed and said, "Well . . . he shot it a lot of times." If tellers laugh at themselves and take everything in stride, the audience will remain relaxed and continue to enjoy the show.

CULMINATION

The more opportunities children have to tell their stories, the more they can perfect their telling and the more comfortable and confident they will become in front of groups. A great way to complete a storytelling project is to have an evening performance for family and friends. We have always done this on a strictly voluntary basis because a group of parents is probably the students' most difficult audience. The kids won't find more supportive or responsive listeners, but the prospect of telling to adults can be unnerving.

Some children rise to the occasion and tell their stories better than ever; others regress. One sixth-grader wrote: "The hardest thing I've ever done was getting up to tell my story all by myself in front of my class and all those parents that night. But it was also the best thing that ever happened in my life when everyone in the audience applauded for me. I felt so good and warm inside. Now I know how it feels to be famous." That kind of confidence lingers and spills over into other aspects of children's lives.

Parental response to the evening of stories has always been very positive. As one mother said, "I can't believe my daughter got up there all by herself and told her story in front of a whole group of people. She didn't even seem scared. I would have been terrified!"

If you can relate to that parent's fear but still want to learn how to tell stories and teach children to tell them, take this sage advice from a second-grader: "Pick a story. Read it three times. Then tell it to someone without the book. It is scary at first, and then you get used to it. You should try it. It's fun!"

Martha Hamilton and Mitch Weiss perform professionally as Beauty and the Beast Storytellers at schools, libraries, conferences, museums, and festivals throughout the United States, Canada, and Europe. They are the authors of Children Tell Stories: A Teaching Guide *(Richard C. Owen, 1990), which won an Anne Izard Storytellers' Choice Award.*

HELPING KIDS LEARN
TO LISTEN

BY NANCY BRIGGS AND JOSEPH WAGNER

Children who are poor listeners frequently have this habit well-established before they enter a classroom. If parents greet their children's efforts to speak with such responses as, "Not now, Junior; can't you see I'm busy?" or "Come back after this program is over" or "Please be quiet; can't you do anything but ask questions?" rejected juvenile communicators may learn to look upon negativism as a normal response as they attempt to communicate orally.

Parents who lack the patience to work sympathetically with children as they struggle for the skill to express their feelings may find themselves rewarded with inattention. They will hear themselves saying, "Can't you get anything right?" "I've told you six times to close the door!" or "Is there something wrong with your ears?" In the last instance the parent might inadvertently have asked an intelligent question.

Assuming that children have normal hearing, they, not their parents or teachers, control the learning process. Children possess the power to "turn off" their ears when they become exhausted or lose interest.

It has been indicated that listening is a reciprocal process between a sender and a receiver. In order to learn to listen, a child must have an attentive listener who is genuinely interested. Kindergarten teachers report that their good listeners usually have a mother or other caregiver who listens sympathetically and carefully when they speak.

The climate for learning established by a classroom teacher has a significant effect on the learning process. Even though teachers are not formally trained in listening techniques, if they develop a warm, friendly atmosphere with their pupils, they find that learning through attentive listening takes place. Children may develop poor listening habits in a hostile classroom environment because they feel threatened by the teacher, the group, or both.

For years it was believed that listening depended on the ability to hear and the child's intelligence and that schools could do little about either. This is equivalent to saying that reading ability depends only on eyesight and intelligence. Equally erroneous was the point of view that practice and intelligence were the only significant components of efficient listening. Although most of a child's day is devoted to activities that require listening skill, there has been inadequate training in this

Effective listening is an important component of literacy. When children lag behind in this area, it can affect their entire educational experience. The best approach to solving the problem may be to adjust one's teaching to meet students' needs. Nancy Briggs and Joseph Wagner discuss some of the causes of poor listening skills and make suggestions for encouraging better listening.

area. Teachers and curriculum builders have assumed that because children could hear, they could automatically listen and comprehend.

Obviously it is an error to assume that listening, especially on complex levels, is something that children do naturally. Training must go beyond teachers' well-meaning admonitions, "Now, children, please pay attention" and "Please listen carefully." Teachers must appreciate some of the problems encountered in listening.

In reading, for example, children are able to adjust their speed to the material's degree of difficulty. When they listen, however, such adjustment is not possible because the speaker sets the pace, and listeners must try to follow.

Another cause of poor listening behavior may be instructional procedure. Children are not challenged and stimulated by a dull rehash of textbook assignments that frequently terminates in a ping-pong–style question-and-answer period. If a teacher can perform the difficult task of personalizing instruction, that is, show children why subject matter is important to them, the teaching of listening is simplified. Although they make up only a fraction of the school day, periods devoted to storytelling, role-playing, and creative dramatics can contribute much toward the growth of good listening habits among children.

TELLING AND LISTENING

Because so much attention is devoted to promoting group-mindedness among schoolchildren, it is helpful to examine storytelling's contribution to acceptable group listening behavior. Those who have worked with children know that they are easily distracted by miscreants in a group. On the other hand, story interest can be so high that the group can exert considerable pressure for conformity upon a mischievous youngster. When listening is the thing to do, more children will listen!

Many factors enter into the degree of empathetic response a class registers for a story. Among these are the several items involved in choosing the right story for a particular age group, the preparation of a story, the mode of presentation, and the use of visual aids. Good listening results from the interrelation of these factors.

The following suggestions will help make telling and listening close companions. Storytellers must be sensitive to signs of poor listening as they tell their story. Shuffling of feet, whispering, and yawning are overt indications that the children's attention has strayed. More subtle signs of inattention, however, are equally important. The vacant stare, although not distracting to other members of the class, indicates a lack of interest.

Teachers who are constantly alert to these and other signs of inattention will be better communicators. They will want to determine why certain children are not listening and will make special efforts to accommodate them in the next story. For example, after school the teller might ask the child if he or she enjoyed the story. Regardless of the answer (which would probably be a defensive affirmative), the teller might ask the student to help choose a story for the next session.

Objective teachers will also analyze their own presentation for possible causes of inattention. The proper technique for storytelling is interpretation rather than acting. Thus, throughout a presentation, the emphasis is on the story and the reaction of those who hear it. Fortunately, unlike actors, who play before a darkened house, storytellers interpret in a well-lit classroom where they can see listeners' responses. If tellers adapt to the needs of the group and are expressive with face and voice, the larger, overt physical gyrations of actors are not necessary to encourage maximum listening.

IMPROVING LISTENING EFFECTIVENESS

Wherever groups of children gather to hear stories, adults discover considerable variation in youngsters' ability to think as they listen, separate key ideas as the story progresses, and relate the appropriate ones to their lives. An experiment in critical listening found that there appears to be an independent ability (or abilities) to listen critically. The study concludes, encouragingly, that listening ability can be improved by practice. The following exercises are designed to assist this process.

- Assuming that there are 24 children, have them form three groups by counting off 1, 2, 3, 1, 2, 3, and so on. Arrange

---

A PICTURE AND A THOUSAND WORDS

Grade level: K–3

Objective: To learn a simple story from pictures

Procedure: Use wordless picture books to stimulate storytelling. Students tell the story using their own words. Some favorite books are

Ardizzonne, Edward, *The Wrong Side of the Bed*, Doubleday, 1970

Carle, Eric, *Do You Want to Be My Friend?*, Thomas Crowell, 1971

Day, Alexandra, *Good Dog, Carl*, Green Tiger Press, 1985

Felix, Monique, *The Story of a Little Mouse Trapped in a Book*, Green Tiger Press, 1980

—, *The Further Adventures of the Little Mouse Trapped in a Book*, Green Tiger Press, 1983

Goodall, John, *The Surprise Picnic*, Atheneum, 1977

—, *Shrewbettina's Birthday*, Harcourt Brace Jovanovitch, 1970

Hutchins, Pat, *Changes, Changes*, Macmillan, 1971

Mayer, Mercer, *Two More Moral Tales*, Four Winds Press, 1974

—, *Frog on His Own*, Dial, 1973

—, *Frog, Where Are You?*, Dial, 1969

—, *A Boy, a Dog, and a Frog*, Dial, 1967

Morris, Terry Nell, *Goodnight, Dear Monster*, Random House, 1980

From Look What Happened to Frog: Storytelling in Education *by Pamela J. Cooper and Rives Collins, published by Gorsuch Scarisbrick. Copyright 1992 by Pamela J. Cooper and Rives Collins. Reprinted by permission.*

each group of eight, one child behind the next, facing the front of the room. Whisper a short message to the first child in each line. Ask him or her to relay the material, in a whisper, to the child next in line. Continue this process until the message has been passed to every child. Ask the last child to repeat aloud what he or she heard and compare it with the original statement whispered to the first child. In this exercise, the listening drill begins with the count-off. After playing this game several times, children call out their number more accurately and quickly, and the accuracy of the whispered message improves.

- Play "find my drawing" (or toy) placed on the chalkboard ledge. One child describes an object, and the teacher permits a volunteer to bring it to its owner.
- Tell a story, and encourage the children to draw a picture of a character, a scene, and so on.
- After playing a song, ask for a volunteer to describe the story behind the song.
- Read a short paragraph that contains an idea that doesn't belong, and ask the children to identify it.
- In all group activities, make a policy of not repeating instructions. If repetition is necessary, call on the children to repeat what was said.
- Give a series of instructions to the group, increasing the difficulty of the action as you go—for example, "Kristi, take the book from my desk, and place it on the table." To the next participant, "Jack, take the book from the table, turn to page 20, and show the picture to Shannon." The game continues until someone fails to follow instructions properly. Teachers should tailor the instructions to fit the intelligence level of the child they plan to call.
- Play a tape of familiar sounds, for example, a boat whistle, a church bell, traffic, ocean waves striking the beach, birdcalls, sirens, and so on. More sophisticated sounds may be played to older children.
- If a story being told contains a repetitive rhyme, encourage children to join in.
- Sensitize children to the daily sounds about them, for example, bird songs, laughter, the sound of a jump rope striking the ground, the sound of skateboard wheels, and so on.

From Children's Literature Through Storytelling and Drama, *second edition, by Nancy E. Briggs and Joseph A. Wagner. Published by William C. Brown. Copyright 1979 by Nancy E. Briggs and Joseph A. Wagner. Reprinted by permission.*

Participatory Storytelling:
A Partnership Between Storyteller
and Listener

By Peninnah Schram

Participatory storytelling is an excellent way to fine-tune listening and concentration skills because of the partnership, the bond, the trust that are established between students and the teacher or storyteller. Not every story can be adapted with the options I present, nor should every story be a verbal or visual participation story. Remember, stories involve active imaginative listening, even when the listener is silent. These creative dramatic suggestions for storytelling can add fun and encourage active learning, as well as release students' excess energy and activate their imaginations even more.

Sound effects

In the classroom, at the moment the storyteller wants the audience to produce a sound effect (which can be introduced before the story begins), the teller should indicate through hand motions or verbal directions what the listeners are to do. For example, if the children should sound like the wind, the teller can practice wind sounds before the story by waving down to indicate lower volume, each hand going to the side to indicate stopping the sound. Students of all ages follow such commands with great eagerness. Rehearsing before the story accomplishes five objectives: getting students to follow directions, to cooperate, to know what to listen for, to feel part of the experience, and to feel responsible for the story.

During the story, at the moment you want listeners to produce a sound effect, use verbal cues (for example, "and the wind began to blow"), or signal with your face and hands so the audience knows exactly when to begin, how long to keep the sound going (even while you continue to tell the story), and when to stop.

Sound effects do involve some risks and must be used with discretion. When they are used too often, they can be overdone or break the story's continuity or even create chaos in the classroom. The interference can cause the children to get carried away. Caution: Avoid the use of sound effects when there is a fragile quiet moment in a story or when the sound is mentioned only once. Do not introduce sound effects every time a sound is indicated in a story.

Here are five possibilities for incorporating sound effects into stories.

Not all stories involve only listening. Many tales in the folklore tradition are participation stories that involve singing, call and response, or listening for the right moment to join in. Storyteller and author Peninnah Schram offers tips on how teachers can invite student participation in stories.

- Animal (including bird and bee) sounds. Children can add the appropriate sound effect whenever the animal appears in the story.
- Weather sounds (especially wind and rain). To produce rain sounds, snap your fingers, clap or rub your hands, rub or tap your thighs. You can add the blowing sound of wind to the rain sounds too.
- Door and window sounds—such as closing, knocking, or tapping.
- Noises such as stamping of feet—to be used whenever a villain is mentioned or to represent a commotion.
- Simultaneous sounding of phrases along with the storyteller. The children can join in whenever these phrases occur. Magical spells and song refrains can also be added when it is appropriate.

MOVEMENT AND GESTURES

As with sound effects, movements can be used to add a physical dimension to the storytelling. The same kinds of word cues or hand signals can be given to indicate what's needed. Students can be very creative in suggesting movements to be adapted for the story. Such an exercise is also excellent for incorporating sign language, improvised sign language, or pantomime for the action that is to be highlighted by movement. Pantomime gestures for birds flying, the sun or moon rising and setting, stars twinkling, candles burning, and so on can be both beautiful and expressive.

Here are some possibilities for gestures:
- Birds or bees flying, spiders spinning a web, fish swimming
- The rising or setting of the moon or sun
- Gesture or sign language used whenever a certain word or phrase is repeated (the gesture can be made simultaneously)
- Pantomime of activities such as picking flowers, listening to seashells, making pottery, kneading dough, and eating
- The character's actions, such as closing eyes, putting hands on head, rubbing forehead, peeling a banana, milking a cow.

MUSIC

Music is an integral part of many cultures, so it is often part of storytelling as well. You may choose to introduce folksongs or melodies from various cultures to the class or to use a song the class knows but in a different context. It is important to be faithful to the spirit and source of the story in choosing melodies. You can be creative, however, when you look for a point in a story where song can be introduced. As is often the case when using sound and gesture, you may first want to teach the children the song or melody. Then indicate, through verbal and nonverbal cues, when the song should begin, whether you are using the melody at the beginning or end or during the story itself, and when you want it to end (either by fading away or abruptly stopping).

A melody can be sung or hummed with great effect at various points during a story:

- When people walk from place to place or ride in a carriage or train, they can be singing (although the song might be a sad one). The class can compose melodies or rhythmic sound effects and use them to segue from one part of the story to the next.

- Many stories include a mother's putting a baby to sleep or children's going to sleep. Add a verse of a lullaby from the appropriate culture.

- Magic formulas can be sung or chanted rhythmically or perhaps told as a rap. The class can compose a melody to the words.

- You and the students can research various holiday songs to add to stories.

- While the characters in a story are hammering, kneading dough, laboring in the fields, gardening, and so on, they could be singing a work song related to the task or what they're thinking and feeling. The song could become a subtext of the story.

- Each time a character comes to the next episode, a refrain or theme song can be repeated as a link between episodes, especially in chain or circle stories (see page 70 for definitions of these story types). The music creates movement into the next episode or the next story in the program.

SUPPLYING ENDINGS AND SOLVING RIDDLES

In a cumulative tale, several characters each help to bring about the resolution of the problem. Such a story has a built-in stopping point at which the storyteller can ask the audience, "Who deserves to win the cow-tail switch?" or "Who should win the hand of the princess in marriage?" In some cultures, members of the audience hear the story often and know the story's ending, yet they are asked to offer their ideas at each hearing. At the beginning you can indicate that you will need listeners' help in completing the story by saying, "Here is a story with a problem or riddle that needs solving. At some point in the story I will stop so you can help solve the problem."

Active listening, an acquired skill, challenges the child. The answers are not as important as the process of determining the answer. Therefore the storyteller should ask, "Why did you choose this answer?" and focus on the reasoning behind the answer. At the end I often add, "All the answers were right; they just belong to another story. So write your own story with those answers, and tell it in your own way." Indeed, older students can do this and share those stories with the class another time. They might also write a modern-day version of a cumulative riddle story.

This method of involving the audience builds suspense, encourages the use of imaginative reasoning and listening, and is indeed very instructive.

ACTIVITIES FOLLOWING A STORY

Discussion or debate following a story, although not part of every storytelling experience, can sometimes be used effectively as an extension of it. Controversial themes and open-ended stories without a resolution serve to stimulate discussion of values and actions. The cumulative or riddle story is one type that can be followed by discussion.

Keep in mind, however, that a follow-up discussion, which needs time, should not always take place after each story. Sometimes such analysis can rob the story and the storytelling experience of their joy and their power for self-discovery.

Several published anthologies offer follow-up activities to stories. They are listed in the bibliography in chapter 13 under the heading PARTICIPATORY STORYTELLING.

Stories and storytelling open up worlds of possibilities to a child. So allow a story, simply told, to be a gift. At other times, however, you may want to explore a theme or character in a story more fully through participatory storytelling. All of these suggestions can help strengthen the vital skills of imagination, listening, and concentration. And most important, through the experience of sharing storytelling activities, a community of friends is created in the classroom.

Storyteller and author Peninnah Schram is an associate professor of speech and drama at Stern College of Yeshiva University in New York City. She travels throughout the United States and other countries, presenting storytelling workshops and performing Jewish stories and cross-cultural tales, involving listeners through the stories' wit and wisdom. Schram has been a featured teller at the National Storytelling Festival. Her books include Jewish Stories One Generation Tells Another *(Jason Aronson, 1987) and* Tales of Elijah the Prophet *(Jason Aronson, 1991). She is the founding director of the Jewish Storytelling Center.*

7

USING STORIES TO TEACH ABOUT PEACE AND THE ENVIRONMENT

USING STORIES TO TEACH
ABOUT PEACE AND THE ENVIRONMENT

Mounting international concern about the condition of the earth and its people has made teachers aware of the need to make environmental awareness and peace studies a part of the curriculum. Yet few standard curricula include the topics. How should teachers approach complex subjects such as military escalation and global warming? Is it really teachers' responsibility to do so?

In traditional cultures young children are routinely taught to understand and be responsible for their relationship to their community, to those beyond the community, and to the earth itself. Taking such responsibility is considered part of being a good person. The traditional storyteller's role in such communities is to teach the members, through stories, how to live. It's not an easy job for teachers in today's classrooms, who must instruct in an environment in which there are few universally agreed-upon truths. Nonetheless, many teachers feel they must do something.

Some turn to stories for guidance. Stories, carefully selected, can present both information and points of view regarding global awareness. More helpful and perhaps more necessary is the fact that storytelling can break down barriers to listeners' understanding and allow them, for the duration of the story, to empathize with events, people, and conditions that would otherwise be beyond their ken.

The articles that follow range widely, but their underlying theme of personal responsibility is summarized in the often-used slogan "Think globally; act locally."

WAR AND LANGUAGE:
A UNIT PLAN FOR ENGLISH CLASS

Can adolescents learn anything profound about the intricate and powerful relationship between language and war? And can storytelling play a role in this process? In a century haunted by such phrases as *acceptable losses* and *mutually assured destruction*, can we as teachers help guide our students to wisdom about violent conflict?

Can we help them make decisions, for example, about the Gulf War? How can they deal with terms such as *carpet bombing*, *softening troops*, and *collateral damage*, which are pumped into our homes via the media? And how can they begin to intelligently enter a national debate on what "supporting the troops" really means?

I've developed a unit for English class that begins to accomplish these goals—a unit in which almost all of my students, from year to year, have worked with dedication and energy. The key feature of this unit is the way it taps the natural human propensity for storytelling.

My "war and language" unit takes three weeks to finish and has two main parts. During the first, students read a variety of written materials about war. During the second, each student assumes a character—soldier, doctor, spouse of a soldier, and so on—and writes about that character's experience in a mock war we hold in class. In other words, the student creates and tells a story. In this way, students begin to consider how words and attitudes influence each other: how, for example, during the Vietnam War both our Vietnamese enemies and allies were called *gooks* and how friend-or-foe decisions were colored by that word or how, as Russell Baker has said, the word *megadeath* doesn't have quite the ring of "a million corpses."

Before either section can begin, of course, I teach the necessary vocabulary. Even eighth-graders are perfectly capable of grasping terms such as *euphemism*, *abstract*, *concrete*, *distancing*, *metaphor*, *jargon*, *technical language*, *dehumanize*, *doublethink* and so on if the teacher's vocabulary instruction is truly effective. (Students can master vocabulary if the teacher presents only five to 10 items a week, explains them clearly, and gives many examples.)

At this point in the unit I introduce the key idea: Language can be used to distance us from the reality of war or to bring us closer to it. The Russians, for example, left "turbulence" behind them as they pulled

Teacher and writer Tim Myers helps his students exhume the truth of war, which is often buried by the use of carefully sanitized language. Having his students tell the stories behind the headlines helps them see the human dimension of war and the risks of continuing to use euphemistic language to describe it.

out of Afghanistan; an article mentions the "effectiveness . . . of non-nuclear bombing." The concrete referents of these words—what it feels like to be bombed or machine-gunned, to step on a land mine, to be orphaned or widowed by the violence of war—are usually lost in the vagueness of such language. As a class, we come back to this fact again and again. And nothing compares to stories in bringing these realities forward because stories, by their very nature, focus on individuals and present human experience in intense and dramatic ways.

Then for a week I have the students read material on war and fill out "read and respond sheets." I present the class with a large collection of writings about war, and students must read a certain number of these articles and fill out one sheet for each. The sheet features two brief questions: What was the attitude toward war in this piece of writing? and What key phrases show this attitude?

I include pieces that reflect every possible level of reading ability. And of course, these writings must interest the students. There's wide variety in my collection: a passage from *The Iliad*, a section from a history book, a G.I. Joe toy-soldier pamphlet, a *Mad* magazine satire on weapons sales, Sergeant Rock comic books, articles on nuclear war, letters from soldiers in Vietnam, encyclopedia articles on weaponry, and so on. I may also require each student to read a book on war, anything from Kurt Vonnegut's *Slaughterhouse-Five* (Delacorte Press, 1969) to *Dear America: Letters Home From Vietnam*, edited by Bernard Edelman (Norton, 1985), to Norman Mailer's *The Naked and the Dead* (New American Library, 1948), depending on the students' reading levels.

The more variety in the readings' readability and topics, the more specifically I can direct individuals to material that will engage them. I may also include heavier, more demanding writings or direct students to them when their interests move in certain directions. These readings provide details about actual war experiences that inevitably show up in the students' stories.

I've invited veterans to come talk to my class too. These sessions have inevitably produced a hushed fascination among the students, and each time storytelling has been the key. The veterans, no matter how skillful they are at narrative, fall into it—and hold my students and me spellbound.

Again, we as a class focus on the human tendency to talk away from the realities of war. What does it mean to say that the improved U.S. military is "tougher"? What exactly are atrocities, in plain English? What underlying attitudes caused an unnamed source to call U.S.–Soviet satellite conflicts "the ultimate video game"? Why did the term *Star*

Using Stories to Teach About Peace and the Environment

Wars become so popular a misnomer for SDI (Strategic Defense Initiative)? Do teenagers fully analyze the meaning of the slogan "Be all that you can be"? Can the word *war* itself, or any other words, really capture the overwhelming reality of combat?

I also ask students to do an adult interview for one of the required sheets, focusing on the cost of war. Films, photographs, and recordings, if available, can reveal attitudes toward war too. This almost automatically means that students experience both actual and fictional war stories. In many cases kids come to school amazed at the true stories they've heard from their parents, relatives, or neighbors.

Once I feel my students have enough background, I bring out maps that represent the imaginary world in which our mock wars occur. I use felt-tip markers and colored pencils on my maps and then laminate them. Showing them to the class for the first time is a motivational high point in the unit: it's crucial in getting the kids involved in the creative writing tasks that lie ahead. Nothing in the unit seems to attract my kids so much as the sight of these maps, the richness of an entire world in which to let their imagination play. As many of us already know, the map of an imagined land seems to cry out for the creation of stories.

The maps must be detailed and visually attractive. The world they represent includes seas and continents, nations, cities, villages, rivers, mountain ranges, and other features, all of which are named. This, of course, is a familiar feature in adventure and fantasy books and one that over time has proved its attractiveness to adolescents—and to adults.

In my world two large nations are fighting over a border province with newly discovered mineral wealth. I use two maps, one of the world itself and an inset that shows the war province and its surroundings. In this province intermarriage between the two cultures has occurred. Primitive hill tribes live in one of the embattled areas. Both of the large nations have specific claims to the province. As tensions mount, an assassination by young hotheads and a massive reprisal from the other side provide the pretext for war. In effect, I give my students a vast story—a history—from which their own stories can naturally flow.

Once my class has some basic information on the state of things, I pass out character lists and hold a "character auction." I choose characters to reflect many different perspectives on war: soldiers, generals, prime ministers, parents or relatives of soldiers, tribespeople, journalists, children, spouses in mixed marriages, military press-release writers, community leaders, doctors or nurses, business leaders, religious leaders, ordinary citizens—even an extraterrestrial observing human behavior from the air and a historian writing about the conflict 50 years later. In each case I ask the students to use the type of language about war that their character would use. How does a soldier's mother or father react to the abstract word *casualty*? What do "tactics" mean to a military thinker? Will an American teenager feel the same way about Conan the Barbarian after he's imagined himself a tribesman whose world is being destroyed in a clash between larger powers?

We then hold the auction, in which students choose their character and any disputes are settled by the "rock, scissors, paper" method— itself an exercise in settling disputes peacefully. Students' finding a way to deal with these conflicts can be a learning experience, a tiny glimpse of the actual meaning of the word *diplomacy*.

During this phase, informal storytelling occurs constantly. As I coach students about their character, I model the creative process by telling anecdotes; by suggesting conflicts, themes, and plots; and by helping students see where the natural drama of their character's experience lies. I act like a storytelling coach, questioning wording or events, bolstering certain ideas with further suggestions, laying out options for mood, voice, and pace. Even more exciting for me is seeing my students spontaneously telling one another their character's stories. Many of them do this with passion and gusto, developing their stories during these live-audience situations and making changes appropriately—a perfect prewriting activity and one that writer–storytellers often use. Students also act spontaneously as one another's critics. Around the room I'll hear such comments as "There's no way he could do that!" "Cool!" "But how many days would it take to get there?" "Why should the soldier care? He doesn't even know them!" Immediate responses such as these greatly strengthen the eventual form of the stories.

Then the mock war begins. Using magnetized colored buttons, I set up on the map simple campaigns and battles. Each student writes about his or her character's experience in the war for each of the next four or five days. I encourage students to write in different forms: diaries, letters, memos, excerpts from novels, sermons, requests for supplies, and so on. We emphasize the range of language these forms produce—from the most specific to the most euphemistic or abstract—and how such half-conscious language decisions influence individual attitudes toward the war.

Using dice, I control troop movement and the outcome of battles. As long as the students follow these basic facts and stick to the setting, they can make up anything else they want. Too much attention to fitting all the stories together inhibits the kind of creative insight I'm looking for.

As the kids work on their daily writings, I circulate, reading, relating

Using Stories to Teach About Peace and the Environment

anecdotes or suggesting plots, pointing out and praising examples of insight or good writing, asking about grammar or clarity, reminding them to fit their language to their character. By the end of the five-day period, each of them has an excellent rough draft. We then talk about turning rough material into a finished piece through selection, compression, summary, polishing, and the like. I've found a very high level of writing in the final compositions they turn in. Many of their stories are compelling and richly realized. My primary evaluation for the unit is based on these compositions.

One of my students developed an elaborate and profound espionage plot in which the reader of his document learns that while reading, he too has been contaminated with poison soaked into the paper—just one more victim in a chain of murder. Another student's story ended with a mother's learning from casual conversation that her son had died in battle, her grief erupting when strangers happen to mention a unique scar on the face of a nameless corpse. The first student was a high-school junior; the second, an eighth-grader.

Four other factors will ensure success with this unit.

A teacher who is well-read in war literature, especially one able to relate anecdotes about war, will engage the students' attention and motivate them much better than a teacher who can provide no examples of what really happens in war. Paul Fussell's magnificent *The Great War and Modern Memory* (Oxford University Press, 1975) is perfectly suited to this aim and is a masterpiece of its kind besides. He writes, for example, of Wilfred Owen's struggle toward concrete language—how Owen writes his mother about the "sufferings" of his men but changes his tone in a letter to Sassoon, another soldier–poet: "The boy by my side, shot through the head, lay on top of me, soaking my shoulder, for half an hour." Well-chosen examples can have a powerful effect on students—and, of course, can be a way of modeling storytelling.

Teachers must also stress their own political objectivity. Students come from many backgrounds and often hold varied opinions about war. From the beginning, I emphasize that I won't try to persuade anyone that war is wrong or right but that everyone should have some sense of the reality of war, of what really happens, through direct language.

I also spend some time talking about the natural human tendency to become desensitized to the horror of violence, and I insist my students realize that even the most direct language cannot capture the actual experience of fighting. Finally, to ensure that my students write about the actual human experience of war—instead of distance themselves from it by treating it as a game—I let them know that we'll write only about the first days of the war and that none of us will ever know who wins the conflict. A game of Risk is hardly the way to encourage accurate language about war; at this point too we discuss exactly what it means to "win."

I always end by discussing with students the ways language is used and misused in the greatest human crisis of all time—the nuclear age. A few years ago an American president referred to the Soviets and their political philosophy as a "cancer," a "virus," and "the focus of evil in the modern world," and I expect my students to identify the dehumanization that such language encourages. We talk about phrases such as *nuclear deterrence*, examining the huge conceptual gap between the cloudiness of the words and the real possibility of massive human suffering much worse than that at Hiroshima—where flesh melted from bone, bodily organs exploded, and broken glass was blasted so deep into the victims that even today survivors must remove slivers that have worked their way up to the surface of the skin.

Looking back, I can see that storytelling could play an even more direct role in the unit. In the future I plan to have students present their stories to the class orally—after, of course, some rudimentary instruction in gesture, voice, expression, and so on. In this way I could formalize the balance of oracy and literacy that has already helped kids come up with such strong narratives.

By the end of the unit I'm satisfied that, as participants in the ongoing human struggle concerning war, my students have begun to see the essential role our use of language will play in its resolution. And I'm confident that stories have brought them closer, as individuals and citizens, to this terrible reality that has so continuously haunted the human race.

Tim Myers of Plattsburgh, New York, is a writer, a musician, a teacher, a father, and an eclectic storyteller for all ages. Myers has a master's degree in literature and 16 years' experience teaching, from sixth grade through university level. He has sold two picture books, published poetry and nonfiction, and won a national poetry contest judged by John Updike. He has traveled widely and lived in Norway, London, and Tokyo.

The Theme of Peace in Folk Tales

By Margaret Read MacDonald

Wondering what our folk wisdom had to say about peace, I began looking for folk tales on themes of peace. Not surprisingly, self-protection and one-upmanship are more popular folk-tale themes than cooperation and peaceful coexistence. However, I did find several interesting tales that may help you think about the possibility of peace. (See the list in chapter 13.)

These tales were selected in the hope that they will give the reader pause for thought. A few are designed for use in storytelling; others might best be shared through reading aloud or silently. All lend themselves to discussion, although there are times when a story is most effective if left to settle into the listener's thoughts on its own.

When I asked other storytellers for peace-story suggestions, they almost always mentioned Bill Harley's "Freedom Bird" right away. It is the story of a bird that cannot be killed and escapes the hunter. The bird really does nothing to bring about peace—he simply escapes with his freedom while taunting the hunter. It is curious that so many folks think freedom and peace are the same thing. In fact, they are probably not compatible concepts. To achieve peace, we must give up some freedoms. The essence of peaceful coexistence probably still lies in the old adage "Your right to swing your elbow ends where your neighbor's elbow begins."

In seeking material for my book, I looked for tales that showed ways to achieve peace. Facile stories suggesting that we all simply join hands and love one another did not interest me, nor did the many stories of peace achieved through the winning of wars. Peace requires constant maintenance. It is hard work—a never-ending task.

In her paper "Stories: The Voice of Peace—An Agenda for Peace and Creative Problem-Solving" storyteller Marcia Lane makes some excellent suggestions:

It is . . . no more useful to tell a child to "think peaceful thoughts" than it is to tell him or her to fly. So how can we promote inner harmony and, eventually and inevitably, harmony between people? By using stories to do three things:

- to encourage children to look inward

Until recently the idea of studying peace was a little like trying to examine a cloud: first you have to catch one. As the need becomes more urgent, however, more information has become available. Folklorist, storyteller, and author Margaret Read MacDonald has turned her hand to peace studies, drawing on the folk wisdom of many cultures.

- to present kids with several possible answers to a problem
- to give children a positive sense of value and purpose—a sense of their own strength and inherent morality.

Most of us have stories in our repertoire that can accomplish these goals. We need to identify those stories, songs, poems, games that work in subtle ways to encourage creative problem-solving . . . . Try to look at your existing materials with an eye and ear to whether they send positive messages, give alternatives to violence, recognize and reject prejudice, and applaud cooperation and collaboration.

One last thought: When we try to tell "peace stories" by eviscerating traditional myths and folk tales, we end up with dishonest storytelling and the inevitable sense that the teller imagines a world without adventure, danger, variety, or disagreement. It is probably undesirable (and certainly impossible) to eliminate conflict in the world. But it is possible, through the stories we tell and the ways in which we discuss them, to expand the choices for living in harmony.

In studying the world's folk tales, I have come to the conclusion that these tales present a mirror of the mind of mankind. Throughout history and wherever humans reside on this planet, their tales speak repeatedly of the same concerns and reach similar conclusions. In the past mankind's tales have stressed trickery and power more often than conflict resolution. Is it possible that by changing the tales we tell we can change our warring nature? It is worth a try.

From Peace Tales: World Folktales to Talk About. *Copyright 1992 by Margaret Read MacDonald. Reprinted by permission of Linnet Books, North Haven, Connecticut.*

Using Stories to Teach About Peace and the Environment

NOT OUR PROBLEM

The king sat with his adviser, eating honey on puffed rice. As they ate, they leaned from the palace window and watched the street below. They talked of this and that. The king, not paying attention to what he was doing, let a drop of honey fall onto the windowsill. "Oh, Sire, let me wipe that up," offered the adviser. "Never mind," said the king. "It is not *our* problem. The servants will clean it later."

As the two continued to dine on their honey and puffed rice, the drop of honey slowly began to drip down the windowsill. At last it fell with a plop onto the street below. Soon a fly had landed on the drop of honey and begun its own meal. Immediately a gecko sprang from under the palace, and with a flip of its long tongue, swallowed the fly. But a cat had seen the gecko and pounced. Then a dog sprang forward and attacked the cat!

"Sire, there seems to be a cat-and-dog fight in the street. Should we call someone to stop it?" "Never mind," said the king. "It's not *our* problem." So the two continued to munch their honey and puffed rice.

Meanwhile, the cat's owner had arrived and was beating the dog. The dog's owner ran up and began to beat the cat. Soon the two were beating each other.

"Sire, there are two persons fighting in the street now. Shouldn't we send someone to break this up?" The king lazily looked from the window. "Never mind. It's not *our* problem."

The friends of the cat's owner gathered and began to cheer him on. The friends of the dog's owner began to cheer her on as well. Soon both groups entered the fight and attacked each other.

"Sire, a number of people are fighting in the street now. Perhaps we should call someone to break this up." The king was too lazy even to look. You can guess what he said: "Never mind. It's not *our* problem."

Now soldiers arrived on the scene. At first they tried to break up the fighting. But when they heard the cause of the fight, some sided with the cat's owner. Others sided with the dog's owner. Soon the soldiers too had joined the fight. With the soldiers involved, the fight erupted into civil war. Houses were burned down. People were harmed. The palace itself was set afire and burned to the ground. The king and his adviser stood surveying the ruins.

"Perhaps," said the king, "I was wrong. Perhaps the drop of honey *was* our problem."

—A tale from Burma and Thailand

Suggestion for telling

Children may want to join you on the refrain "It's not our problem," though this is a quiet, thoughtful story rather than a rowdy audience-participation tale.

"Not Our Problem" is retold by Margaret Read MacDonald. Variants may be found in *Burmese and Thai Fairy Tales* by Eleanor Brockett (Follett, 1965), *A Kingdom for a Drop of Honey and Other Burmese Folktales* by Maung Htin Aung and Helen G. Trager (Parents' Magazine Press, 1969), and *Tales From Thailand* by Marian Davies Toth (Charles Tuttle, 1971).

From Peace Tales: World Folktales to Talk About *by Margaret Read MacDonald.*

Green Grow the Stories

By Suzanne Martin

What should teacher–tellers look for when choosing stories for environmental education? Writer Suzanne Martin's article surveys several storytellers to find out how they select stories and what suggestions they have for telling.

As long as people have been around to create stories, they've found inspiration in nature's every sight and sound. Notes Berkeley, California, storyteller Nancy Schimmel, "Every indigenous people has stories about the environment and about noticing things." Lots of contemporary storytellers are noticing too—going back to nature for their material and finding it a rich lode.

The growing tradition sparks interest in listeners and tellers alike. "Stories can address any environmental issue," says John Porcino, a storyteller based in Amherst, Massachusetts. "Conservation is one. Recycling is another. Preservation of the land and caring for endangered species are others." Porcino's work is included in the book *Spinning Tales, Weaving Hope: Stories of Peace, Justice, and the Environment* (New Society Publishers, 1992). Of the collection's 29 stories, Porcino says, eight specifically address ecological issues.

But simply setting a story in the deep dark woods does not give it ecological significance. To be successful, such stories must somehow awaken wonder at the world around us. And like all memorable stories, they must offer new insights that can be taken to heart and explored.

Diane Edgecomb of Boston has been telling nature-oriented stories for the past nine years. Her audiences include children and adults, and her stories weave together such environmental issues as habitat preservation, water conservation, and recycling. Most of all, she says, her material encourages listeners to take a personal look at nature. "The people in the audience have to find their own connection to the natural world," she says. "They have to find what astonishes them, what they value in nature." Two of her favorite stories are *Who Speaks for Wolf: A Native American Learning Story* (Tribe Two Press, 1991) by Paula Underwood and "The Garden" from *Frog and Toad Together* (Harper & Row, 1972) by Arnold Lobel.

Schimmel shares Edgecomb's view and has added a bibliography of ecology stories to the third edition of her book *Just Enough to Make a Story* (Sisters' Choice Press, 1992). "I want stories and songs that show our connection to nature, stories that empower people," she says. "You don't go out and look for an ecology story. You find one that touches you and addresses people's concerns."

But finding the right tales can be difficult. Tellers borrow from folklore, use contemporary literature, and often develop their own stories. Still, says Edgecomb, "We need to create more material. The fact that there's a tree in the story doesn't make it an environmental tale." Although she has been researching nature stories for eight years, she says she's discarded "tons of stuff" because it didn't have a strong enough environmental emphasis. "This is like any other kind of storytelling," Edgecomb explains. "You can't look for an easy fix. Environmental stories should include the human angle, the spiritual angle, and practical applications. It takes time to develop stories."

Edgecomb finds much of her material in ancient myths and in the folklore of various cultures. "From the older folklore we get a more spiritual look at nature," she says. "We can become inspired in a mystical way." She also discovers the ecological perspective she's looking for in Native American stories.

Doug Elliott draws from the nature lore of North Carolina, his home state. A storyteller for 12 years, Elliott, based in Union Mills, is perhaps best known for his raccoon and possum tales. But his work also encompasses birds and bears, weeds and herbs, and assorted bits of wild wisdom from the mountainous backwoods of his state. Elliott shares his personal interest in the natural world via lighthearted stories, songs, and jokes. His work grows from his own observations of plants and animals and is nurtured by Native American lore and conversations with his mountain neighbors.

"The material pulls different cultural experiences together," he says. "Then when I'm telling a story, it triggers all kinds of memories and recognitions for people listening. Somewhere in the story, they'll hear something they can relate to."

In their search for ecology-related material, storytellers are also tracking down nature themes in traditional tales. Old standards are being told with new twists that add environmental emphasis. Schimmel points to stories featuring Br'er Rabbit and Coyote that are being told as part of environmental programs.

But asking old tales to perform new tricks can stretch the stories too far, some tellers argue. Tweaking them into environmental messages could be viewed as a disservice to both the stories and their culture.

Other tellers disagree, asserting that environmental themes often run subtly through folklore and that such themes can be emphasized without altering the tales' original intent. Porcino, for example, mixes contemporary stories with traditional lore to give voice to environmental themes, drawing on African, black American, and Yiddish folk tales.

"Many stories that don't look like environmental ones on the surface really are," he says. "You give stories an environmental slant by showing people that they can make a difference—that it takes everyone doing a little bit to make something work."

For people not yet bitten by the environmental-awareness bug, stories can bring the natural world closer to home. They illustrate the relationships between human behavior and the state of the environment—serving as a kind of ecological consciousness-raising. And through stories skeptics can be converted: those who believe that environmental issues are political rather than personal can be moved to action.

One of Edgecomb's most empowering tales, she says, is "The Boy Who Loved the Swamp," a piece she wrote after reading an article about a boy who saved his neighborhood swamp. When developers planned to drain the site and build on it, the youngster marshaled enough community support to stop the project. "The important thing to the kids is that the story is true," she says. "They just love that."

Successful environmental stories can charge audiences with enthusiasm and a sense of victory. But, some performers warn, tellers should keep in mind the danger of coming across as too heavy-handed—of the message's overpowering the story. Listeners who feel preached to and put upon will end up irritated rather than inspired.

Doom and gloom about the world's environmental situation don't play well either—harping on the "too little, too late" theme only instills fear and intimidates listeners. That's particularly important for those who tell stories to children. Says Edgecomb, "We can't take our own seriousness about environmental problems and put it in a kid's world. The best thing we can give children is stories that help them connect with nature. If storytellers can't give hope, what are we here for?"

Instead of browbeating listeners about their lack of action and failure to save the earth, stories should raise hope, emphasize the joys of our relationship with nature, and challenge members of the audience to take whatever personal actions they can. "At some level, that's what storytelling is—a call to action," says Elliott. "If it touches you, that's a call to action. Any action that will help save this world is appropriate right now. And by telling interesting stories about nature, you turn the occasion into environmental education."

From global warming to deforestation to recycling, environmental issues are being raised and examined in classrooms across the country. "The environment has become a real kid issue," says Schimmel. "It's very empowering and can be very positive." Children may lack the means to stop world hunger, but they can recycle aluminum cans and avoid littering. They know they can help make the environment a cleaner, safer place, and they're looking for ways to do more.

For storytellers that means receptive audiences for ecology tales and nature programs, from grade school on up. But environmental storytelling is also sneaking out of the classroom. Park rangers, scout masters, and environmental educators now regularly show up at storytelling workshops, and they're taking notes about how to incorporate stories and storytelling techniques into their programs.

Whether told in classrooms or around a campfire, stories add a dynamic dimension to environmental education. "Storytelling accesses more than the brain," says Elliott. "It hooks into the heart, into the sensual side, into our spirituality."

As a teaching tool, environmental storytelling can capture a young imagination quicker than any science lecture. Through stories the natural sciences can come alive with humor and suspense and joy. Facts can be surrounded with fantasy, and imaginations can wander and wonder. Stories can lay a foundation of interest in the natural world.

"Our society has lost its connection to nature," says Edgecomb. "But science has shown us that our environmental problems are a major issue. As storytellers we can help bridge the gap between science and nature. But the stories must be more than a call to action. Through the stories the listener must be able to experience some kind of transformation and a philosophical shift."

For all that storytelling can do to reveal nature's mysteries, gray areas exist, and not all environmental complexities lend themselves to easy explanations. Children frequently want clear-cut solutions to muddled adult problems, and for those telling ecology tales, the end of a story is often the beginning of a surge of questions. "We don't have all the answers," says Schimmel, "and it's important to let children know that. As storytellers we can only open up ideas and stimulate imaginations.

"Looking at and listening to nature before we go charging in, that's the message," she continues. "Through stories we can bring people into a mood where they can appreciate their natural surroundings. The way a story affects your mood can be very powerful."

Where the spirit moves, mind and body follow. So be still and listen. The stuff of stories surrounds us, telling of plants and animals, plains and mountains, sea and sky. They flow with the rhythms of nature and answer the call of the wild.

From *Storytelling Magazine*, spring 1992. Reprinted by permission.

Teaching environmental stewardship with stories can lead students into a deeper understanding of the web of life and help them create a lasting ethical framework. Sixth-grade science teacher Pamela Bomboy explains how she does it.

TEACHING KIDS TO CHERISH THE EARTH

Stories and storytelling activities can help build a classroom ethic of preservation and conservation of our earth and its resources. Here are some ways to start.

- Immerse yourself in Native American stories, myths, and legends. Many of these tales rejoice in and explain the natural world. As keen observers of nature, Native Americans believe all natural things have spirits. Honoring their part of the whole is an integral aspect of the Native American way of life.

- Learn about the geological and human history of your area. How has it changed with human habitation? What environmental problems could occur in the future? If you can, find a local-history story that reflects an ancestor's use of the natural world.

- Find an area outside the school that can serve as an outdoor classroom. It should be easy to get to and, if possible, should have a variety of plants and animals. If you don't have a wooded area nearby, your school's front yard or a neighboring park or garden will do.

- Teach your students the scientific skill of making good qualitative observations, using the five senses. Allow your students to see, hear, touch, smell, and taste the world around them.

- Have each child begin a naturalist journal. This can be a sketchbook, a spiral notebook, or simply composition pages tied with yarn. On the first page, have the children write "A Naturalist Journal by (child's name)." Then have them draw and color something they've always enjoyed in nature. Provide your students with crayons or colored pencils. For future entries, have them include an entry number and date.

- Initiate a discussion on the relationship between science and stories. Discuss how ancient peoples often used stories to explain natural occurrences they didn't understand. Then tell a Native American "how and why story" such as "How the Chipmunk Got Its Stripes" from *Seneca Indian Myths* (E.P. Dutton, 1951).

- Take your children to the outdoor classroom for their first visit, and tell them a Native American creation story. Then ask each child to find a special place there. This should be done individually. Ask the children to make observations about their special place, using the five senses, and then write them down. Next have them sketch something they found in their special place that's pleasing to them.

Every visit to the outdoor classroom should begin with a story and include an environmental activity and writing or recording in the children's naturalist journals. Finally, as your students begin to fully celebrate the natural world, encourage them to use their journals as the basis for stories, poetry, plays, banners, or posters that can be shared with others.

—Pamela Bomboy

From the Yarnspinner, *May-June 1993. Reprinted by permission.*

Using Stories to Teach About Peace and the Environment

8

USING STORIES
TO TEACH HISTORY

USING STORIES TO TEACH HISTORY

Teaching history is essentially story-making. How could it be otherwise when so often we don't really know the moment-by-moment details of past events? The best we can hope for is to get the facts straight and tell what happened without imposing our own ideas too often. And it is the facts of history that students are most often asked to remember—not the story that frames the facts, not the complex interweaving of human characters on the loom of time.

"The facts" can be slippery too, as indicated by the recent reappraisal of the discovery of the Americas by Columbus. For the native peoples who lived here, the experience of being "discovered" was very different from that of the explorers. Obviously interpretations of such events can vary greatly.

Storytelling can help by furnishing a context for the facts, breathing life into events that may seem dry and dusty in a textbook, and providing opportunities to explore different points of view about the same event. Storytelling allows students to make a living connection to the past—and for a moment they can hear the gunfire through the trees at the Battle of Bull Run or taste the salty tears of a captured Ashanti warrior as he lies in chains in a slave ship bound for the Carolinas.

The following articles define the task of making the facts of history come alive. They also offer suggestions on how to begin.

MAKING HISTORY COME ALIVE

BY BARBARA LIPKE

I once had a professor of European history who made history almost interesting. He wrote the date 1666 on the blackboard, then said, "The Great Fire of London—you can remember the date because the sixes look like leaping flames."

I did remember the date, but it was several years before I realized the drama of that event.

Who remembers the date of the Great Chicago Fire? (October 8, 1871.) Not many people. But the story of Mrs. O'Leary's cow's kicking over the lantern? Now, that we remember. This and other tales can be the key to making history come alive in the classroom. Most history texts have managed to make the whole thing dull and dry as dust, and that's a crime.

One dictionary defines history as "narrative of events; tale, story." So there you have it: permission to use stories in your history curriculum. Your students are much less likely to be bored with your lessons if you include stories in the teaching process. History *is* story and won't be boring if told as such.

A couple of years ago Ken Burns did a public-television series that made the Civil War come alive. What made this production so different? Burns told us the stories of the conflict, using the letters and photographs of some of the individuals and families involved. He personalized the Civil War.

Through educational research, we've learned that telling stories and reading from good, well-researched historical fiction are two ways to make history come alive.

Making history into story requires research, but the dividends are golden. For example, a curriculum in American history, 1850 to the present, would minimally encompass the Gold Rush, slavery, the Civil War, waves of immigration, westward expansion, the advent of big agriculture, the growth of industry, the Spanish-American War, World War I, World War II, the Great Depression, the Holocaust, the nuclear age, the civil-rights movement, the Korean War, the Vietnam War, and the Persian Gulf conflict.

Having your students simply recite the dates and events of this era would be terribly boring. Instead, select some high points, and concen-

Storyteller Barbara Lipke was a classroom teacher for 24 years. Along the way she picked up many ideas on how to teach history to young people. Here she offers suggestions on humanizing history, creating historical stories, and sparking students' interest in the subject.

trate on those. What you want your students to remember is up to you. Suppose it's the Great Depression. One or two stories, stories found in history books or even better, in primary sources—such as letters, diaries, or the reminiscences of students' older relatives—will make the historical event become vivid. It's the detail, the sense of immediacy, that can re-create the scene for you and your listeners.

Here's a sample story:

I remember one bitterly cold day in 1934 when I was 9 years old and on my way to school in New York City. Jobless and homeless people were everywhere. Grown men were selling apples for five cents each on nearly every street corner. It was at the corner of 10th Street and Sixth Avenue that I found a $5 bill. To me it was a fortune—more money than I had in the big bank around the corner. I looked around. No one was nearby. The closest person was half a block away. I picked up the bill and put it in my pocket, feeling half elated, half guilty. All day long that $5 bill lay in my pocket like a guilty secret, an undeserved bonus. Someone couldn't pay the rent, buy shoes, or pay the doctor because I had that money. When I got home, I told my mother about my good luck. We had a long talk, and in the end I sent the $5 to the Red Cross. Then I felt better . . . and worse.

A whole range of stories—many of them even more dramatic than this one—could make the Great Depression come alive for your students. You just need to search them out.

But what about the Spanish-American War? Or the presidential election of 1876? Or other historical topics that aren't so familiar? Start with your own knowledge. Decide what your students should learn about these subjects, then look up the information. The election of 1876—wasn't that the one that was thrown into the House of Representatives, the one that led to the withdrawal of federal troops from the South, to the end of Reconstruction, to the beginnings of Jim Crow laws, and to the rise of the Ku Klux Klan? A little more research should reveal the answers and some stories.

FINDING AND TELLING A STORY

Let's go through the steps, using as our topic the Battle of Salamis, 480 B.C.E., when the Greeks defeated the Persians. First, go to your social-studies book and get the background facts. Next, invent a hero or a heroine, but if you take the latter, be sure you understand the role women played in Greece at that time. Give him (let's say he's male) a name and an age (about the age of your students), and make him a boy of Athens. Perhaps he knows Themistocles (the Greeks' chief strategist and commander) or is on board a Greek trireme (the battleship of the time) as flute boy. A flute player's job was to help keep the 170 rowers moving in unison.

You now have a hero who is both excited and fearful about the coming battle. His mother and younger sisters have been sent off with the other women and children, and he is soon to have his first taste of battle. The Persians show up. They're a formidable force, but the triremes prove so maneuverable and so good at ramming the clumsy Persian ships that the Greeks win, and Athens is saved. Meanwhile, you've re-created the salt smell of the sea, the sound of gulls wheeling overhead, the rhythm of 170 oars rowing in unison to the piping of the reedy flute (played by your hero), the crash and splintering sound of the rams' hitting the hulls of the Persian ships, the battle cries, and all the blood and gore your students can take.

It took me 15 minutes to find the necessary information, using the encyclopedia and a good travel book on Greece, and create this story. Simply use your own textbook, or ask the school librarian to help you find resources. A good atlas will help you accurately visualize the scene.

Once your story is developed, try it through once or twice. Ask yourself these questions: Do I have a good, clear beginning? Do I have a strong ending that pulls the story together but doesn't preach or moralize? Do I know the sequence of events? Can I see each incident in my mind's eye? If you can answer yes, you're ready to go.

Whatever you do, please don't memorize the story. If possible, don't even write it down. Tell it to an audience—best of all, an audience of one supportive person. Explain that you're trying out new material and want to know if it works. Then get some feedback.

Tell your story with feeling and as though you were right there, living it. Watch your students' faces. Are they with you? I'll bet they are, and they will probably never forget the Battle of Salamis.

Storytelling enhances history, making the subject come alive for both teachers and students. Remember, print is but 500 years old and writing a mere 5,000, but people have told stories forever, using them to pass their history and culture from generation to generation.

From the Yarnspinner, *August 1993. Reprinted by permission.*

The Civil War as Seen Through Story

By R. Craig Roney

Once you've developed a historical story, what do you do with it? Craig Roney, a professor of children's literature at Wayne State University in Detroit, tells a haunting tale about the Civil War and describes his step-by-step approach to expanding the story into a unit.

Storytelling enables students to interact with culture (past and present) through narrative, which is the major means by which children make sense of the world around them. As such, storytelling is a natural way for students to explore the historical past, the belief systems of varied societies, and diverse factual information as well. A story I tell, an adaptation of a ghost story originally written by Ambrose Bierce, provides an example. It is called "A Cold Night."

The scene is a broad, frozen, cadaver-strewn plain spanning the Stones River near Murfreesboro, Tennessee—the aftermath of one of the Civil War's bloodiest days of fighting. For the living, the fight for survival continues throughout the night as the men contend with bitter cold and the persistent fear that they might be killed during the next day's fighting. In the midst of this numbing carnage, a simple act of kindness and respect is acknowledged in a rather eerie fashion.

A Cold Night

Late in 1862 the Union forces were divided into three armies. The Army of the Cumberland, 45,000 strong, under the command of Major General William S. Rosecrans, was situated just south of Nashville. The general's main objective was to march on Chattanooga and take that city, which served as a major railroad supply hub for the Confederacy.

Standing between Rosecrans and Chattanooga was General Braxton Bragg and 38,000 seasoned Confederate soldiers, encamped just north and west of Murfreesboro, all up and down the Stones River.

The battle of Stones River (Murfreesboro, if you favor the Confederate cause) began on December 31, 1862. Rosecrans' men had marched from the north and west. Bragg and his troops defended from the south and east. The strategy favored by both armies was identical: Hold with the right line of forces; attack with the left line. Had both plans been carried out simultaneously, the armies would have swung around like a huge revolving door. But as was typical of most early Civil War battles, the Confederates struck first and drove the Union troops back and in on themselves so that by day's end, the Union position was shaped like a giant jackknife with the blade partly exposed.

Perhaps as a result of the confusion, the Confederates were unable to drive the Union forces from the field. Still, the fighting had been fierce. The volleys of musket fire alone had been so loud that soldiers on both sides of the line had plucked cotton bolls right from the plants and stuffed them in their ears to stave off the awful noise.

Now, for some unexplained reason, Bragg failed to capitalize on his victory that first day. His army sat idle on January 1 and the morning of January 2, but he took up the fight again on the afternoon of January 2 and was repelled by savage cannon fire. Fifty-eight Union cannons lined up in a row tore Bragg's line to shreds—one of the few instances during the war when cannon fire played a significant role in turning the tide of a battle.

Two days later Bragg retreated to Tullahoma, Tennessee, 36 miles to the south, and Rosecrans walked into Murfreesboro. The Battle of Stones River was over.

Both armies would be immobilized for several months. And it is an axiom of war that if you cannot fight, you cannot win. And the casualties? The dead and the wounded? Thirteen thousand for the Union, 10,000 for the Confederates—well over a quarter of the strength of both armies.

Now, one of the Union soldiers still alive at the end of the first day's fighting was Ambrose Bierce, the noted Civil War chronicler and a captain in an Indiana regiment. That day Bierce and his companions had taken refuge behind a railroad embankment that served as a breastwork, staving off the repeated charges of Confederate infantry. Before the embankment lay the dead of both armies, piled two or three deep. Behind the embankment the ground was flat, broad, open, and strewn with sizable boulders. Next to nearly every boulder were dead Union soldiers who had been dragged out of the way during the battle.

When the fighting subsided late that day, the heat of the day was replaced with piercing cold—a crystal-clear night despite the clouds of gun smoke created earlier that day, a night frozen and unyielding.

Among the dead lay one whom no one seemed to know, a sergeant, flat on his back, his limbs outstretched, rigid as steel. He had died on the spot where he lay . . . or so it seemed.

He had been shot squarely in the center of the forehead. One of the Union surgeons (perhaps out of idle curiosity, perhaps to amuse the still-living soldiers gathered nearby) had pressed a probe clean through the sergeant's head until it struck dirt at the base of the skull.

The night had grown so frigid that frost had formed on the grass around the sergeant, on his ashen face, his hair, and his beard. Some Christian soul had covered him with a blanket, but as the night turned colder and unrelenting, a companion of Bierce's approached the body,

took hold of that blanket, and said in a solemn voice, "Please forgive me, sir. But I fear I'll be needing this more than you tonight." He took the blanket, and then both he and Bierce wrapped themselves in it and suffered through the night.

That night every man lay still and silent. Pickets had been posted well out in front of the railroad embankment. These soldiers were permitted to move to ensure the security of the army, but movement by all others was prohibited. Conversation was strictly forbidden. There was to be no movement, no sound, no light, no heat. To even have lit a match would have been a grave offense.

Stamping horses, moaning wounded, anything that made noise had been sent well to the rear. All the living suffered the bitter cold in silence, contemplating the friends they had lost that day or perhaps the imminence of their own demise on the morrow. I tell you this to suggest that it was not a scene for a ghastly (or perhaps I should say ghostly) practical joke.

When the dawn broke, it broke clear. "It's likely we shall have a warm day of it—the fighting and all," remarked Bierce's companion. "I'd best return the poor devil's blanket."

He rose and approached the sergeant's body. It was in the same place but not in the same attitude. Instead of lying on its back, it was on its side, the chin tucked to the collarbone, the knees pulled up tight to the chest. The collar of its coat was turned upward, the shoulders hunched, the head retracted into the collar, and the hands were thrust to the wrist into its coat. This was the posture of someone who had died of extreme cold, not a gunshot wound. And yet there was the unmistakable evidence, the bullet hole through the head. But within arm's reach of that young dead sergeant, etched in the frost in the grass were written the words YOU ARE FORGIVEN.

The story is captivating; it never fails to appeal to audiences in upper elementary school through high school. Beyond being entertaining, however, the tale is also edifying. Woven into the fabric of the text are facts about the battle: the dates, the setting, the nature of the fighting that took place. Through the story, students encounter the commanders of both armies and their battle plans. Terms such as *picket* and *breastwork* are introduced, their meanings clarified by the context. Embedded in the story are elements sure to rouse discussion and clarify values: the merit of war, the dehumanization of combatants, the necessity for maintaining humane behavior in an uncivilized world. Introducing children to history through stories such as "A Cold Night" involves emotional as well as intellectual response on their part and thus transforms the study of history from the memorization of facts or analysis of irrelevant abstractions to relating past events to one's own life today.

Reprinted by permission of the publisher from Blatt, Gloria, Once Upon a Folktale *(New York: Teachers College Press, copyright 1993 by Teachers College, Columbia University. All rights reserved), chapter 1 (pages 10–13, 22).*

A FIFTH- THROUGH 12TH-GRADE STORY SESSION

1. Students write for information about the battle (National Park Service, Stones River National Battlefield, Rt. 10, Box 495, Old Nashville Highway, Murfreesboro, Tenn. 37130).

2. Teacher tells "A Cold Night."

3. Follow-up discussion

   a. Recall battle facts: when and where it took place, how long it lasted, size of armies, number of casualties.

   b. Determine from context what *breastwork* and *picket* mean.

   c. Recall facts about the ghostly incident: where it took place, who was involved, any unusual behavior.

   d. Discuss implied personalities of Bierce, the surgeon, and Bierce's companion and the effect the war had on them.

   e. Discuss the pros and cons of war.

4. Using troop-movement maps of the battle, have students locate where the ghostly incident likely took place.

5. Extension activities

   a. From various accounts, report on who won the battle, its significance, and the reasons Bragg chose not to attack on January 1.

   b. Students learn to tell stories from *The Civil War, Strange and Fascinating Facts* by Burke Davis (Fairfax Press, 1982).

   c. Students create dioramas or drawings of scenes from the story.

   d. Students write and illustrate a Civil War alphabet book.

HELPING STUDENTS CONNECT
WITH HISTORY

BY REX ELLIS

Educator and storyteller Rex Ellis recognizes how tough it can be to motivate students to learn—especially when they see the subject matter as irrelevant. Here he offers tips on helping them feel a sense of connection with the past.

Wham! A book hits the floor. The entire classroom erupts in laughter as you turn to see a student mimicking how you, the teacher, will respond. In spite of the caricature, you notice that his portrayal is laughably accurate.

You have two choices: You can admonish the student for being disrespectful, or you can ignore it and try your best to make a smooth transition back to the topic at hand—American history.

How do you make this stuff interesting to a class of young adults who seem to be more interested in the fascinating way their hormones have kicked in at this point in their lives? How do you talk about Thomas Jefferson, George Washington, Simon Gilliat, Sukey Hamilton, Betty Wallace, Phillis Wheatley, Yarow Mamout, and the complex circumstances that led to the building of our nation when the prevailing prose of the day is rap and popular songs are being sung by groups with names like Snoop Doggy Dogg, En Vogue, Blind Melon, Guns N' Roses, and Meat Loaf?

Many educators say that motivating students to learn is their greatest challenge. Running a close second is finding ways to reach an increasingly diverse student body. Although the difficulties vary according to students' grade level, demographics, and socioeconomic background, such problems remain the bane of most teachers.

Many learning theorists believe that motivating students to learn is easier once you establish contact. They assert that high-quality learning is a result of connecting students with activities, environments, and methodologies that match their abilities, interests, and experiences. Mihaly Csikszentmihalyi, a psychologist and a professor at the University of Chicago, believes that motivation to learn can be stimulated either extrinsically or intrinsically. Extrinsic factors are most common in formal learning environments such as public schools. Students pay attention to the teacher so they will get a good grade or because they will be tested. Intrinsic learning occurs more often in informal learning situations. That is, the activity or experience itself is so interesting, entertaining, or positive that people voluntarily focus on it. For some it's horseback-riding, playing a sport, playing or composing music, or even telling stories. Whatever the activity, something about it makes the person want to participate. In the book *Optimal Experience: Studies of Flow in Consciousness* (Cambridge University Press, 1988) Mihaly and Isabella Csikszentmihalyi describe this as "the state in which people are so involved in an activity that nothing else seems to matter; the experience itself is so enjoyable that people will do it even at great cost, for the sheer sake of doing it."

When this happens, learning becomes self-directed and is rewarding in itself. Although this may not always be possible in the classroom, it is a goal to strive for. As Judith Renyi puts it in her introduction to the book *Fire in the Eyes of Youth: The Humanities in American Education* (edited by Randolph Jennings, Occasional Press, 1993), "If we truly honor the minds of all our children, we will encourage them all day and every day from first grade through 12th to read and observe, to analyze and hypothesize, to answer back and to argue, and to create something new out of the voices of others so as to create a new set of voices to add to our culture."

Literature, art, and the performing arts are mainstays of educators trying to make connections with bored students, to help them enjoy learning and develop critical thinking skills. Although history is particularly useful in aiding students who have trouble with abstract thinking, they are often bored or turned off by the rote-memory approach to history taken by most public-school systems.

The last two decades have seen a revival in the art of storytelling, and many teachers now use it to help them reach students. Countless museums also see the benefits of storytelling. The Smithsonian Institution's National Museum of American History, Colonial Williamsburg, Greenfield Village, Shadows-on-the-Teche, Sturbridge Village, Plymouth Plantation, Mystic Seaport, and many others are using storytelling techniques to teach history.

Storytelling can help teachers provide students with alternative ways to learn about the people, places, and events that make up history, but it is important to remember a few points. In order for storytelling to be more than an entertaining respite in an otherwise uneventful day, teachers must determine objectives, devise related activities, and target specific outcomes. In addition, I advise teachers to

- Use multiple sources of information. Don't rely exclusively on one text. Texts may include poems, novels, and historical documents.
- Concentrate on history as a process rather than fall prey to the "great men" syndrome. Discuss and find stories to accommodate all the players within the historical period you want to discuss.
- Try to connect storytelling to your students' lives, families, experi-

ences, and environments. It can be frustrating trying to teach history in an exciting and interesting way, especially when you consider that the bulk of information to be communicated was accumulated before the students were born and therefore seems to have little immediate relevance. But dig deeper, and you'll find connections, parallels, and models of behavior that are astoundingly relevant.

- Complement your storytelling by using primary documents as well as artifacts and reproductions in order to give alternate perspectives on the topics under discussion. They are interesting and provide interactive learning opportunities that enhance the story and invite students' involvement.

- Remember that history is like a puzzle. Not even the most objective historians have a complete picture. At best, historical research is an attempt to provide a perspective, based on the most current and reliable information available.

- Encourage students to offer their own views on and perceptions of what might have taken place. Use their natural storytelling skills to motivate them to tell their own version of historical events when knowledge about them is incomplete.

- Remember the rich quilt of history, and include Indian, black, Mexican, Chinese, Japanese, Irish, German, and other perspectives as you tell the story of how America developed. (See Ronald Takaki's book *A Different Mirror: A History of Multicultural America* [Little, Brown, 1993].)

When telling a story, be sure to think about organization and sequence (what takes place first, second, third, and fourth and whether it will make sense to your listeners). Don't forget the theme. Why are you telling the story? What is the point? What's in it for your listeners? They will want to know why they should listen to you and what relevance your story has to their lives and experiences, so be sure to establish common ground.

Good stories are built around conflict. What are the opposing points of view, and are the characters dynamic enough for the average audience to care about them? Finally, does the story have substance? Is the story one that the audience can get caught up in? Does it say something important?

Using storytelling to accompany a history curriculum can provide students with an alternate way of looking at the past. Although they may have viewed history as pertinent only to a time and place vastly different from their own, storytelling can stimulate their imagination with fascinating, three-dimensional objects and people. You may want to try creating stories that play up local history. That sends a clear message to your students that their history is important.

A word about props. Don't be afraid to use them. Encourage students to experience history from multiple perspectives, using all of their senses. We are tied to objects that provide, represent, or express something important to us.

Be sure that those perspectives are historically well-balanced. Avoid the tendency to discuss only what you feel comfortable with. History is complex and cannot be grasped completely if we do not discuss the good, the bad, and the ugly.

Make sure you understand the content, but don't assume that because you know the history, you are ready to teach it. It is important to put just as much effort into the way you present the information as you do into what you teach. Ask yourself which techniques or ways of delivering the information will be most beneficial to the students. Try to create a sense of time and place that is different from the present. Too often we expect students to visualize different times and places but don't equip them with the tools to do it.

If you're talking about the 18th century, for instance, ask questions such as If you lived during the 18th century,

- What would you do in your spare time?
- What games would you play?
- What kinds of clothing would people wear?
- Where would a boy take a girl he liked?
- How far could you travel in an hour?
- How did people get from one place to another?
- What happened when people got sick?
- What kind of food did people eat?
- What kind of work did people do?
- What did people do to entertain themselves?
- What was important in their lives—money, clothes, power, family?

It's also important to do simple research that will help you with the content.

- If possible, visit the sites you discuss in class. If that's not possible, at least use maps, pictures, and other graphics so that students can get concrete images of as many aspects of the period as possible.
- Have the kids do a series of oral histories from their own community, and challenge them to try to make their own connections.
- History is best seen as a series of puzzle pieces that are still being

found. Students should not see history merely as observers but should realize that they are part of history and have the power to influence it just as the people they study did.

- Students should realize that our history is incomplete. Although we know a great deal, there is a great deal we do not know, especially about ordinary people and everyday life.

- Remember that historical stories can be told and performed most accurately when both you and the students have a detailed idea of what life was like, how people interacted, and what was important to them. And the lessons to be learned from mistakes made throughout history—no less than the good things that happened—teach students to think critically.

- The best gifts you can give your students are the tools and empowerment they need to become historians, curators, archaeologists, paleontologists, and scientists.

A word about multiculturalism and diversity: If you've had a student tell you, "You can't teach me anything about my history because you're not black," challenge the student to teach it to you. Any student who tells you that you can't understand another group's perspective because you are not a member of the group should be able to back up that charge by taking the lead in teaching the rest of the class what you "cannot" teach.

All of us are laboring under the mystery of history. Although we should all seek to understand the motivation behind such statements and discuss them openly and honestly, the worst we can do is become convinced that indeed we have nothing to offer because we are not Jewish, Irish, Latino, or black. Getting along with one another requires self-recognition as well as self-acceptance.

Dr. Rex M. Ellis is the director of the Office of Museum Programs at the Smithsonian Institution in Washington, D.C. Before coming to the Smithsonian, he directed the Department of African-American Interpretation and Presentations at Colonial Williamsburg. He studied at Virginia Commonwealth University, Wayne State University, and the College of William and Mary. Ellis is an educator and storyteller who uses his museum experience and knowledge of history to underscore the contributions made by the African-American community.

Dramatic plots make stories compelling, but it's the details that help listeners see, smell, taste, hear, and touch the action. Storyteller Karen Golden explains why it's so important to add the texture of every-day life to historical tales and offers some tips on getting started.

HISTORY HAPPENED A DAY AT A TIME

By Karen Golden

When I was in high school, I had a history teacher who loved to spice up his lectures with stories rather than simply recite an endless flurry of names and dates for us to memorize. On those story days, we sat on the edge of our seats. But our teacher never finished his tales in one day. He always ended with "to be continued." Though we begged him to tell us what happened next, his final words were always "come back tomorrow, and you'll see."

We did! I remember very little of what he said about the details of this war or that—unless the information was part of a story. I do remember his telling us about his experiences fighting overseas during World War II and writing love letters to his wife-to-be, and I'll never forget the details of John Wilkes Booth's harrowing escape from the Ford Theater after shooting President Lincoln.

I learned that one of the best ways to teach history is through stories, in which the facts are woven into the backdrop. These historically based stories can educate listeners on more than one level by teaching both a lesson or moral and teaching about the past. We remember stories because the description of characters and settings forms pictures in our minds that are easier to recall than lists of disembodied facts. Whenever I tell stories, whether folk tales or personal, family, original, or historical narratives, I infuse them with the details of place and time. Skipping the details and going directly to the meat of the story leaves the story void of nourishment on a human level. We are all voyeurs who want to know the interesting details of how others lived.

Information about day-to-day life can be gathered from history books and biographies, encyclopedias, diaries, interviews, and even historically accurate movies. Following is a checklist of items to include in stories whenever possible. In all cases, be specific rather than general, and use language that activates all the senses: sight, sound, smell, taste, and touch.

- Historical context. Weave into the story information about political situations, natural disasters, wars, world leaders, and so on—for example, "Back in 1838, when Martin Van Buren was president, there lived a young girl . . . "
- Foods. What did people eat? What did they call the foods they prepared? Use the original names for specific dishes, and then describe the food in terms the audience will understand: "Mrs. Sherman loved to make gefilte fish, which tastes like boiled fish meatballs."
- Expressions and manner of speaking. These can provide a sense of time and place: "When the children walked into the classroom, Mrs. Smith always said, 'Put your wraps in the closet, and leave your galoshes in the hall.'"
- Cost of living. How much did things cost? How

much money did people make? "Aunt Mary was only 8 years old in 1875, yet she worked in the sweatshop for 10 hours a day, making $1.50 a week."

- Transportation. How did people get from one place to the next? Did they travel by wagon train, Model T automobile, or steam locomotive?

- Housing. What did the houses look like? How many people lived in one room? "In 1889 Luke and Maggie moved west to Nebraska. Like everyone else, they built a house out of thick sod and called it a soddie."

- Games. Children love to know how other children lived long ago. What games did they play? What did they do with their time before the days of television? "I can still smell the cornhusk doll that Mama made for me when I was 5. She made the nose from a clove."

- Tools and household appliances. It's hard to imagine what life was like before electricity and running water, but people lived under those conditions and used a variety of tools and household items that are now obsolete: "Eloise loved to trick her older sister by putting cooking oil in her wash-basin water or on her shoe-button hook."

- Styles of dress. What styles of clothing were worn in different periods of history? Who wore what and where?

These are just a few of the categories I search in order to find details that put stories into a particular time and place in history. When I teach students how to create historically based stories, I suggest that they find at least 10 items from these categories and add them to the story. I often run a brainstorming session to see how many different items we can come up with for a given time and place.

Learning about history one day and one person at a time rather than in huge chunks will grab your listeners and keep them asking for more. Just think—we are now living the history of the future. Look around the room, and notice all the things that typify this time and place in history—the computer, microwave, electric juicer, fax machine, and so on. Stories about the past can and should breathe with as much detail, as much texture as is present to us today.

Storyteller, musician, writer, and workshop leader Karen Golden of Los Angeles specializes in Jewish, multicultural, personal, and historical stories. In 1993 Golden was featured in the Los Angeles Times *and on National Public Radio. She has produced one audiotape,* Tales and Scales: Stories of Jewish Wisdom, *and six of her original stories will be published in 1994.*

9

USING STORIES
TO TEACH SCIENCE AND MATH

USING STORIES TO TEACH SCIENCE AND MATH

The role of imagination in science and math curricula is usually seen as minimal, despite the fact that abstracts such as math problems and scientific formulae originate in the right side of the brain—the same place music, art, and poetry come from. This view, that only logical, sequential thought is valuable for scientific inquiry, is firmly entrenched in most curricula.

Kieran Egan, the author of *Teaching as Story Telling* (University of Chicago Press, 1989), offers quite a different viewpoint:

"An impoverished, empiricist's view of science has misused the authority of science to promote in education a narrow kind of logical thinking at the expense of those forms of thinking which we see most clearly in children's imaginative activities . . . . We in education might sensibly establish a more balanced view of children's thinking and learning [and see that] . . . imagination is a powerful and neglected tool of learning."

Egan sees the whole curriculum as one great story we have to tell children. He argues in favor of the need to meld imaginative play with the adventure that is the heart of all experiment and inquiry—and to show through story the drama of learning.

Albert Einstein called imagination the greatest power of the human mind. By incorporating storytelling into the teaching of math and science, teachers harness one of the strongest and potentially most useful skills their students have—the power to imagine.

The articles that follow shed light on many uses of story and storytelling as means of sparking students' interest, engaging them in inquiry and experiment, and helping them understanding difficult concepts.

TELLING TALES ABOUT
SCIENCE AND MATH

BY JENNY NASH

Larry Johnson's storytelling and video class emphasizes student participation, but he recalls one boy who never got up to tell a story of his own. It was something of a mystery, though, because Johnson knew the youngster enjoyed being in the class and listening to the stories spun by the teacher and the other children.

"I don't make the kids get up and tell stories," says Johnson, who teaches at Pillsbury Math/Science/Technology School in Minneapolis. "I encourage them and let them find their own time."

One day the boy told Johnson why he wasn't participating. "I don't need to be a storyteller," the child said. "I'm going to be a scientist." It's not difficult to see why the youngster felt as he did. After all, the conventional wisdom holds that storytelling concerns itself primarily with the fuzzy stuff of mythology, folklore, and magic, whereas science reveals clear, immutable facts.

Fortunately teachers and tellers are chucking that outdated view. Today they're marrying the humanities and sciences, using innovative programs that entice children (and adults) into the subject matter of science rather than bombard them with isolated facts. Educators are trying new approaches because many of the old ones no longer seem to work. While our world grows more technical, young Americans are losing ground, as more than 300 educational reports attest.

One report—based on the results of exams given to 9- and 13-year-olds from 20 countries—indicates that among the 15 countries that tested representative samples of children, U.S. 13-year-olds came in 13th in science and next to last in math. These dismal statistics are challenging educators to come up with new methods of teaching science and math, and storytelling seems to be a winner. Schools such as Pillsbury, museums, and even college campuses are hosting storytellers turned teachers and educators turned storytellers.

The phenomenon seems natural to Mary Budd Rowe, a professor of education at Stanford University in Stanford, California. "Science is a special kind of story-making, with no right or wrong answers, just better and better stories," Rowe says. And stories can hold students' interest, she adds, long after the memorization of facts has left them glassy-eyed.

"When you study a textbook," she says, "the amount of time that you

Writer Jenny Nash surveys a range of approaches to using stories to teach science and math to students from first grade to college. The teachers and tellers she interviewed see storytelling as an interdisciplinary approach that succeeds because it treats the curriculum as a whole rather than as a collection of discrete units and disciplines.

can stick with it is relatively small. But the same kinds of information can be woven into a story. When you pick up a good adventure story, you may be really tired, but two hours later you're still reading. We educators haven't taken advantage of the fact that plot is a very important way of helping people tie ideas together and stay interested."

Joan Leotta, a storyteller and writer in Burke, Virginia, uses stories to spark children's curiosity about science. "I use stories to give a context for scientific facts and to excite kids' interest in the subject. Then, when they have the facts, these stories strengthen their imagination."

She believes that a good scientist must have a lively and flexible imagination and that the imagination needs exercise, just as muscles do. "Scientists who have made breakthroughs have made a leap of faith from the known to the unknown," she says. Storytelling, she believes, can help train future scientists to make that leap.

Leotta became interested in combining stories and science after taking her children to a program by Mona Enquist-Johnson. Enquist-Johnson, a naturalist with Virginia's Fairfax County Park Authority, used the story of a snake, Crictor, who lives in Paris with an old lady, to introduce the program. "She talked about such things as the fact that snakes are good, that not all snakes are dangerous, and that when a snake has its tongue out, it's sniffing you," Leotta says. "We made snakes out of chenille sticks and puffballs, and since the program took place at the nature center, we saw and handled real snakes. I still remember that program years later because it was such fun."

Many educators say fun is what's missing in contemporary science and math education. When at age 11 Mary Budd Rowe came upon Albert Einstein staring intently at a fountain at Princeton University, the great physicist showed her how to move her hands quickly to see the separate drops of water as they spurted upward. As they walked away from the fountain, Einstein said to her, "Never forget that science is just that kind of exploring and fun."

Those were the qualities the Miami Museum was looking for when it hired storyteller Judy Gale to create programs for schoolchildren and the public. Several years before, Gale had put together and performed a series of concerts called Wonder With Me—dealing with the kinds of questions people have wondered about since time began—for the Rockland County, New York, school system.

She and anthropologist Linda Houlding, the natural-history curator for the Miami Museum, used that same concept for the museum's Wonder With Me shows, after overcoming some initial resistance from other museum employees. They complained that anthropology wasn't a real science, and storytelling certainly wasn't, Gale says, but the director at the time persevered and pushed the project through.

In each program the two would focus on a question such as What is thunder? How do birds learn to sing? or What job does the sun do in the food chain? They'd do a brief experiment illustrating the question and talk about what we know today on the subject. For example, to illustrate what creates the northern lights, the women used electricity to ionize nitrogen, oxygen, and neon in glass tubes—which causes nitrogen to glow violet and neon to become orange. Then Houlding would discuss a specific culture, and Gale would come on and tell a story from folklore that the culture would've used to answer the Wonder With Me question.

HOLISTIC APPROACHES

Interdisciplinary is the name of the game in using storytelling to teach about technical subjects, and nobody takes the concept more to heart than Sam Yada Cannarozzi, an American storyteller living in France. Cannarozzi wrote and performs a unique program he calls Nursery Rhymes From the Periodic Table, which consists of short poems, myths, and anecdotes about the elements and their discoverers.

In Cannarozzi's introduction to Nursery Rhymes he states that "the magic of the world is slowly dying because of the compartmentalization of the sciences." He's doing his part to end the division and unite the world of words and stories with that of atomic weights and numbers.

Cannarozzi became interested in the periodic table when he came upon a reference to the element tantalum. He discovered that it was named after Tantalus, who in Greek myth was punished with eternal thirst while standing neck-deep in water that receded whenever he stooped to drink from it. "I looked up tantalum's chemical properties and found that it's often used for surgical and dental tools because it rejects water," Cannarozzi says. Next he looked up the element niobium. When he found that it was named for Niobe, Tantalus's daughter, and that niobium is extracted from tantalum, he was hooked.

So are his audiences, who range from young schoolchildren to university professors. One of his first performances of Nursery Rhymes From the Periodic Table was for doctoral students and professors of biology and chemistry at the university in Lyon, France. Afterward several members of the audience came up to Cannarozzi to share their own elemental anecdotes. Often, though, he says, listeners are wistful. "The most common response I hear to my evenings with adults is 'If only they had taught me that way when I was in high school.'"

Fortunately the students of teachers like Larry Johnson are enjoying a more holistic approach to learning science. Johnson, a professional storyteller and certified master gardener, used to do storytelling and video work part time in the Minneapolis public schools. But Teri Edwards, the principal of the magnet school where Johnson now works full time as a storyteller/whole language/video teacher, created the position in order to hone students' communication skills. Doing that, Edwards felt, would directly benefit the way the children think and therefore their scientific skills.

Johnson, who teaches children of all ages, has also been good for their gardening ability. The school has a garden that often figures prominently in the kids' stories and video work.

Fran Stallings, a professional storyteller based in Tulsa, Oklahoma, incorporates another kind of green in her program Stories for a Green Earth. Stallings, who has a doctorate in biology, performs the ecology-oriented stories for several school districts in the Tulsa area. "I've always had an interest in stories that would convey a heart—as well as a brain—understanding of the basic concepts of ecology and science," she says. "Science tells how, but stories tell why. *Why* is not a science question; *why* is a human-heart question. It represents the human, emotional entry into a scientific area. You shouldn't approach young learners with a lot of facts. That kind of approach doesn't connect. But stories have the emotional hooks to get people interested."

Unfortunately, though, a strictly factual approach is the only kind many young learners see. "High-school science is apt to be taught like this: 'Here it is, kids; swallow it down. It's eternal truth, and it'll never change.' That's not science," says Stallings. "That's archaic dogma. A research scientist is constantly finding more questions than answers. That's what is exciting—and frustrating—about science. To be a good scientist, you have to be playful. You have to get wild ideas."

FINDING MULTIPLE SOLUTIONS

Sure, storytelling helps develop the imagination. It also strengthens divergent thinking: the ability to come up with different answers to the same question. Both capabilities are important components of creativity, says Deborah Tegano, an associate professor of child and family studies at the University of Tennessee at Knoxville. "Creativity is an important part of the entire curriculum and an integral part of everything a child does."

Tegano and other researchers study young children's potential creativity, for example, their ability to solve problems innovatively. When such skills are cultivated in children, the result is adults who can think well and create, whether their area of endeavor is painting or space travel.

Too often, she believes, children are taught convergent thinking instead—that there's only one correct answer to a question. But that doesn't encourage students to think for themselves. "Even in early math and science education, we tend to teach convergent thinking," she says. "That's antithetical to science and math—probably the most open-ended disciplines in the world." —Jenny Nash

From Storytelling Magazine, *winter 1993.*
Reprinted by permission.

Using Stories to Teach Science and Math

LIKE KEYS TO THE MIND

In Jackie Easley's first-grade classroom, math concepts are anything but dull. The texts Easley uses for class gave her the idea of using story cards and small objects, or manipulatives, so the children can see mathematical concepts in action. "I start by telling a story about the children or animals in the picture, and I give them names and a problem," says Easley. "Then the children add or subtract the manipulatives according to the story."

She uses a variety of story cards and objects to nudge the children's imagination: a polar bear sitting on an ice floe eats, or subtracts, little fish crackers that swim by; a picture of a playground is the backdrop to photocopied class pictures. A little nudge to the imagination goes a long way. Once the kids get started, their stories can get wild, as they try to think of more and more outlandish reasons for fish or friends to increase or go by the wayside—for instance, the fish that left to go surfing in Hawaii rather than swim with its friends.

The kids themselves are their favorite subjects, she finds. "They enjoy telling stories about their friends and classmates. Both their oral-language skills and math skills are developed by such activities."

Alan Davis uses stories and numbers in a different way, for learners a lot further along in the educational system. Davis, who teaches statistics at the University of Oklahoma Health Sciences Center in Oklahoma City, uses myths and legends to get his point across. He began trying this approach after a particularly discouraging day in the classroom.

"I was demoralized after I delivered a statistics lecture to medical students that had the effect of confusing them even more," he says. "So I decided that I would try a storytelling approach." Davis had two good reasons for trying it. First he points to the Jungian idea, popularized by Joseph Campbell, that certain symbols, or archetypes, can be understood by everyone. Says Davis, "Myths are like keys to the mind that can unlock doors because they've been around for so many centuries."

Davis's second reason for using stories was to put unfamiliar or, to some students, scary concepts in a familiar setting: mythology and the classics. "Plato said that perceiving truth is like being in a cave. Human beings are in a cave, and from the shadows on the wall we have to perceive the truth. But we never actually see the fire that casts the shadows. In a nutshell that's the statistical method: by looking at the samples we draw and the data we have, we make conclusions."

So Davis began creating stories with mythic characters to help illustrate statistical problems. "I have a story about Apollo, who is concerned because people have headaches. He comes up with a cure and

starts testing it on people. But when he tries to report his results to Zeus, Zeus keeps questioning the validity of what Apollo's done. Between them they work out all of the protocols to a clinical trial."

Davis then presented these ideas and some mythological stories at an American Statistical Association conference. His presentation generated a lot of interest, and a Swedish statistical journal asked him to write an article on his method of using myths to teach statistics.

College professor James Liles of the University of Tennessee at Knoxville also relies heavily on narrative—but he gets his points across with true tales and anecdotes. Liles, who has taught human biology and physiology for nearly 40 years, has always told stories to add spice to his courses. "When students hear about an actual thing that happened or that might happen, I always feel that it cements the idea much more firmly in their minds than if they just hear the facts—which can be rather dull at times," he admits.

Liles tells the story of a colleague's experience to illustrate the paralyzing effects of curare, a drug that certain South American Indians apply to their arrows when hunting game. Liles's colleague was set to have abdominal surgery, and he had been given the medical equivalent of curare to paralyze his muscles as well as anesthesia to knock him out so he wouldn't feel pain. Unfortunately the curare took effect about three scalpel cuts before the anesthesia did. But since he was utterly paralyzed—a person under the influence of the drug can't so much as twitch an eyelid—he couldn't let the surgeon know that. A student who recently heard the anecdote attests, "After listening to that story, I couldn't forget about curare if I wanted to."

Storytelling has become even more important to Liles's teaching as his classes have grown. "For the last 10 years I've been teaching primarily large classes," he says, "and it's more difficult to keep the students' attention. You have to be a bit more of an actor and raconteur with a big class."

Whether their listeners are preschoolers or Ph.D. candidates, more educators are becoming raconteurs, using stories to pique interest, illustrate hypotheses, or highlight points. Who says stories and science must be poles apart? Quoting from an old high-school chemistry book, Sam Yada Cannarozzi says, "Why not tell the tales of chemistry, the captivating birth and development of the periodic classification of the elements?" Such tales can spark "in the eyes of young and old alike the natural curiosity so important, so fundamental for all the sciences."

From *Storytelling Magazine*, winter 1993. Reprinted by permission.

Using Stories to Teach Science and Math

Storyteller, writer, and educator Joan Leotta offers a unique perspective on the scientific process as story and argues that imagination is the heart of scientific discovery.

STORIES PLUS SCIENCE EQUALS DISCOVERY

By Joan Leotta

When preparing the bookshelf for your science classroom, be sure to leave room alongside Edison and Einstein for Aesop, Jules Verne, and plenty of folklore. Storytelling in the science classroom? Most definitely! Story and science both seek to answer the question What if? Each takes us on a road to knowledge, to answer the why as well as the who, what, when, and where of the unknown. Storytelling can be a servant to the science teacher in the work of helping students learn.

The word *science* comes from the Latin word *scientia*, meaning knowledge. Many of humankind's first efforts to construct a body of knowledge are immortalized in story—in legends, folklore, myths. Storytelling and science are on the same quest—the quest for knowledge. Each demands insatiable curiosity and limitless imagination. Science teaches about the world around us, and storytelling teaches us what the world around us could be. Putting the two together demonstrates the old adage "two heads are better than one."

Storytelling's relationship to science is as old as the human race. Humankind has often sought to explain why with a story—about the origin of the

world, why leaves change colors, and so on. Stories help make complex scientific issues and principles more accessible to even the youngest student.

Stories about the natural world, such as pourquoi tales that seek to explain why or stories that deal with future possibilities, can pique curiosity and get students' creative juices flowing. Stories and anecdotes about science and from the lives of scientists and inventors do the same.

In addition, the scientific method of observing, classifying, using logic, conducting experiments, and forming hypotheses is paralleled closely by story construction. Ideas for stories come from observing what goes on around us. The storyteller must sort out the characters in the story and classify them by type and development within the story—good, bad, stays the same, changes. Folk tales were often developed based on people's observations of animals' activities and human nature, which were woven together to teach a lesson.

Logic draws the story from a beginning that engages the listener, marries the scene to the action of the story—that is, the process or the experiment of the piece—and then moves us to the ending, where everything comes together. By its very nature, story calls us into the realm of the abstract. We are called to ask What if? and to create a new world to answer our question.

To answer the question Who is the fastest? science says, Have a race over a given course, and document the results. Story says, Let's answer this by having two animals race each other—two very different ones, a tortoise and a hare—but let's also weigh overconfidence against persistence.

Process, the part of the experiment that today's instant-oriented students have the least patience with, is the heart of story, the plot. The execution of plot is analogous to the process of experimentation.

In tales the effect of each part of the process on the outcome can be clearly seen. Pourquoi tales, though light on scientific accuracy, are great for teaching this process—every trait and action of the creature that is transformed plays a part in creating that transformation. Thus, the story's plot describes an experiment. Students can practice the skill of attention to process by making up their own stories, listing plot and action sequences (sequencing being a basic skill for this exercise). Some might even benefit from taking a real experiment and making it into a pourquoi tale or a transformation story, giving names and characteristics, heroic and villainous aspects to the various neutral elements of their scientific experiment.

All good things must come to an end, and a story needs a defined ending, just as an experiment does. A hypothesis is sometimes put forth at the end of a story, just as a scientist may form one after observing the results of an experiment. In story this hypothesis is in the guise of a moral to be learned or a change explained (as in pourquoi tales). Or perhaps a group gets to live happily ever after as a result of the incidents in the tale. Science often expresses conclusions with the precision of a mathematical formula or a hypothesis (an educated guess) about the way the world works, whereas storytelling often overlays its message with emotion and its results with irony and a hypothesis about the way the human heart and mind function.

Storytelling exercises many skills, including probably the most important one for scientific advancement and discovery: imagination. Without imagination, a sense of wonder about relationships, the ability to see beyond what one's physical eyes and the laws of physics allow, there would be no light bulbs and no theory of relativity. Stories plus science equals imagination plus facts, and imagina-

tion plus facts leads to discovery. Geniuses such as Einstein and Edison often attribute their ability to move into new levels of thinking to their sense of wonder.

Many great scientists and inventors, grounded in a solid base of knowledge, leaped to greater heights because they had imagination. Montgolfier, the inventor of the hot-air balloon, was fascinated with flight, steeped in all the knowledge of his day. But what triggered his successful experiment with hot air? Legend has it that he was sitting inside his house in front of the fire while his wife dried one of her wide-skirted frocks. As he pondered his problems, he watched the skirt of the dress fill up with hot air, billow out, and rise. He had seen it many times—so had others. But at that moment, his imagination took over, and he saw that the dress could be a balloon, which could carry him to the heavens and the fulfillment of his dream.

Storytelling has the final advantage of keeping at the forefront the principle that ideas are meant to be communicated. Just as a story has an audience, an experiment has an audience and a purpose. The scientist does not work in a vacuum.

Storytelling in the science classroom doesn't guarantee that all of your students will chart new courses in the world of science. But it will at least create a wider range of interests among students. Interested students are motivated students. And motivated students are the ones who learn.

Joan Leotta of Burke, Virginia, tells stories in schools and libraries, on television, and at festivals and fairs. She is also a poet and an award-winning author. A Virginia Touring Artist and an Artist-in-Residence for the Virginia Commission on Fine Arts, Leotta lectures on and teaches writing, storytelling, and dramatics to children and adults.

Using Stories to Teach Science and Math

Science, Technology, and Contemporary Legends

By Gail de Vos

Contemporary legends, stories that many people believe describe events that happened to a "friend of a friend," are constantly being told by young adults. Listening to the legends, many of which are horrific, gross, or just plain silly, is not thought of as listening to stories. In fact, members of this audience may think they're too old for stories. Yet they sit spellbound when presented with modern horror tales and stories full of dark humor.

After being introduced to the idea that listening to stories is appropriate (and deliciously fun) behavior, young adults soon discover that storytelling is a natural part of their lives. As a teacher and storyteller, you can help them discover that contemporary legends have many functions other than pure entertainment. Contemporary legends can also be harnessed to many areas of the curriculum, igniting students' enthusiasm and providing relevance.

One of the primary functions of contemporary legends is to explain or "handle" anxiety created by the misapprehension and misunderstanding of science and technology. By telling and listening to these stories, people are able to articulate their fears and share them with others. Although the stories may not actually solve their quandaries, they do allow people indirectly to face their fears. Creating and telling stories to aid in this operation is nothing new—the earliest tales were stories told to explain natural and scientific phenomena and help a fearful audience cope with the terrors of everyday life.

In his book *Curses! Broiled Again! The Hottest Urban Legends Going* (Norton, 1989) Jan Harold Brunvand writes that in our modern tales, fear of technology may be a substitute for the supernatural fears expressed by myths from earlier times. As a result we hear horror stories "concerning microwave ovens, fast foods, and elevators rather than monsters, omens, or evil spells."

A recurring theme of the legends is trouble with technology: people having their insides cooked while acquiring a tan at a tanning salon; contact lenses fusing to eyes as a result of radiation; puppies, kittens, and occasionally babies placed in microwave ovens; and organ transplants involving stolen kidneys. The stories can be collected, told, discussed, and related to developments in technology. These tales can also

Storyteller and educator Gail de Vos provides food for thought on today's urban legends. Such tales belong in the classroom, she says, not only because adolescents are familiar with this genre of storytelling about fast food and phantom cars but also because the stories often deal with important scientific and technological themes.

spur discussion of the fears invoked by the popular-culture character of the mad scientist.

Research shows that contemporary legends evoke different responses from various age groups. The story about the poodle in the microwave was believed by younger children as scientific fact if the tale was related by someone in authority, whereas young adolescents treated the story as a gross joke to be told to their peers, Betty Belanus reported ("The Poodle in the Microwave Oven: Free Association and a Modern Legend," *Kentucky Folklore Record*, volume 26, 1980). Older listeners, skeptical of the safety standards of the microwave companies and the U.S. government, tended to believe that the stories were plausible. Students can investigate the possibility of such legends' actually occurring and the use of cautionary tales about scientific discoveries.

In the classroom the telling of contemporary legends can spur dialogue that can be channeled in specific directions. For example, a discussion on changes in modes of transportation can begin with the telling of the story "The Vanishing Hitchhiker." The story of the hitchhiker who vanishes from a vehicle and is subsequently identified as a ghost has been told for centuries around the world. The earliest stories show the hitchhiker on horseback; later versions involve horse-drawn carriages and then roadsters. Now the vanishing hitchhiker appears on deserted highways, in airports, and on the backs of motorcycles. Students can also explore the role of the automobile in modern society by following this discussion with other car tales, such as "The Boyfriend's Death," "The Porsche," "The Death Car," and "The Dead Cat in the Package."

After listening to the story "Southern-Fried Rat," students can not only discuss the phenomena of fast-food restaurants and prepackaged meals but also the changes technology brings to a society. Chemistry classes can investigate the hows and whys of contaminated-food tales; physics classes can explore the phenomenon of "Gravity Hill." Through

TANNING-SALON TORMENTS

People become anxious when they don't have a clear understanding of the events, people, and technological advances around them. Such was the case when tanning salons started to dot the landscape. Countless young people, it was said, began using the salons to acquire exquisite tans. It was also soon claimed, however, that countless young people with beautiful tans were dropping dead, just like that.

When autopsies were performed, it was said, doctors found that while these young people were acquiring their tans, they were cooking their insides! No one stopped to think—cooking one's insides, microwaves, tanning salons, ultraviolet rays—they simply reacted to their fear and passed the warning on to whoever contemplated entering a tanning salon's doors.

The same thing happened when microwave ovens first appeared. Most people didn't understand the technology involved, and because this incomprehension made them anxious, legends about "the pet in the microwave" started to circulate.

—Gail de Vos

Using Stories to Teach Science and Math

telling and exploring contemporary legends, students begin to see the connection between the legends and the technological and scientific aspects of their lives. They also begin to understand that science and technology influence not only the content of modern folklore but also its methods of transmission and therefore the narrative style.

Stories transmitted as "Xerox lore," defined by Brunvand as "a category of folklore that circulates in the form of copy-machine duplicates" (*The Vanishing Hitchhiker: American Urban Legends and Their Meanings*, Norton, 1981), can be written or drawn as are stories transmitted by way of computer networks. Entire computer bulletin boards are dedicated to urban legends (Freenet: alt.folklore.urban).

The legends are also transmitted by electronic mail as in the case of the story "The $25,000 Cookie Recipe." The legend of the "free" recipe from Neiman-Marcus exploded throughout the E-mail of North American telecommunications companies in 1989. The same tale has appeared several times in the newspaper column of Ann Landers. This resurrected tale is believed again and again because it deals with the delicious taste of revenge.

Teachers can find a ready supply of these tales in Brunvand's five books of urban legends, in *Scary Stories to Tell in the Dark* (Lippincott, 1981) and the two additional similarly named books by Alvin Schwartz, and in the works of Daniel Cohen. A recent treasure-trove is *The Scary Story Reader* (August House, 1993) by Richard and Judy Dockrey Young.

The best source, however, is students. Tell them a few such tales and let them tell you the ones they know. Instantly the classroom has a storytelling atmosphere in which students realize that the tales they tell and the scientific principles you're teaching are all part of the real world of modern adolescents.

Gail de Vos of Edmonton, Alberta, Canada, specializes in telling stories to young adults. Her first book, Storytelling for Young Adults *(Libraries Unlimited, 1991), is the result of her research for her master's degree in library and information studies. A former history teacher, de Vos has taught junior high in Australia and Laos. She teaches storytelling for the School of Library and Information Studies at the University of Alberta and conducts workshops and tells stories across Canada. Her second book,* Tales, Rumors, and Gossip: Contemporary Legends in Grades 7–12, *will be published by Libraries Unlimited.*

At first glance Hughes Moir, a storytelling college professor, and David Mastie, a science teacher and magician, seem an unlikely duo. But Mastie saw the connection between science and storytelling and invited Moir into a delightful adventure in combining stories and experiments.

ADVENTURES
IN SCIENCE MAGIC

When Hughes Moir and David Mastie join forces for their unique school program, anything can happen. They've created ghosts, blown out candles from 30 feet away, and fascinated everyone from kindergarten kids to high-school teachers in the process. Their flashy performances combine modern-day Mr. Wizard–style science demonstrations with the ancient tradition of storytelling. Call it educational entertainment, or as Moir puts it, science magic.

"The programs are incredibly fast-paced and heavy on science presentations," he explains. "Storytelling is the connector. It helps solidify the students' memory of the science and helps focus the scientific concept."

Moir's storytelling and Mastie's science demonstrations take the spotlight in rapid-fire succession during programs that generally last two to three hours. Moir begins by telling part of a story for about five minutes. Then, playing off something mentioned in the story, Mastie creates a short, attention-getting science display that also lasts about five minutes.

Moir takes the lead again, continuing the story for a few more minutes, and then Mastie interjects another scientific feat.

The program goes full-speed ahead as stories flow into science and science connects with stories. Both men frequently move into the audience. They encourage participation during break-out sessions that allow audience members to perform some of the science demonstrations themselves. They also encourage further study by providing written outlines of the stories and the science presentations, hoping that children will create their own projects.

"We're after modification of the teaching method," says Mastie. "Once you do it, you own it. If you blow the bubbles or make the gas, you own it, and you've learned it."

Oddly enough, the stories themselves seem to have little or nothing to do with science. Moir draws most of his material from folk ballads, urban legends, even stories about Winnie-the-Pooh. For  instance, in one tale Moir recounts a family's difficulty in trying to blow out a candle. With the lights dimmed, Mastie moves slowly up the aisle with a candle, then proceeds to use compressed air to blow it out from a distance of 30 feet. Several other quick demonstrations show alternative ways of blowing out a candle.

"David's demonstrations are very dramatic," Moir says. "They're quick and effective. The stories get the kids to see the connections. Most of the stories have no connection to science on the surface. They're just traditional and familiar tales."

Forging the connection between science projects and storytelling happened quite by accident for the two men. After they performed separately for a gathering of librarians, one of the event's organizers suggested the two try working together on a program. Moir lived in Ohio at the time and Mastie in Michigan. Without ever meeting face-to-face, the two developed their first program over the telephone.

"I would ask Hughes about the stories he was telling and then build a piece of science around something in the story," explains Mastie. "He told one story that had a monk and an apple in it. So I created a piece of science that used an apple. If a story included a lot of colors, I would build something that worked with colors. Almost anything in the story could be used as a connection to the piece of science."

The unexpected collaboration worked, aided by their experience and backgrounds in classroom teaching. Moir is now retired from teaching and liv-

ing in rural Colorado. Mastie is a high-school science teacher in Ann Arbor, Michigan. Together the two have given programs primarily for elementary- and middle-school assemblies. They've often followed presentations for the schoolkids with special performances for families and teachers.

No matter what the age group, audience responses to the unusual program are similar. Between the imaginative stories and action-packed science demonstrations, listeners come away with a new appreciation and knowledge of science—and a clear memory of how that science related to the story.   —Suzanne Martin

10

STORIES AND HEALING

THERAPEUTIC STORYTELLING IN THE SCHOOL SETTING • 149

TELLING SECRETS • 154

ENCOURAGING CHILDREN'S PERSONAL STORIES • 156

GETTING KIDS HIGH ON LIFE • 159

STORIES AND HEALING

In the story collection "The Arabian Nights" the narrator, Scheherazade, a beautiful maiden in the court of King Shahriar, saved herself, her king, and the kingdom with her storytelling. The story tells us that when King Shahriar discovered his wife's infidelities, he killed her and afterward revenged himself for her offenses by nightly marrying a virgin and killing her in the morning.

Scheherazade asked to be married to the king, saying, "I can deliver the land from trouble." On her wedding night, when the king came to her, she asked permission to tell a story, and he settled in to hear her words. She told her tale of love so compellingly that as the night wore on, the king's anger softened. She broke off the tale at morning light, asking the king to return the next evening to hear the rest. The king agreed, and so began the thousand and one nights. Each night he would come to her, and she would resume the tale, always breaking it off before morning.

On the thousand and first night Scheherazade actually finished her story of love. The king embraced her, saying, "Scheherazade, you have delighted me, and your tales have instructed me. My heart is mended, and the evil nights are gone. Stay with me always."

By modern standards, King Shahriar was severely psychotic. Yet, the tale tells us, the healing presence of stories brought about an inner transformation.

The relationship between stories and healing is receiving serious attention today. Indeed, Richard Hillman, a noted psychologist and the author of *Healing Fiction* (Station Hill Press, 1983), found that patients who had had stories read or told to them as children got better faster than those who had not.

The most basic means of therapeutic storytelling is simply making sure that young children hear stories. Many therapists, ministers, and educators go further, though, using students' own stories, folk literature, and original tales to help children address issues that are often difficult to confront head-on. The following articles look at these methods and shed light on the sometimes troubled lives of schoolchildren.

Therapeutic Storytelling in the School Setting

BY SARAH MALONE

Sarah Malone, a clinical social worker, works daily with children referred to her for evaluation or counseling. In this essay she communicates her respect for the children and their stories and her careful use of therapeutic tales. She offers many suggestions for incorporating therapeutic storytelling into school settings.

One evening after tucking my 6-year-old son into bed, I heard him singing an impromptu song about heart attacks and triple-bypass surgery. I instantly recognized the story line as a takeoff on his beloved grandmother's heart attack and surgery six weeks earlier. Now, after the crisis, he was dealing with the event by inventing a story song in the privacy of his darkened room. In the process I was privileged to witness the power of storytelling to help a child achieve mastery over emotional distress. My son's song was a therapeutic story.

But how is storytelling therapeutic, and how can schools use storytelling to promote emotional health in children?

Storytelling has been an important communication tool from time immemorial, its power lying partly in this history. It is, in the Jungian sense, archetypal—so intrinsic to the human condition that it resides, to quote a Spanish expression, in the bone marrow (*en la medula*). Each time we answer such routine questions as "How was your day?" and "What happened when . . . ?" we tell a story.

An important reason stories are healing is that they use metaphor. Instead of confronting an issue head-on, thus raising the listener's anxiety and defenses, a story's lesson enters through the subconscious. Metaphor allows the listener psychological distance from emotionally threatening content, increasing the likelihood that its message will be received. The story, therefore, may work a magic that translates into improved self-image or various feelings or behavior without ever directly receiving credit for such transformative powers.

Of further therapeutic value is storytelling's ability to encourage relationship-building and trust. The moment the teller and listeners jointly enter the story world, an intimate bond is formed, allowing both parties briefly to drink from the same cup. Toward such an end, I have regularly told stories to the same group of 90 students, from kindergarten through third grade, for four years. These children have developed a sense of trust and rapport with me as "their" storyteller.

Health-promoting strategies for teachers and counselors alike include bibliotherapy and therapeutic storytelling; telling role-model stories about historic figures and people from one's cultural or family tradition; and encouraging individual or group story creation.

Bibliotherapy and therapeutic storytelling • Bibliotherapy refers to the oral reading or telling of published stories that the teller believes to have therapeutic value for a specific child or group's emotional needs. Careful story selection is the key to gaining the greatest therapeutic value from this approach. It is important that selected stories metaphorically address the experience that the teller hopes to influence.

An example of this approach is the use of a children's story with a 3-year-old girl whose mother had died in an automobile accident. Friends and relatives were concerned about the child's lack of emotional expression regarding the loss. An aunt related Arnold Lobel's simple tale "Tear Water Tea" (from *Owl at Home*, Harper & Row, 1975) to the child and her siblings. The teller described Owl's filling the teakettle with his own tears as he recalled such sad things as "chairs with broken legs" and "mashed potatoes left on a plate." Next she invited the children to help Owl think of other sad things. The 3-year-old immediately said that "it was very sad when Mommy died." The storyteller incorporated this information into the story without pause, eliciting more tears from friend Owl. After gathering additional sad thoughts from the other children, the teller ended the story with Owl's acknowledging that "tear-water tea is always very good." In this example, the story subtly evoked an initial and spontaneous verbalization of the child's loss and sadness. This story also acknowledged the healing power of expressed grief as tears become warm, comforting tea. If Owl could cry, perhaps she could too.

Children's librarians are trustworthy resources for stories addressing specific topics or life events. I encourage teachers and parents to select stories appropriate to the emotional age of the child—not his or her biological age. Regression is common when children face life crises. Older children and teens can, when under emotional stress, readily gain therapeutic value from stories that on the surface appear geared to a younger audience. And many stories that do not at first glance appear to address a specific concern may nonetheless bolster a child's sense of mastery and hope. Fairy tales, myths, and legends are good examples.

Role-model stories • Stories that illustrate the moral character of role models build ego strength and self-identity in children of all ages and from all cultural backgrounds. Story selection for this purpose should include both male and female figures from a variety of ethnic and social groups. The stories should emphasize the role model's ability to overcome adversity appropriately, focusing on the model's courage, innovation, and perseverance. In selecting models, the storyteller should honor the children's requests. This will enhance their identification with the role model and involvement in the story. Hearing about the life history of famous athletes, political figures, and so on encourages the child to integrate the strengths of the hero or heroine.

Children may also wish to "adopt" a hero. To do so, each child draws a card-sized depiction of the adopted hero or heroine to carry in a wallet or book bag or tape to a school desk. Children may then consult with the hero when confronted with difficult choices, guessing what the model might do under similar circumstances. In this way, the hero or heroine acts as an "inner guide," gradually fortifying the child's own conscience or superego and improving the child's behavioral choices.

Other models may come from one's own or family stories. Probably each of us can recall a "perfect" moment from our past: a time when we felt at an all-time emotional high. We can probably also remember a moment when we overcame adversity after some struggle. A storyteller using this approach encourages children to recall such moments and tell their stories. Next children identify character attributes that helped them achieve that perfect moment. Examples include times of creativity, daring, commitment, courage, and so on. Encourage the children to develop an "I" statement, incorporating an assertion of character. While looking in a mirror or drawing a self-portrait, each child should state or write affirmatively, "I am creative, daring, courageous," and so on. Also ask the children to visualize themselves enacting the quality in a real-life situation. Finally, have the children express the intention to honor this trait in the future.

Family members can be valuable resources for family-history stories, and research shows that parental involvement at school supports student achievement. To help encourage such involvement, a special-education teacher and I invited parents and grandparents to share a life story that included a value they wanted to transmit to their children. Guest tellers were instructed to tell a story of any length from their own experience or from their family's oral tradition. Children took pride in introducing their relative, and children whose parents were unable to participate "adopted" a substitute. The school counselor, principal, and others readily accepted invitations from such children.

After each story the children asked questions and made comments. A videotape was made, with copies available for the children to keep as a record of the entire project. In subsequent class periods with their teacher the children drew a picture for each story they had heard, assigning to each a title and a lesson learned. Once compiled into a colorful book, the drawings served as a pictorial record of the many stories shared over the two-week project period.

An example of one such story was that of a great-great-grandfather whom the teller had never known. Family lore had it that the grandfather wished to buy a barn located on a neighboring farm. Having agreed upon the price, the two parties sealed the deal with a handshake late on a Friday afternoon. Given the distance from town and the time of day, however, the grandfather agreed to pay his neighbor the following Monday. The barn burned down on Saturday. As onlookers watched the debacle, some remarked to the grandfather that he was fortunate not to have paid for the barn since it had now burned to the ground. The grandfather replied, "I don't see why I'm so lucky. As far as I'm concerned, I've just lost myself a barn." Monday he went to town, withdrew the agreed-upon sum from the bank, and paid his neighbor for the barn. The teller shared this story as one that had deeply influenced her respect for commitment and personal responsibility.

Individual or group story creation • Story creation helps children master traumatic events, as my son did with his song. Methods abound for helping children create therapeutic stories. (I encourage those interested to explore the work of Richard Gardner and N. Kritzberg. Jerrold R. Brandell gives an excellent summary of therapeutic storytelling strategies in "Storytelling in Child Psychotherapy," published in *Innovative Interventions in Child and Adolescent Therapy*, edited by Charles E. Schaefer [John Wiley & Sons, 1988].)

One approach I have used successfully in school is to invite a child to develop a story about a drawing or sand-tray scene that he or she has just completed. The counselor acts as scribe, writing the story verbatim from the child's dictation, finishing with the title. This technique provides insight into the child's world-view and coping mechanisms. It also assists the child in mastery of life challenges. Play-therapy approaches are also very helpful, with the child leading and directing the story theme. As in other storytelling approaches, requests by the child to replay the same tale repeatedly should be honored; gradually, as mastery over the underlying psychological issues is achieved, the child will move on to new material.

In group settings the entire group can be invited to develop a story together. Members are asked to make up a story about an animal or aspect of nature that overcomes adversity or one that explains how an animal or entity acquired a specific trait. Group process is as important an aspect of story development as the story itself. Children must take turns, negotiate one another's editing recommendations, and reach consensus about plot and outcome. The counselor or teacher may guide group members toward more socially adaptive outcomes, if necessary. Finally group members choose a means by which to share their story with others. One popular avenue is to illustrate the story and make a book for presentation to their classmates. Puppetry, dramatization, video productions, and other avenues are additional possibilities.

When using any of the methods described here, storytellers should refrain from elaborating on the psychological meaning of the stories. They should also resist the temptation to secure conscious acknowledgment by listeners of a story's therapeutic meaning. First, the meaning is often different for each listener. Second, overt discussion may undermine the power of the metaphor by bringing its meaning into consciousness. Once the cat is out of the bag, the listener may well resist integrating the story's message.

I hope these examples illustrate some useful ways therapeutic storytelling can occur in a school setting. One important outcome is that children (and their parents) become empowered to tell their own stories. Each person is, after all, the author of his or her own reality—and each of us can choose at any point to alter the story line. Skills gained through school storytelling serve children well into the future, as they learn to reinterpret life's experiences. Even the most dismal experience can be related in a lifesaving way for the benefit of one's development and that of one's children.

I end with an example of this process that occurred in December 1982, when I visited my 87-year-old grandmother a month before her death. She had lived a long, challenging life and was bewildered to find herself in a nursing home following a sudden stroke. As we walked down the white linoleum hallway toward the dining room, Grandma looked at me and said, "I didn't ask to come along on this trip, but now that I'm here, I might as well make the most of it." As always, that is exactly what she did. I might add, she went out like a true light.

Sarah Malone, A.C.S.W., L.I.S.W., is a clinical social worker who lives with her husband and son on an organic farm near Moriarty, New Mexico. She first told stories as a volunteer at her son's preschool but soon found storytelling of value in her work as a child and family therapist. Now employed as a school social worker, Malone uses stories—her own, those of the children she serves, and published tales—as tools for achieving therapeutic goals.

Homeless children and those who are at risk for any reason are nonetheless children, with hopes, dreams, loves, and fears. In this interview, Melissa Heckler describes her work with such children and the richness that stories can bring into their lives.

TELLING SECRETS

About eight years ago storyteller Melissa Heckler of Armonk, New York, arrived at a school ready to tell a few tales. Her classroom audience included homeless children and children at risk because of abuse, family drug use, learning difficulties, racial tension, poverty, and other problems. The school suggested that Heckler not tell any family stories, assuming that the last thing such kids wanted to hear or talk about was family life. So Heckler told the students folk tales.

"To everyone's surprise, the kids who were most at risk were the most responsive," says Heckler. "They were riveted by the tales. We found that they used the stories as a mask—as a way to tell their own secrets."

Since that experience Heckler has seen at-risk children respond to stories in ways she never imagined. She now takes her tales to homeless shelters and works as an artist in residence for the Westchester County Council for the Arts, telling to all ages of schoolchildren. She also visits classes through the state's Board of Cooperative Education Services. And in every classroom she watches as storytelling works its magic with at-risk children.

"In a third-grade class I once told a very compli-cated African tale," Heckler recalls. "Afterward a boy stood up and retold the tale from beginning to end. The teacher was amazed because this boy could barely read or write. It was clear that he was an auditory learner. So here was a way to begin working with this child."

Through her work Heckler has found that kids' favorite tales are those of indigenous peoples and hunter-gatherer cultures. She avoids stories such as the Grimms' fairy tales and traditional giant stories that present a hierarchical view of families and life. Native American stories catch the students' attention, as do trickster tales and African and African-American stories.

But Heckler's repertoire doesn't stop with folk tales. She also uses personal stories, her own and the children's, to draw the kids out. She may take an object from her childhood—a doll, a rock, a photograph—to class and encourage the children to ask her questions about it. Through that exercise she teaches them to ask open-ended questions that will lead to the telling of stories. She urges the kids to close their eyes and picture a special object of their own. Then they take turns telling stories about the objects.

One of the most important parts of the storytelling process, she says, is telling the children her own story. She may have them ask her questions, or she may simply tell a tale about herself. She encourages teachers to do the same in order to help develop a rapport with the kids. "It doesn't matter whether you've had a rough life or a privileged one. What matters is that you're telling them your story," explains Heckler. "They have to sense that what you're telling them is real. They need to see you as a person. That will help them open up and tell their stories."

Heckler also asks the kids to collect stories from

family members and friends. To make telling those stories a playful activity during class, she sometimes has the children present their stories as if they were doing a radio program, complete with a student moderator and guest appearances by student storytellers. Or they might act out a TV show and tell the tales to a video camera. Other times the kids simply share the stories with their classmates. Regardless of how the stories are staged, the children continually surprise Heckler with their honesty and their revelations.

"One boy's father was a firefighter," remembers Heckler, "and he told a story about his father's being injured on the job. The father had fallen from an icy ladder and broken his back. When the boy told the story, the teacher said that he had never shown so much dignity, and from that day, the other kids treated him differently, more kindly. There is so much focus on the weaknesses in these kids and their lives. Telling their own stories gives them a chance

to express their heart and their strengths. They begin to see their own richness."

Given the opportunity through storytelling, at-risk children eagerly respond with stories of their own lives, no matter how desperate or traumatized those lives seem to be. Heckler's only advice to teachers is that they must recognize that such children have been placed at risk through no fault of their own. If they are homeless or abused, it is by chance, not choice. Educators need not shy away from this special audience for fear of intruding on a child's personal plight.

Heckler stresses that no specific stories are required to reach these children.

"Teachers need to find stories and ways of using storytelling that are comfortable for them," she says. "That's the most important thing. The kids will let you know what they want to hear and what they want to tell."

—Suzanne Martin

ENCOURAGING CHILDREN'S
PERSONAL STORIES

BY ELAINE WYNNE

Sometimes children's personal stories seem shocking or inappropriate for classroom sharing. Elaine Wynne, a Minneapolis therapist who works with children and families, offers advice on coping with this sometimes touchy area.

I can't do storytelling with the students anymore. The last time I did, a terrible thing happened—a boy talked about his penis."

This is an approximate quote from a high-school teacher. I've often wondered if this kind of event is not a major reason why storytelling and oral literacy are so neglected in most school curricula.

There's no question that this situation might shock or surprise the teacher or the other students. Of course, if such a story came to the teacher in written form, he or she would be the only one to see it. When it's told in a story, the whole class hears it, and the teacher must deal with the repercussions.

I'd want to ask why the boy felt a need to tell this story and to tell it in the way he did. My response to the educator who told me about the incident was that I felt it would be unfortunate to give up on storytelling altogether. Now that the situation had occurred, I had several recommendations:

- Before students tell stories again, talk with them and set some guidelines for what is appropriate in the classroom. If they are telling personal stories, urge them not to tell anything that would make them or others feel too embarrassed.
- Have a talk with the boy in private, and express concern about the way he told the story. Try to determine his motivation.
- Talk with the school social worker or psychologist about the incident and enlist his or her help.

The teacher could also stipulate that only traditional and literary stories may be used. I would like to explore, however, the valuable learning experiences that can come from children's telling stories from their own life.

Before I became a psychologist in Minnesota, I did many school residencies as a storyteller. In one residency I had two groups for kids. One was a group that used stories to teach relaxation skills; the other, a dream group. Each child would tell a dream, and the other children might act it out, with the dreamer directing the drama. Sometimes we drew the frames for a film, and other times I told stories that the dreams reminded me of.

Some children became so excited about the class that they started dream journals. Sometimes the dreams tumbled out rapidly, and the child needed to ask a parent to write down the dreams. We never interpreted the dreams and instead saw them as dramatic material.

At the same time I was doing stress-reduction work that used stories about QR, the "quiet response." One girl in that group, whom we'll call Mary, arrived at school one day telling of a nightmare she'd had the night before. She had been telling the dream over and over in school and by the afternoon was more agitated than she had been in the morning. One of the teachers knew of my work with dreams and recommended that Mary come early to relaxation class and tell me the dream. She did. In the dream Mary kept falling into a lake or ocean, and her girlfriend kept saving her, but the dream ended with her falling in again and with Mary's being afraid that the friend would not be able to rescue her.

I validated her feelings, and then, because the class had arrived, I said, "Why don't you draw a picture of how QR can help you with something difficult in your life?" Mary began to draw QR as a rust-colored elliptical shield (there was no single description of QR; all the children had their own image of how QR looked). The shield slipped between Mary and the water and now had the potential to save her. After doing the drawing and telling the other kids about it, Mary appeared to relax considerably. Later, when I visited the school psychologist and explained what had happened, I said I had a hunch that Mary felt uncertain about whether a female figure could help her. The psychologist then told me that Mary's parents were in the process of getting a divorce and that Mary was going to stay with her mother. She began to wonder if Mary was afraid that her mother couldn't care for her, as her mother had a fairly extensive disability.

The psychologist subsequently set up a meeting with Mary and her mother, during which Mary was able to share her feelings and her mother was able to reassure her. Mary began to settle in more comfortably at school. Even though her parents were divorcing, she now felt more secure about her mother. If the disturbing event had not occurred and had not had a place to reveal itself, Mary might have continued to worry, and it's very likely her schoolwork would have suffered.

Sometimes teachers express fear about what children will reveal if they tell personal stories in class. Here are some suggestions:

- If a child tells a story about physical or sexual abuse, in most states the teacher is required to report the abuse. The teacher certainly should not be faulted if the topic comes up in class.
- When hearing their peers' stories, children often find that others'

experiences are much like their own, which can enhance self-esteem.

- If a child begins to tell something that sounds as though it will involve too deep a self-disclosure, the teacher can respond by saying, "Good story, James. Let me talk with you after class, and we can see if there are other ways to tell your story." After class the teacher should speak with the child about self-protection or about telling the story to other professionals.

- If a support group is possible or indicated, the teacher might suggest it. Of course, any such support group must have confidentiality rules.

- If a child experiences deep emotion when telling a story, a teacher can say that we can't always predict how we will feel when we tell a story and that he or she sometimes finds that happening too. The teacher might add that the student's response probably means it's a very good story but perhaps this is not the right time to tell it. If the story brings out only a small expression of the emotion, the teacher can simply allow the story to stand. After all, many artistic representations bring about the expression of emotion. The teacher can talk with the student and reassure her or him after class.

It is in some ways unfair that teachers today have such great responsibility in children's lives, but it is also a great challenge and an opportunity for educators to be present to children who express important needs. It is not likely that the harshness of some children's lives will change soon, and it is not possible for us to close our eyes and ears to that reality. It would be a great tragedy if storytelling, an excellent aid to developing oral language, were neglected simply because it can be an expression of children's difficulties.

When children tell stories from their own experience, teachers may be challenged in ways they haven't been trained to handle. I suggest that rather than see these situations as negative, teachers use them as opportunities to teach storytelling techniques, to help children learn appropriate boundaries in the classroom, to get to know the children more deeply, and to offer acceptance.

Elaine Wynne, M.A., of Minneapolis is a freelance storyteller and a licensed psychologist in private practice who works with adults and children. For six years she worked at Minneapolis Children's Medical Center, using story and metaphor to work with children who had cancer, asthma, and other disorders. She has taught workshops in metaphor and story for several universities, and for 10 years she's taught storytelling at Metropolitan State University.

GETTING KIDS HIGH ON LIFE

BY STACIE MARINELLI

"With addictions, it's not enough to say no. You also have to say yes to something," Buckfield, Maine, performer Rick Adam tells a middle-school audience, describing how learning to play the electric guitar and joining a band helped him break a teenage food addiction. Storytelling can help young people say yes to healthy habits, believe tellers, therapists, and educators who are using the art to help prevent substance abuse and aid in recovery.

How? Stories can play an important part in both education and therapy—by communicating the devastating effects of addiction in ways that strictly factual presentations can't and by giving kids a means of expressing their own fears and troubles via metaphors and symbolic language. And storytellers, some of whom have conquered addiction themselves, can serve as role models of healthy, fun adulthood.

"Addictions are about isolation and denial, resistance to change, and being cut off from your inner source of life," says Brattleboro, Vermont, storyteller Mary Sinclair. "Healthy life patterns have to do with spontaneity, flexibility, intimacy, and the ability to draw on one's imagination." Stories, she says, can help promote these traits and give young people the inner strength to fight the lure of addiction.

Sinclair, who has a master's degree in counseling, once worked at Spofford Hall, a New Hampshire treatment center for alcoholism and drug abuse. Since 1986 she has directed Serendipity School, an East Burke, Vermont, summer storytelling camp where mythic tales, the arts, and body work—including deep-breathing and movement techniques—are used as vehicles for healing. The combination of approaches, Sinclair believes, can help participants feel happy, creative, and naturally high. The campers, some of whom are troubled children, range in age from 8 to 17.

Before they begin the camp, the youngsters choose a tale from the oral tradition, guided by a book list Sinclair provides. During the program the children work intensively on their chosen story. "That means they walk the walk of the characters and go into the caves and smell the smells, and they really work the story," Sinclair says. "There's a super-conscious part of us that guides us to stories."

Partly funded by Vermont's Alcohol and Drug Abuse Prevention Ser-

It isn't always easy for children to resist the lure of drugs and alcohol. Here storyteller and writer Stacie Marinelli describes educational programs that use storytelling, music, and theater to educate young listeners about addiction's pitfalls while encouraging them to stay on a positive path.

Tales as Tools

159

vices, the program involves some direct teaching about addictions as well as discussion of healthy and unhealthy behavior. The kids might talk about story characters who avoid violence, stay calm in times of crisis, or collaborate to get a job done. They also discuss real-life situations—for example, why kids tease one another and what effects such behavior can have.

Although the children's story choices are not analyzed, they often seem revealing. An 11-year-old boy from an alcoholic family who didn't pay much attention to him selected an African story about King Leopard, whose throne is usurped by Dog. Leopard goes into the world to find a new voice and new strength and later returns to fight Dog for the kingdom. In Sinclair's view, the telling of tales that the children have chosen themselves is healing. "In order to really learn to tell a story," she says, "it has to unfold and become real in you. As that happens, chaotic material is organized into patterns, which then can be integrated into who you are. When you can name and organize what is true for you, you begin to be able to live with it."

UNTYING LIFE'S KNOTS

In many communities schools have become frontline fighters in the battle against drug and alcohol addiction. Such schools often sponsor organized prevention programs involving outside entertainers and speakers as well as small-group activities and discussions about such topics as peer pressure, stress, healthy relationships, and communication.

Granted, entering an auditorium full of hundreds of roughhousing, giggling youngsters can be daunting for the visiting storyteller. Performers must both entertain and motivate students who may have been hearing the "just say no" message all week. That's one reason Portland, Maine, storyteller Jackson Gillman begins with "The Perfect High," a humorous story complete with music and special effects, in which he pokes fun at all kinds of addictions and portrays such zany characters as a new-age guru who tries to advise a seeker that "the perfect high comes from within."

Gillman goes on to tell "Hard Knocks," a realistic one-hour story of a family crippled by alcohol. This tale of a troubled youth, his deaf younger sister, and his alcoholic father spells out the characteristics and emotions of an alcoholic family as well as the road to recovery. After the performance students break up into small groups with teachers and counselors to discuss how they feel about what they've heard, with the help of a study guide Gillman provides. The guide's questions help draw out students' responses, and it lists resources for further information—

for example, Alateen, a 12-step group for teens who live with or are otherwise involved with an alcoholic.

Rick Adam's school program, Singing in the Darkness: A Journey Through Addiction, is presented as personal testimony. Although Adam's tale touches on drug dependency, eating disorders, and a suicide attempt, it is ultimately a story of recovery, and he lightens the mood by building in music, mime, juggling, and even rope tricks.

Adam conveys his message with unique wordplays and metaphors. Describing a bad day when he was a kid and couldn't get the knots out of his sneaker laces, he mentions what he calls "not-good-enough knots." During his performance he places a beer bottle on the table of a set that depicts a 1950s-era kitchen and says, "We looked like a regular family, but we had a secret. My father drank. Now, don't get me wrong. My dad wasn't a bad man. Alcoholics are just regular guys. They just have too many not-good-enough knots inside them."

As the character's father's alcoholism worsens, the boy gains weight, which he loses through his dedication to the guitar and a diet and exercise. Later, though, he descends into drug addiction and attempts suicide before entering a drug-treatment center. The rest of the story describes how he found the way out of his private hell and into a life of balance and positive choices. "Healthy choices don't hurt anyone. When you start making good choices," Adam tells students, "the not-good-enough knots start disappearing."

New York City's Karen DeMauro, an actor and an acting coach for more than 25 years, brings her own brand of prevention-based story theater to schools, working with kids from elementary grades on up. Using participatory storytelling, she hopes to promote a sense of wellness in children that will help them shun drugs and alcohol.

DeMauro creates plays with the kids, using stories to open up their creativity and provide material for scripts. She tells the children, "We're going to build a story about the things that matter most to us about being healthy people who can create and do things in the world." In one play the children encounter a magic mountain made of addictive substances, and they must decide whether and how to avoid them.

DeMauro always begins her programs with movement exercises because she believes strongly in the concepts of kinesthetic learning and embodiment—that children will remember what they've physically experienced. She then takes them on a guided visualization in which they meet the "wise person within," who gives them advice and a gift to help with their problems. The visions the kids share of the wise person and his or her gifts become chain stories, in which each student adds

something to the tale. In the process, DeMauro believes, problems and memories are released, and the children gain the experience of discovering some answers from within.

"The more we eliminate the root causes for substance abuse"—problems such as isolation, denial, boredom, low self-esteem, and a lack of coping skills—"the more kids are connected with life," she says. "When you feel fully alive, like when you're telling a story, you have in your body a memory of what it's like to be totally functioning and healthy."

This work isn't just good for kids—it's healthy for its practitioners as well. Says Rick Adam, "Doing this show keeps me straight because I can't teach this to others and not follow it myself." DeMauro adds, "I have personal issues I'm working on, and this is a perfect opportunity for me to keep dealing with those things."

Storytellers don't pretend that the path to healthy living is easy, though, or that recovery from addiction is instantaneous. Rather, the process is an unending healing journey.

"I still get not-good-enough knots," Rick Adam tells students near the end of his show, before disappearing backstage and emerging in the costume of his character Professor Paddywhack, supporting on his back a one-man band that took him 15 years to create. Young listeners react to the bizarre contraption's music with laughter and applause. "And I still have a band," he adds, alluding to the band he joined as a kid.

"Whatever your dreams are," the teller concludes, "they're *your* dreams—no matter how crazy they may seem to other people. Say yes to yourself. No matter what anyone says, go after your dreams."

From Storytelling Magazine, *spring 1993. Reprinted by permission.*

11
TOWARD COMMUNITY IN THE CLASSROOM

Toward Community in the Classroom

We live in a culturally rich society. The U.S. Department of Education projects that by the year 2000 more than half the students entering our schools will be children of color, originating from many different cultures. Through storytelling, teachers can reflect this diversity in the curriculum, using tales from various cultures to enhance every content area.

The storytelling teacher is in an ideal position to introduce a climate of understanding and tolerance in the classroom, especially because of the recent increase in folk-tale collections written for oral retelling (see chapter 13 for a list of recommended books). In retelling such stories, teachers can communicate a great deal of information about the lifestyles and beliefs of different cultures. And in their deceptively simple manner, these stories can help us appreciate the diversity of other traditions while they reveal the common threads and universal themes that unite us—that enable us to build community.

Frank Ettawageshik, an Odaawaa (Ottawa) Indian from northern Michigan, offers a note of caution, however, for those who tell folk tales from other cultures. He points out, for instance, that storytellers tend to use past tense when describing Native Americans, yet his people's culture is a living one. "There is even a word for pizza in our language," he notes. Ettawageshik suggests that those who tell stories from cultures other than their own should also try to communicate how the story's people live today and how their traditions fit into their present life.

The following articles address the topics of researching and telling stories to teach about the value of both diversity and community. Storytellers and educators from several different cultural groups offer background, suggestions, and food for thought.

More Cultural Than Thou?

By Doug Lipman

Well-meaning people are often deceived by the fallacy of "plain vanilla." An aspiring storyteller might say to me, for instance, "You're lucky. You have those great Jewish stories to tell. I'm just a WASP. I wish I had your kind of culture." Or I'll get a call from a library or school system: "We really need your program on individual differences because we don't have much diversity in our rural white region."

Please remember: vanilla is a flavor. Vanilla ice cream has a color. Every group of well-to-do, white male middle-managers—just like every group of poor female Navajo weavers—contains an astounding diversity.

So I tell the aspiring WASP teller to reclaim her own experience: she lives stories every day. When I go to the rural white third-grade classroom, I start by helping the kids to discover and value their differences from one another. Only then can they reach out to people from other geographic areas and ethnic backgrounds with respect and love.

In the storytelling community controversy rages over the propriety of telling traditional stories that come from outside the teller's culture of origin. The one point everyone can agree on is that such stories need to be treated with respect. People seldom realize, however, that if the teller does not truly accept his uniqueness, he can't possibly give full respect to a story from another tradition. If he accepts the fallacy that he has no culture, he can't relate to another culture as equal to his.

Prompted by ecological awareness, I might want to tell certain Native American stories because they speak of a connection with the environment that's missing from my European-American culture. But wait a minute. What is the story of the European connection with the environment? Aren't there two trends—one to plunder colonies, the other to nurture gardens? Identifying the neglected trend means we can bolster it in the future—and come to Native American stories as allies, not parasites. If I do not learn my heritage, I will be using the Native American stories to cover up my severed relationship to the earth.

Once I performed in a rural area where Jews are uncommon. Afterward a woman came up to me and told me her story. She had grown up nearby in a town with no Jews and had been a teenager before she realized that Jews existed. She told me that my Jewish stories had moved her, and she thanked me for coming. Her manner and words suggested that

Anglo-Saxon teachers and students may feel left out of discussions on ethnic heritage because they feel as though they don't belong to any particular group. Storyteller and storytelling coach Doug Lipman of West Somerville, Massachusetts, takes the refreshing point of view that everyone has such a heritage—some traditions are just more apparent than others.

we were people with different experiences that could enrich each other.

After the same performance another woman spoke to me. She smiled rigidly and said, "It's so nice to have a Jew here. I've always liked Jewish stories. We need to hear you people more." Her manner and words suggested that *she* was a person but *I* had interesting stories.

If I were to learn that the first woman was telling Jewish stories she'd learned from me that day, I'd be pleased and honored. If I learned the same of the second woman, I'd feel like a witness to a theft.

Groups who receive less than their share of wealth and power shouldn't be expected to bear the burden of providing feelings and experiences for the rest of us. Instead, if we explore and celebrate our unique selves, stories, and heritage, we'll be able to reach out to other cultures with a true sense of reverence, excitement, and compassion.

From Storytelling Magazine, *winter 1992. Reprinted by permission.*

THE MULTICULTURAL CHALLENGE

When preparing multicultural story programs, tellers must give an accurate portrait of the cultures involved. Here are some tips to help you in the process.

- When selecting each story, carefully consider the source. The 398 library classification is full of story books from many lands, but many don't give a high degree of respect to origins. It's a good idea to find books that have cultural notes and glossaries because these indicate a concern for accuracy and documentation.

- When you find a story, check out its source. Look for the tale in other books. Research the author and the culture or ask a representative of the culture to determine how accurate the story is.

- Establish a cultural context for the story. Research ways in which tales, folk stories, legends, and written literature and history are used. Even though you may not use all the information you uncover, it will help you convey to listeners an impression of that culture. Make the 970 classification at your library as important as 398.

- Don't violate cultural taboos. Some stories are meant for telling only by men, for instance; some only in winter.

- Put the tale into an accurate cultural context during your program's introduction or finale. If you change significant parts (for personal reasons or to suit audience needs), relate that information.

- Learn the correct pronunciation of character and place names in the given language. Be able to accurately describe the setting of the story.

- Use participation and follow-up activities to expand the cultural experience. Have your audience guess word meanings, examine or work on a map of the country, or take part in a craft typical of the culture.

—Joan Leotta

From the Yarnspinner, *August 1991. Reprinted by permission.*

STORYTELLING AND THE SACRED:
ON THE USES
OF NATIVE AMERICAN STORIES

BY JOSEPH BRUCHAC

There is a great deal of interest in American Indian stories through-out storytelling circles, and almost all storytellers seem to know and tell at least one such tale. Often these tales are among their favorites. Storytellers also usually find that audiences ask for and respond to them with enthusiasm.

It is understandable that there should be such an interest in Native American stories: after all, this country was founded on "Indian land." The stories of the many native nations of what is now the United States speak to both Indian and non-Indian in ways unlike those of any other tales. Moreover, the many Native American tales already collected and in print constitute one of the richest bodies of myth and legend found anywhere in the world. There are currently to be found in books tens of thousands of Native American tales from the more than 400 oral traditions of North America—tales filled with memorable and exciting details that attract both storytellers and audiences. Iroquois stories, for example, abound in such wonderful creatures as stone giants, monster bears, flying heads, magical dwarfs, vampire skeletons, and more than a dozen different trickster figures.

For many storytellers American Indian tales are untapped and fertile ground. A storyteller first finding an American Indian story that speaks in that special voice to him or her must feel as Balboa (not Cortez) felt on that peak in Darien when he first saw the Pacific Ocean. There are, however, a number of problems related to current uses—and misuses—of American Indian stories by non-Indian storytellers. These problems stem in part from that very newness, that undiscovered quality, that makes the stories so attractive and exciting to a storyteller seeking new ground. Not only are the stories new to the potential teller, so too are all of the real (rather than stereotyped) aspects of Native American culture, past and present. Difficulties also arise because the majority of non-Indian storytellers encounter the stories first in a book rather than from the lips of an American Indian. Unfortunately, many written versions of Native American stories that are still alive in the oral tradition of a particular people have been incompletely or inaccurately recorded.

It is a sad truth that the average non-Indian American today knows less about the American Indian than did the first European settlers on

Many storytellers feel an affinity with Native American stories and eagerly share them with students. Teller and author Joseph Bruchac applauds this effort, offers insights into what the stories mean to Native Americans, and gives suggestions for telling the tales responsibly.

the continent—who survived because of the help and friendship of Native Americans. Even people who live within a few miles of large and active American Indian communities know little about their Native American neighbors or express disbelief that they even exist. The myth of the "vanishing red man" is more alive in the minds of most Americans than the vital continent-wide, growing population of Native Americans that prompted Simon Ortiz, Acoma storyteller and poet, to say in one of his poems, "Indians are everywhere."

Along with the lack of knowledge about present-day Native Americans goes ignorance of the place and proper use of American Indian stories. No story—in any culture—exists in isolation from the life of its people. The problems of the rationale, effectiveness, and validity of transplanting stories from one culture to another do not relate just to American Indian tales. The best storytellers are usually aware of those problems and may even engage in heroic efforts to understand the origins and cultural contexts of the tales they use. Yet many storytellers—including some of the best—know only that the American Indian stories they tell came from this or that book or were told by this or that non-Indian teller. Ironically, they may know less of the origin of an American Indian tale—which grew from this soil—than they do of one from ancient Babylon or the Fiji Islands. Almost universally the non-Indian tellers using an American Indian tale have never heard a word spoken in the particular American Indian language from which that tale comes, have no knowledge of the intellectual or material culture of that Indian nation, and have never met a living American Indian from that nation. In many cases they don't even know where the story comes from—other than that it is Indian. And they almost certainly do not know the strong relationship between storytelling and the sacred that exists throughout the many Native American nations.

Before I go further, let me make clear that my aim is not to discourage non-Indians from telling American Indian stories. The stories of Native American people are, to a degree, now part of the heritage of all Americans. The lessons they teach—and I will speak more about the lesson-bearing qualities of Native American tales—are probably more needed today by all of us than they were hundreds of years ago by those who first told them. These are powerful stories, powerful as medicine or tobacco. But like medicine or the tobacco whose smoke was used to carry prayers up to the Creator, stories must be used wisely and well or they may be harmful to both tellers and hearers alike. Every Native American storyteller I have spoken to about this agrees that there is no reason why non-Indian storytellers who understand and respect American Indian tales should not tell them. But there is a great deal to understand, and respect implies responsibility. It is my hope that this article may lead non-Indian tellers to a better understanding of American Indian storytelling and suggest some directions they may follow to develop the proper relationship with the stories they wish to tell.

NATIVE AMERICAN USES OF STORIES

Native American stories have traditionally been used to teach the people those lessons they need to know to cooperate and survive. American Indian cultures throughout the continent placed high premiums on both the independence of the individual and the importance of working for the good of all. Coercion was seldom used to force an individual to conform, and the lack of police, strict laws, and jails was often remarked upon by European travelers, who noticed that the American Indians they visited also seemed to have no crime. This lack of coercion was particularly evident in the child-rearing practices of Native American peoples. Universally it was regarded as deeply wrong for any adult to strike a child. The European rule of "spare the rod and spoil the child" seemed perverse to Native Americans, who believed that beating children would produce only negative results. Striking a child could serve only to break the child's spirit or stir resentment. Such a cowardly act was a terrible example.

Instead, when a child did wrong, the first thing to do was use the power of storytelling to show the right way. If a child was disobedient, rude to an elder, or doing things that might be dangerous to the child, he or she would be told one or more lesson stories designed to show what happens to those who misbehave. The power of the stories—which are told to this day—was usually enough. If stories and other measures, such as throwing water on the child, did not work, various shunning practices—pretending the child did not exist or (in the case of the Abenaki) blackening the child's face and sending him or her out of the lodge to be ignored by all in the community—were used. As soon as the child indicated willingness to behave properly, the shunning ended. Adults too were told stories to help them see the right paths to follow.

Because such lesson stories were of great importance to the welfare of the individual and the nation, they had to be charged with great power. A good story, one that is entertaining and creatively effective, is more likely to affect its hearer. The role of the story as social guide made it all the more important that the story be memorable. Because of this, it is important that non-Indian tellers understand clearly the message a particular story is meant to convey. If you are unaware of the way the story was used, you may be more likely to misunderstand or misuse it.

It is no exaggeration to say that all American Indian stories, when used in the right context, can serve as lesson stories and important tools of communication. That is still true among Native American peoples. In fact, even jokes may be used in that fashion in Native American communities. If an American Indian tells you a joke, listen closely to it. Invariably that joke applies to something you have done or said. The joke may be intended as a lesson for you or even a reprimand if you have overstepped your bounds in some way. But because Native American people still believe in noninterference in others' actions—except in indirect ways—telling a joke may be the chosen way to point something out.

It is important to remember too that Native American culture is holistic. By this I mean that there is no separation between church and state, none of the convenient pigeonholing we find in Western culture that makes it easy to separate the sacred from the everyday. In the American Indian universe, everything is sacred. A book I strongly recommend to anyone interested in the role of stories in contemporary Native American life is *Wolf That I Am* by Fred McTaggert (Houghton Mifflin, 1976). It chronicles the efforts of McTaggert, then a graduate student at the University of Iowa, to collect and write about the stories of the Mesquakie people, whose settlement was not far from Iowa City. Although he thought he would be collecting quaint folk tales from the remnants of a dying culture, he soon found himself confronted by people who believed strongly in themselves, their language, and their religious rituals. Far from dying, the Mesquakie way was very much alive. Far from being ready to share their stories with the tape recorder–bearing graduate student, the Mesquakie people were protective of their traditions.

At the advice of a Mesquakie friend, also a student at the university, McTaggert once trudged through a snowstorm to reach the house of a man who was said to know many stories. But when McTaggert knocked on the door and Tom Youngman stepped out, closing the door behind him, this is what happened:

"I was told you might be able to help me out with some information about stories," I began.

The man's deep brown eyes looked into mine for several minutes. I sensed in his eyes a power and a calmness that I was not at all familiar with. He was wearing only a flannel shirt, but he did not even shiver in the cold, piercing wind. As he stood in front of the closed door, looking deeply into my eyes, he somehow put me at ease, and I felt neither the fear nor the guilt that I usually felt when first meeting people on the

Mesquakie settlement. His silence was an adequate communication, and when he finally spoke, I knew what he was about to say.

"I can't tell you stories," he said softly. I had no trouble hearing him over the whistling wind. "I use my stories to pray. To me they are sacred."

I thanked him, and he opened the door again and retreated into his small lodge.

Later McTaggert realized that he had been tricked by his Mesquakie student friend. At first he was angry and confused. Then he realized that by being tricked—as in the Mesquakie story "Raccoon and Wolf," which he had read in an old collection—he had learned a lesson.

There are also stories, and this varies from one Native American nation to the next, that are part of healing rituals. The most obvious example may be the Navajo stories that are part of the various healing-way ceremonies. Figures from those stories are made in colored sand on the earth, and the person to be cured is placed on top of that sand painting—made a part of the story—in a ritual that may go on for days. In other Native American nations, some stories are to be told only to certain initiated people and even then only at certain times. What responsibility does the storyteller have when he or she discovers one of these stories and wishes to tell it outside of the original context?

I am not sure I know the right answer, but I do know that taking sacred things lightly is not a good idea and that caution is more advisable than foolhardiness. Stories are told about characters, Coyote, for example, who take the sacred too lightly and do things the wrong way. Within the stories, they always pay for their mistakes.

It appears to be a continentwide tradition that all Native American myths and legends are to be told only at certain times and in certain ways. Keewaydinoquay, an Anishinabe medicine woman and storyteller, has a song that begins each storytelling. She always offers *asseyma*, or tobacco, for the ancestors during its singing. Those who have studied with Keewaydinoquay do the same.

In most parts of North America stories were to be told only during the winter season. In some cases a story may be told only at night. Further, to mention the names of certain characters in stories—Coyote, for example—outside of the stories is an invitation to bad luck. Coyote, say some of the California Indian people, might hear you mention his name and then come to visit you and do mischief. One can, I suppose, find logical reasons for these prohibitions. To engage in storytelling during the growing season when one should be working in the fields or gathering food might be seen as counterproductive. People have greater need for stories in the winter when food may be scarce and nights are long and cold; then a good story helps keep up one's spirits. But the prohibitions against storytelling out of context are, I have been told, not enforced by human beings. Instead, the powers of nature step in. Tell stories in the summertime, the Iroquois say, and a bee will fly into your lodge and sting you. That bee is actually one of the Little People, the Joge-oh, taking the shape of a bee to warn you that you are doing wrong. The Abenaki people say that if you tell stories during the growing season, snakes will come into your house.

For whatever reasons, I tell certain stories only in the months between first and last frost. A non-Indian friend of mine who wanted to tell Indian tales, however, neither knew nor cared about such prohibitions. He looked up some stories from a 19th-century text and began to memorize them. Finally he learned them well enough to tell them in public. But the first time he told one of those stories, he became ill. I advised him to learn more about the native people who told them. His response was that he now had to find out whether this was just a coincidence. Quite deliberately he told another of the tales in public. This time he became so ill that he almost died. He concluded that he did need to know more about the stories, made a trip to Oklahoma to visit some old people from that Native American nation, and discovered the stories he'd been telling were nighttime stories, only to be told at a certain time of the year and never (as he had done) in the light of day.

SOME DIRECTIONS FOR NON-INDIAN TELLERS

What I share here is not a set of hard and fast rules but some possible directions for non-Indian storytellers to follow when they wish to use Native American tales. They come from my own approach to the stories I tell, ones that come from the traditions of my own Abenaki ancestors and the other Native American people from whom I have learned.

• Instead of learning Native American tales solely from books, learn them from the life of the people. Visit American Indian people; try to find out more about their ways of life and their languages. When using written texts, fully research the versions of the story if more than one version exists. A knowledge of the language and people from which the story comes should help you develop a version truer to the original.

• When visiting Native American people, remember that listening and patience are cardinal virtues. The old stereotype of the stoic Indian comes in part from the fact that all too often non-Indians monopolize the conversation. It is common practice in Western culture to interrupt others when engaged in conversation. Such interruptions effectively terminate conversations with Indian people. When asking questions, avoid leading questions or ones that can be answered with a simple yes or no. Native people place great value on politeness and will often say yes just to avoid disagreeing with you.

- Know what type of story you are learning. Find out if there are certain times when it is to be told, and be aware of the way the story's construction fits into the culture and world-view of that native nation. If you are not certain of a story's uses or origin, don't tell it. Furthermore, if you wish to use a story you have heard from a Native American teller, always get that person's explicit permission to tell it.

- When telling a Native American story, try to avoid subtly racist language or language that stereotypes. Many non-Indians, for example, do not realize that it is deeply insulting to refer to a woman as a "squaw," a child as a "papoose," or a man as a "brave." Remember that Native American cultures, rather than being primitive or ignorant, were often politically and culturally more sophisticated than most European nations at the time of Columbus. As Alvin M. Josephy Jr. writes in *The Indian Heritage of America* (Knopf, 1968), "Belief in the freedom and dignity of the individual was deeply ingrained in many Indian societies." (His book should be read by any teller using Native American tales.) Moreover, Native American women in many tribal nations—such as that of the Iroquois, where they owned the houses, controlled the agriculture, and both chose and deposed chiefs—played central roles.

One of my favorite Iroquois stories is about the Storytelling Stone. The tale tells of how the first myths and legends were taught to a boy by an ancient rock. In exchange for each story, the boy gave the stone game that he had shot. It is an important story for anyone who wishes to tell Native American tales to remember, for it reminds us of the principles of reciprocity and the right relation to the earth, which are at the root of Indian stories and Indian culture. Storytellers, whether Indian or non-Indian, who keep those principles in mind will be well on their way to making use of Indian stories as they were meant to be used—for the people, for the earth.

From The National Storytelling Journal, *spring 1987. Reprinted by permission.*

Introducing African Storytelling

By Charlotte Blake-Alston

African stories are often full of wit and beauty and can be readily found in collections. Story-teller and former teacher Charlotte Blake-Alston offers tips on introducing the stories and the role of the griot, or traditional African teller, into the classroom.

Help your students appreciate storytelling's place in African societies. A channel for communicating the values and beliefs of the people, storytelling forms the basis of African-American literature. Getting in touch with the storytelling tradition can encourage your students to preserve and pass on their own history and culture, as Africans have been doing for thousands of years.

GETTING STARTED

- Tell your students that African storytellers, called griots (*gree*-ohs), have long told stories, legends, and poems. Through them the community passes on its history, traditions, and rules of behavior to children and tries to explain the unexplainable (such as how the moon got in the sky).
- From Ghana come popular stories of Anansi, the spider. Read "How the World Got Wisdom," then ask your children how Anansi was selfish. In groups they can invent their own reasons why wisdom is found everywhere, then create group stories using the Anansi character.
- Brainstorm for a list of "unexplainables" such as why spiders hide in corners, elephants have long noses, grass is green, pigs like mud. Write each one on a sentence strip to post in a line around the classroom. Have each child select a title and create a story to explain it.
- Designate your students the official griots of their families. Ask them to list some stories that are told and retold in their families, such as "The Time Grandpop's Bow Tie Fell in the Soup." What special things about their family do they want others to know? At home each child can discuss the list, then pick one story to share in class.
- Appoint each child as an official classroom griot. What stories would they share with the rest of the school? How would they tell the class's history?

BRANCHING OUT

- Though stories may be used to get people to examine their own behavior, the characters are often animals or insects. Ask the children why. Next, have them think of behaviors that can lead to problems among friends, such as teasing, unfairness, jealousy, or exclusion. Can they recall such a situation—or a story in which someone learned an important lesson? Ask them to write the stories, substituting animal characters for people.

- Form a storytelling troupe. Urge each child to learn one story (not necessarily word for word) and to practice telling it to a classmate. Then invite other classes in, or send your children out in small groups. They can create 3- by 5-inch business cards advertising their services.

- Stage a readathon. Stock your classroom with African folk tales, books by African-American authors, and books that feature African-American children as main characters. Read or tell one story or poem a day.

- Make a story cloth. Africans do this to depict the lives of chiefs or other members of the nobility, with each appliqué representing a life event. On construction paper, felt, or cloth children can draw pictures of items from their family stories, then sew or glue them onto a large piece of felt or burlap. They can display the cloths or use them when telling family stories.

HOW THE WORLD GOT WISDOM

Nyame (nee-*ah*-may), the sky god, was searching for a creature to look after the world's wisdom and distribute it fairly. Nyame decided to entrust the wisdom to Anansi, who put it in a large pot and kept it in his house. He put a lid on the pot so the wisdom would not spill. The longer he kept it, the more he thought about keeping all the wisdom for himself.

Looking for a place to hide the wisdom, Anansi ran through the forest till he came to a very tall, wide silk-cotton tree—the perfect hiding place. Anansi ran home and got the pot of wisdom and some rope. He tied the pot onto his stomach and began climbing the tree. This was very difficult. Anansi tried several times, but each time he fell to the ground.

Anansi's son had been watching and said, "Father, I think if you tied the pot on your back, you would be able to grip the tree much better." Upon hearing his son's wise words, Anansi realized that wisdom was not something he could keep all to himself. In anger, he threw the pot to the ground. It broke, and all the wisdom spilled out. People came from the four corners of the earth and scooped up the wisdom. And that's why wherever you go, wisdom can be found. There is enough for me and enough for you.　　　　　—An Ashanti folk tale

Collections From the People of the Story

By Peninnah Schram

In the last three decades a treasure-trove of tales from the rich Jewish oral tradition has been preserved in print. Storyteller and author Peninnah Schram discusses some of the best books for tellers.

Beside my childhood bed stood a bookcase filled with the books I loved to read—including a book of Jewish folk and fairy tales that seemed to have been there since my earliest memories. I was also fortunate in having storytelling parents: my father, a cantor, told me biblical and Talmudic stories, while my mother taught me through proverbs and teaching tales. Those early stories, the many I have discovered in my reading and research since, and those that I now tell have given me a greater sense of my people and myself.

The Jews have always loved and told stories. The rabbis understood the importance of story in teaching and transmitting values and traditions. A story is a beautiful means of teaching religion, values, history, traditions, and customs; a creative method of introducing characters and places; an imaginative way to instill hope and resourceful thinking. Stories help us understand who we are and show us what legacies to transmit to future generations.

Since the focus of the Jewish world is story, we have gathered a great many stories: those found in the Bible, the Talmud (the Oral Law), the Aggadah (the stories, legends, folk tales, animal tales, allegories, parables, and maxims that convey the spirit of the Oral Law), the Midrash (the interpretation of the Law, often in story form), medieval collections of tales, Hasidic stories from the 18th century, Yiddish stories from the 19th century, and the folk tales that have been retold through the centuries in the Middle East and Eastern Europe.

In the past 30 years a renaissance of Jewish storytelling has taken place, as numerous collections of stories from Jewish sources have been published. Although the Hasidim must be credited with the 18th-century revival of Jewish oral storytelling, it was folklorist and professor Dov Noy who spurred the preservation and perpetuation of Jewish stories by founding the Israel Folktale Archives (IFA) in 1956. Through the work of volunteers, more than 17,000 stories have now been transcribed after being collected from those who have immigrated to Israel. Noy classified the stories' motifs and variants and assigned each story an IFA number, thus converting an oral tradition into an accessible written resource for future generations.

In 1963 Noy's best-known book, *Folktales of Israel* (University of

Chicago Press), was published. This volume includes 71 representative tales from the archives, and the brief introductory notes to each tale indicate the IFA number, the narrator's name and place of origin, and the story's main type and motif. Noy also cites parallel versions of each story. Everyone who's published stories from Jewish sources during the past two decades owes a great debt to Noy's pioneering labors—as well as to the monumental work of Louis Ginzberg, Moses Gaster, and especially Micha Joseph Bin Gorion.

The next milestone in the renaissance was the publication of Howard Schwartz' several books of selected and retold folk tales: *Elijah's Violin and Other Jewish Fairy Tales* (Harper & Row, 1983), *Miriam's Tambourine: Jewish Folktales From Around the World* (Seth Press, 1986), *Lilith's Cave: Jewish Tales of the Supernatural* (Harper & Row, 1988), and *Gates to the New City: A Treasury of Modern Jewish Tales* (Jason Aronson, 1991). Schwartz has earned the right to be called America's foremost Jewish folklorist and anthologist, and his books are a gold mine of tales. Always careful about documenting his tales, Schwartz includes extensive notes and bibliographies at the end of each volume.

Having met both Noy and Schwartz, I was encouraged to write in my own voice the stories I had been telling. My goal was to capture an oral style of telling on the printed page, and in 1987 my first collection, *Jewish Stories One Generation Tells Another* (Jason Aronson), was published. I introduced each story with a one- or two-page commentary, explaining how I found the story (or how it found me) and telling something about the story, the sources, the variants, the motifs, any changes I'd made, and so on.

In 1990 I co-authored with Steven M. Rosman *Eight Tales for Eight Nights: Stories for Chanukah* (Jason Aronson). Because of my fascination with Elijah the Prophet since childhood, I often told stories about him, and in 1991 my book *Tales of Elijah the Prophet: Master of Miracles* (Jason Aronson) was published. The collection's introduction explains the strong appeal of this ancient biblical and folklore hero.

In 1988 Beatrice Silverman Weinreich's *Yiddish Folktales* was published as part of the Pantheon Fairy Tale and Folklore Library. Translated from the Yiddish by Leonard Wolf, these 178 stories were gleaned from the archives of the YIVO Institute for Jewish Research. Many of the tales were collected during ethnographic expeditions to Eastern Europe in the early part of the 20th century—long before the days of tape recorders and video cameras.

In 1989 two comprehensive anthologies, each containing more than 250 stories, were published. The first, *Jewish Folktales* (Doubleday,

1989), selected and retold by Pinhas Sadeh and translated by Hillel Halkin, draws heavily on the oral-tradition stories collected in the IFA, as well as from Eastern European literary sources. (The book was originally published in Israel in 1983.) The second anthology, Ellen Frankel's *The Classic Tales: 4,000 Years of Jewish Lore* (Jason Aronson, 1989), is modeled somewhat on Nathan Ausubel's classic anthology, *A Treasury of Jewish Folklore* (Crown), first published in 1948. Frankel's volume is different, though, because its stories are arranged in chronological order—from biblical and Talmudic narratives through Hasidic and folk tales—and it includes indexes for further research.

In addition to these outstanding collections of Jewish folk stories, three wonderful books geared for young people have been published. Howard Schwartz and Barbara Rush have compiled a book of 15 folk tales, *The Diamond Tree: Jewish Tales From Around the World* (Harper Collins, 1991), drawn from all of the various Jewish sources. In *The Answered Prayer and Other Yemenite Folktales* (Jewish Publication Society, 1990) co-authors Sharlya Gold and Mishael Maswari Caspi have retold traditional tales brought by Jews arriving in Israel from Yemen via Operation Magic Carpet. The book includes a helpful glossary and pronunciation guide. And in *My Grandmother's Stories: A Collection of Jewish Folk Tales* (Knopf, 1990) Adèle Geras frames 10 stories with a dialogue that takes place between grandmother and grandchild.

Continued interest and research in the Jewish oral tradition promise to keep it vital and vibrant. In this way the ancient stories will continue to serve as links between young and old. As the stories are retold and rewritten for each new generation, they will help keep alive the Jewish people's values and traditions. And through books, words, and tales, the Jewish people will retain their legacy as the people of the story.

This article is adapted from the author's essay "Current Collections of Jewish Folktales," which appeared in *The Jewish Book Annual*, volume 49, 1991–1992, edited by Jacob Kabakoff and published by the Jewish Book Council.

From Storytelling Magazine, *winter 1993. Reprinted by permission.*

12

TAKING STORIES
BEYOND THE CLASSROOM

SUPPORTING SCHOOLWIDE STORYTELLING • 181

TURNING PARENTS INTO TELLERS • 184

Trading Places, Sharing Tales • 186

STUDENT FESTIVALS: A TAPESTRY OF TALENT • 187
Festival Fund-Raising • 193

Taking Stories Beyond the Classroom

Previous chapters explored the rainbow of possibilities for using stories in the classroom and the many benefits for students' intellectual and emotional life. Taking storytelling outside the classroom is a natural next step for teachers and students. In many schools enthusiasm about stories and storytelling bubbles over into such activities as student storytelling festivals, parent-teacher meetings, teacher workshops, and ultimately community events.

Every school district looks for high-quality, low-cost programs that will enrich the curriculum. Storytelling programs are ideal because they are generally low-cost, low-technology, high-visibility, high-involvement events. And parents' perception that good things are happening at their child's school can pay off when they are voting for tax hikes to fund the education budget.

Many teachers and school officials would like to do more with storytelling but aren't sure where to begin. In the following articles educators and storytellers share their insights into taking stories outside classroom walls. Their ideas are meant to suggest possible directions and can be adapted to each school's needs and goals. The possibilities for storytelling events are limited only by a school's imagination and the supply of willing volunteers.

Supporting Schoolwide Storytelling

By Jay Stailey

How can I make storytelling feel at home in a school setting? That's what I asked myself when I left an assistant principal's position at an elementary school in Baytown, Texas, to become principal at George Washington Carver Elementary in the same school district. In my former job I had completely separated my life as an administrator from my storytelling work. But I knew as principal I would have to meld the two or risk seeing my time and interest in storytelling swallowed up by my new responsibilities as school instructional leader.

It was natural that the first step on my new journey was to bring stories to Carver—stories from both the principal's office and the storytelling community. With this in mind, I set forth for myself the task of making sure that every child heard stories from me in a formal setting at least twice each school year. With Halloween on the horizon and too many of my children talking about Jason (from the *Friday the 13th* films) and wanting to celebrate by wearing hockey masks to school, we chose to focus the day on the oral tradition.

More than 850 kids heard scary stories. This was followed by the predictable oral-tradition process of kids' telling scary stories to one another at lunch, in the classroom, and on the bus. I took the opportunity to assure nervous teachers that the true gift of stories was the children's ability to create images that were just the right level of frightening or weird or fun to meet their emotional level.

Through the rest of the year I used awards assemblies, graduation exercises, and grade-level celebrations to spin tales to the kids of Carver. In the final month of school we organized and celebrated our first Write Way Day, now an annual event. On this day a featured author–storyteller appears, and regional and local tellers share their tales, along with guests who express their stories in song and art.

Over the past four years our guests have included author–storytellers Lynn Moroney, Carmen Deedy, Patricia McKissack, and Angela Medaris; storytellers Elizabeth Ellis, Joe Hayes, Jeannine Beekman, James Ford, Charlotte Byrn, and Mary Ann Brewer; and a variety of local tellers, including members of the Houston Storytellers Guild and students from my class on storytelling and education at the University of Houston at Clear Lake. Singer–songwriters Bob Danaher and Mike

Principal Jay Stailey not only supports student and teacher storytelling but also tells tales himself. Here he describes how he encourages storytelling and why being a visible role model for teachers and students is important.

Lewis have helped children tell their stories through song.

In addition to bringing stories to the children, I worked to present to faculty and staff the justification for the educational, social, and emotional value of stories. I told stories to make specific points, set a tone, or provide diversion in faculty meetings, employee celebrations, and staff-development workshops. I also brought in speakers to discuss the value, purpose, and methods of using stories to promote, among other things, language development and the writing process. Patsy Cooper, the author of *When Stories Come to School* (Teachers & Writers Collaborative, 1993), worked with primary and language-arts staff members. Lynn Moroney did workshops for teachers and students on how stories leap from the spoken word to the pages of books. Moroney and Carmen Deedy told stories to parents and discussed the important role of stories in building family values and traditions.

After I began teaching at the University of Houston, I shared much of my university work with interested grade-level teams. These staff members took storytelling from an "outside" interest to the next level, making it a live and vibrant part of the classroom experience.

The fourth-grade team, using Martha Hamilton and Mitch Weiss's *Children Tell Stories* (Richard C. Owen, 1990) as a guide, created a six-week language-arts unit that exposed children to the art of storytelling through tapes and live tellers, taught them specific storytelling skills, and helped them choose and learn stories. The unit culminated with student tellers' visiting the primary classrooms to share their tales.

The primary teachers began employing some of Cooper's emergent-literacy techniques to everyday language-development activities. The second-grade team and multi-age classrooms set up listening centers, using audiotapes, and included specific stories in many of their thematic units. Stories have become prevalent at Carver, and a day seldom passes that I don't enter a classroom for any number of reasons and hear a request (from a child or a teacher) for a story.

Now that we have brought stories to Carver and continue to create and use stories throughout the curriculum and the school, the natural next step will be to share our stories with others. We are planning to do so in the upcoming school year. Our new librarian has an acute interest in storytelling and is looking at models of student storytelling troupes in hopes of giving the fourth- and fifth-graders, trained in the classroom, opportunities in special settings to continue to enhance their skills and share their stories at Carver and in the community. Through my work at the university, with the children's museum, and with the Houston Storytellers Guild's festival, we hope the Carver kids will be able to share

Taking Stories Beyond the Classroom

their tales and gain more experience telling stories in the community with professional tellers and other students.

For teachers and administrators wishing to replicate the Carver model or create a similar "school of stories," the challenges are many, but the journey is rewarding and the destination well worth the effort. The research points clearly to the many positive reasons for telling stories with children. Start with this book and the books listed in chapter 13, set your course, and don't turn back!

As for the continual concern about available funds and diminishing resources, I emphasize that everyone has a limited budget and sets priorities based on funds available. Make storytelling a priority, start small, plan and promote well, and back up your results with research. Finally, network with storytellers from local, regional, and national organizations, use existing and successful models, and be creative and flexible in your approach. As stories come to live in your school, celebrate their arrival, give them a place to grow, and be prepared to share them with your community and the world.

The other challenge at our school and at others is to find storytellers and stories that can reach the children in their own world and carry them off to story worlds where they can learn about the strengths and weaknesses of humankind in ways that will help them survive and grow. At Carver Elementary, 89 percent of the students come from backgrounds of poverty, and many struggle to find their way, using the language of survival in a school world that speaks the language of negotiation. Ninety percent of the students come from minority cultures, more than 50 percent from homes where English is not spoken or is spoken as a second language. It is important for students to experience and learn to value stories and storytellers from a variety of cultures.

If you are in the Houston area and would like to visit George Washington Carver Elementary School, please know that you will be welcome. If you bring your stories and are willing to share, you will become part of our storytelling community.

Jay Stailey is principal at Carver Elementary School in the Goose Creek District, Baytown, Texas. He has appeared as a featured performer at storytelling festivals and at the Exchange Place at the National Storytelling Festival. Stailey has served on the National Council of Teachers of English storytelling committee and is a member of the National Storytelling Association's board of directors.

TURNING PARENTS INTO TELLERS

BY JUDY SIMA

Judy Sima, a storyteller and middle-school media specialist, felt that bringing stories to every student in the Fitzgerald Public Schools stretched her too thin. Drawing on the resources present in the community, she trained a group of parents who now volunteer their storytelling skills.

Storytelling has been part of my life for years, in my work as a media specialist and a freelance storyteller. I've long been aware of the importance of storytelling in the classroom, but I found myself increasingly frustrated with my own limitations of time and energy. In 1987 I decided to take action by forming a corps of parent storytellers called the Fitzgerald Parent-Tellers. The program involves systematically training parent volunteers to become classroom storytellers in the Fitzgerald Public Schools of Warren, Michigan.

Getting parents to volunteer is the first step. I began by telling stories and sharing my vision at parent-group meetings. This approach brought four moms into the program. Now we have 10 committed parent-tellers.

Who can join the group? Anyone with an interest in stories and a desire to work with kids. Adults who work part time or are retired are good candidates. Our current parent-tellers come from a variety of backgrounds. Some have a good deal of drama experience, and others have performed as clowns. We even have retired teachers. One parent knows French and Spanish, and her French tellings of "Goldilocks and the Three Bears" are favorites. In another case, a mother who is talented in costume design teams up with a parent who does terrific accents. Together they never fail to surprise and delight the kids.

Parent-teller meetings are held for one hour each week at the middle school's media center. After the parent-tellers select stories for telling, I take them step by step through the story-learning process. During these sessions, I stress story visualization as well as the importance of telling in our own words. We devote a considerable amount of time to practicing before the group. I routinely give positive feedback, offering suggestions for improvement only upon request.

After the parent-tellers have prepared a couple of stories, they are given opportunities to present several half-hour performances for groups of 80 to 100 students. After this initiation, the tellers are ready to fill teacher requests for classroom visits. On a request form, teachers can indicate what they're currently teaching, what maps are available, and when the tellers can come to their classrooms.

To better connect the stories with classroom studies, we've developed a follow-up activities sheet. Using the sheet, the tellers develop one or two activities to go with their stories, then leave the sheet with the teacher. They also leave forms the teachers can use to evaluate the tellers' visits.

We schedule teacher requests for storytelling by sitting down with our calendars. Programs are approximately 30 minutes in length and are scheduled back-to-back at the same schools. Beginning tellers are usually paired with experienced ones.

The cost of the parent-teller program is minimal, with the main expense the pot of coffee served at our weekly meetings. Parent-tellers can borrow from a large cart filled with folklore collections, picture books, and storytelling audiotapes (on loan from the school media centers). A copying machine is also available.

EXPANDING THE CIRCLE

Making the parent-tellers part of the school community is important, so I give each one a monthly calendar of the school media centers' events and invite them to attend. I also relate information about local storytelling events and encourage the tellers to attend with their families. If there will be a story swap, I invite them to move beyond their comfort zone and participate.

My dream of expanding the circle of storytelling in the Fitzgerald Public Schools has been successful—and it extends even beyond the classroom. Several parent-tellers have been invited to perform at bookstores, public libraries, and neighboring schools. Some have influenced their own children to join my middle-school storytelling troupe (see the related article that follows). Best of all, our storytelling efforts have culminated for the past two years in a Fitzgerald Family Storytelling Festival, where parents, students, and teachers can perform for the community.

From the Yarnspinner, *December 1993. Reprinted by permission.*

TRADING PLACES, SHARING TALES

When Warren, Michigan, school media specialist Judy Sima started the after-school Chatterton Talespinners club six years ago, she gave her suburban Detroit students a way to learn about storytelling, have fun, and practice public speaking. Three years ago Detroit reading teacher Karen White formed a similar storytelling group for her inner-city students after hearing about Sima's Talespinners.

Then the two educators came up with an even better idea: why not get the two groups together so that the youngsters could deepen their understanding of storytelling while getting to know one another? Since then they've put the notion into practice, giving the white suburban students and inner-city African-American students the opportunity to discover their common ground.

At Chatterton Middle School, Sima's sixth- to eighth-grade performers learn the fundamentals of storytelling and later go into the community to share their tales with senior citizens, middle-school kids, and preschoolers. White teaches reading to fourth- and fifth-graders at Keidan Elementary School. Her lunchtime group, the Keidan Storytellers, learns African-American stories and teaches them to younger students.

Sima and White met through the Detroit Story League, and as they became friends, they decided to create a multicultural storytelling exchange program between their schools. Says Sima, "Our goal was to provide a positive way for kids of different backgrounds and from different parts of the city to get together through storytelling."

The two hoped the students would make friends, share stories, and learn from one another—and they did. Says White, "The exchange promoted real cultural understanding between the two groups."

For the first storytelling exchange, held in January 1992, White brought 30 of her students and some parent chaperons to Chatterton to meet 30 of Sima's students. The adults encouraged each student to find a partner from the other school who shared the same birthday, family birth order, or favorite television show. After the students paired off, they interviewed each other and then introduced their partners to the rest of the group.

The Keidan group told a story about Kwanza, an African-American cultural festival. In turn, Chatterton taught Keidan "The Mosquito," a Hawaiian string story. Then both groups performed the "Jazzy Three Bears" group chant. After eating a pizza lunch, White's group returned to Keidan.

Three weeks later Chatterton visited Keidan. The students found their partners and played group and individual story games. The Storytellers demonstrated the use of the kalimba, an African thumb piano, and the Talespinners performed a story-song in sign language. A local fast-food eatery provided lunch for a nominal charge and donated T-shirts imprinted with KEIDAN STORYTELLERS. When the meeting ended, many of the tellers exchanged addresses and phone numbers.

Sima and White hope their idea catches on. "Storytelling broke the ice and helped the students feel less awkward when meeting new people," says White. "Stories are a natural way of helping people get to know one another." —Debbie L. Feldman

From Storytelling Magazine, *spring 1993. Reprinted by permission.*

Taking Stories Beyond the Classroom

STUDENT FESTIVALS:
A TAPESTRY OF TALENT

BY GAIL NEARY HERMAN

In order to acquaint students and teachers with the benefits of story-telling, I began working with teachers in 1984 to produce the Tapestry of Talent Student Storytelling Festival in Connecticut. To support the festival, I wrote a small grant to a local teachers' enrichment organization and the state arts council. In the following years we received mini-grants from local arts councils.

Since 1985 I have directed 18 storytelling festivals in three states. The festival in Connecticut continues each year, with Rosalind Hinman as artistic director and Claire Krause and other teachers assisting.

GENERATING INTEREST

First I advertised with a flier to teacher organizations and directly through the schools to interested teachers who had attended one of my storytelling workshops. Offering a workshop for teachers and parents is a good way to develop interest in a festival. Any adult who thought children might benefit encouraged and supported students' storytelling efforts and talents. The flier invited students to tell short original or family stories as well as stories adapted from literature. Students could perform alone, in pairs, or in small groups of three to eight.

At the bottom of the flier was a registration form for teachers or parents to return with a small registration fee (usually between $4 and $8) to cover the cost of performers, refreshments (fresh fruit or ice cream), and students' storytelling certificates, which were given to a school chaperon at the end of the day. In order to avoid overrepresentation of any school, we limited the number to eight children from each school. We have not found this necessary in the more rural festivals.

Some years the registration fee was larger to help defray the cost of hiring the adult storytelling-workshop leaders and performers. Some years an evening performance by adult storytellers was also advertised to the public. Parents or teachers brought the students to the festival (and the evening event, if any).

THE FIRST STEPS

When we found a school (or a college) that had at least 10 to 15 rooms for sharing circles composed of seven to 10 students and several parent

Gail Herman believes in taking student stories statewide. Her program for organizing children's storytelling festivals has been taken up by schools and community organizations in three states. Here Herman describes her step-by-step plan.

or teacher onlookers—as well as several larger rooms for workshops—we submitted news releases, along with photographs, to newspapers throughout the state. Photographs help get your release published. You need to submit the release at least a month in advance, however, and newspaper editors have a hard time understanding this time frame. They usually want to publish your release the week before the event. You must speak to the news editor or include a note explaining that students need time to prepare their stories.

The facility should also have an auditorium for the final main-stage storytelling performance. In the early years fewer than 100 students attended, with an additional 30 to 50 adults and onlookers. You can limit the number to what you feel is a good-sized group for your space. We find between 50 and 150 students is workable.

After students register, send them a letter that congratulates them for participating. This letter should list all the schedules and should include a map. Allow parents, teachers, and students the chance to give feedback by providing an evaluation form. You can give these out at the festival or mail them afterward. Our evaluations show that adults enjoy the events as much as the students.

STORY SHARING, NOT COMPETITION

"Will our stories be judged?" asked one student. "Absolutely not," I responded. "Storytelling is a communal event, and every story is special." Call it narrative, storytelling, or even yarnspinning; everyone has a story to share and a way of preserving the significant life events that make up the human experience. So in student storytelling festivals everyone tells a story in a 45- to 60-minute story-sharing circle. These are small, "safe" groups of seven to 10 students and their parents or teachers, who serve as story-sharing leaders. The most important attributes of a sharing-circle leader are friendliness, enthusiasm, and an ability to keep people at ease and focused on active listening.

When students arrive, they receive name tags marked with a designated sharing-circle room. Unregistered last-minute call-ins (expect some pleading phone calls) can be grouped in a newly designated room if necessary.

If your festival is statewide, students will arrive in late morning (around 11 or 11:30) to register. You might invite them to bring their lunches and eat during the story-sharing period (11:30 to 12:30).

After everyone has shared a story, the leader asks who might enjoy telling on the main stage. Students who wish to, and not all will, should write their name, story, and school on a card. These are given to the

Taking Stories Beyond the Classroom

director or master of ceremonies, who will select from them at random during the two-hour-long main-stage event. Some years I have asked sharing-circle leaders and students to decide which story from their group should be heard by everyone first. Usually the story chosen is told by an expressive individual who is able to hold a large group's attention. The leader marks that card with a star, and the director chooses from these first. If there are 10 sharing circles, the 10 tellers designated by their groups will go first in random order. The other tellers follow, also in random order.

WORKSHOPS

Each year I invite or hire several professional communicators to give two 30- to 40-minute workshops each. Mimes, dramatists, magicians, storytellers, puppeteers, voice teachers, dancers, and others have given workshops to 20 to 50 students, depending on workshop room size and the topic. Some years I have had little or no money with which to pay professionals; other years I have had grants that paid small amounts. Each year a storyteller is invited "from far away" to give workshops and perform a story or two during the main-stage event or a special evening performance.

The National Storytelling Association (formerly the National Association for the Preservation and Perpetuation of Storytelling) publishes an annual directory of storytellers and storytelling organizations, listed by state, that can serve as resources. If you live in a rural area, as I do now, and have little money to start with, I suggest you mine talent from among your teachers, community theater groups, radio announcers, local youth leaders, and others. You will find a gold mine of people ready to assist you. Involving the community at the beginning of your festival activity is an excellent way to encourage people to help spread the word. If they do not feel comfortable leading a workshop, ask them to lead a sharing circle instead.

Remember, the people who lead workshops should be good with students. They might be performing artists, teachers, or hobbyists, but they must relate well to children. Primary-grade children enjoy being actively involved. Creative drama and story-theater workshops work well, as does storytelling with mime and puppets. Students can become involved vocally or physically or, in the case of puppet storytelling, at least visually. Help the workshop leader focus on several things the groups can learn about the art form. What helps the professional communicate well? Is it voice, visuals, facial expression, body movement, mime, or gestures? Is it a special way of finding family stories or a technique for remembering a story found in folk literature?

I assign students to groups depending on the topic and their age or grade. I group together grades one through three; four and five; and six through nine. In Connecticut the festival grew so much that a separate day was added just for older students.

MAIN-STAGE TELLING

Students who choose to tell on the main stage enjoy using a microphone, although this is not essential in smaller auditoriums. In smaller rooms you may not need a microphone, but I recommend that you ask for a small raised platform about one foot high. This keeps the teller in view and therefore helps the teller keep the audience's attention.

The master of ceremonies welcomes students, parents, and teachers and explains the audience's role in making the storytelling successful. He or she can mention the importance of making eye contact with the storytellers. The audience's attention tells storytellers that people are interested and listening and thus helps tellers do their best. The emcee should also point out where the bathrooms are and ask that people leave only during the applause.

The emcee introduces each student and arranges the microphone, chair, or whatever the child needs. After each student's story the emcee can encourage the audience to appreciate the teller's efforts. Clapping is the most common form of acknowledgment, although there are others. After a mimed story without words, we use "mime applause," clapping without sound. If a student forgets to mention the source of the story, the emcee can ask the teller whether the story is original. The emcee can also say a few words about the story or its style. For example, if a teller used a musical instrument, the emcee can mention that many story-tellers around the world have traditionally used musical instruments to emphasize a mood or accompany a song within the story. If students tell a story in tandem (with two people sharing the narration), the emcee might mention that this style is used by modern tellers such as the Folk-tellers of North Carolina. If a group tells a tale in story-theater style, the emcee can call attention to the fact that Broadway actors use the tech-nique from time to time. A helpful book for the emcee on the history of storytelling around the world is Anne Pellowski's *The World of Story-telling* (H.W. Wilson, 1990). (Adding extra commentary on the history of storytelling helped me obtain a humanities council minigrant for several years.) Finally the emcee thanks each student again for his or her story and introduces the next teller.

I use a bongo drum to hold the names of all the students who have

Taking Stories Beyond the Classroom

volunteered to tell. In the large side of the drum I hold all the volunteers' names; in the small side, the names of those whose stories have been chosen by their group to be told first. I choose at random from each side. Students are told ahead of time that main-stage performers are chosen at random. The telling takes one to two hours. Students who have younger sisters and brothers or who are in first or second grade often leave early because of the length of the day. I always stay until everyone who wants the chance to tell on the stage has had one. We find that this informal way of conducting the main-stage event is less frightening for students—and that even those who were adamantly opposed to volunteering often raise their hands and ask to tell at the very end. For some students this is a great breakthrough.

After the festival, be sure to send out a news release, including some students' names and story titles, as well as photographs. If you can entice local reporters to cover the event, do so.

FORMATS

Formats and schedules can be varied to fit your group's needs, size, and budget. Sharing circles are very informal and therefore help students overcome stage fright. For this reason we have held them first on festival day. With larger numbers of students (150 or more), however, sharing-circle time can be divided and the workshops scheduled to take place between sharing times. Only a professional storyteller then tells on the main stage, in a short performance of 20 minutes.

In the rural western Maryland festivals, storytelling parents and teachers are frequently the workshop leaders. We often have an evening performance by a storyteller in addition to the day's events. The audience for the evening performance includes families of student tellers and nontellers. Sometimes we invite a few student story-theater groups or individual student storytellers to perform for the evening along with the professional storyteller. Flexibility is the key.

Since Connecticut's population is large and the state is small, what was once a one-day festival for children grades one through 12 now takes place during a series of days at Wesleyan University and meets the needs of a variety of students in grades three through eight. One day involves students who have prepared stories to tell. After the second workshop all students meet to view a professional performance on the main stage. On another day groups of students work with two or three artists to develop a student performance. At the end of the day these groups perform for one another for about 10 minutes each. This event, Make a Play Day, has become extremely popular with students. A third

event is a storytelling field trip for students who are being rewarded for some special achievement and for those who are not yet sure they want to perform. The trip involves attending a performance by professional storytellers in a theater and a picnic lunch with entertainment by roving mimes, balloon storytellers, and musicians. The cost is $6 per child, and the students bring their own picnic lunch.

In rural Appalachian Maryland the community holds a yearly festival of bands, fiddling contests, and craft sales. I've added a Tall Tale Liars Festival to this Autumn Glory weekend of traditional arts and crafts. Children perform prepared stories early in the morning, followed by adults. Because this is a traditional tall-tale event, residents enjoy the idea of competition for the best or most outrageous tall tale or lie. The nature of the event is not competitive, however; it is fun and promotes community spirit. The names of local places, lakes, bridges, and mountains infiltrate the stories, and the exaggerations rival those heard at any town's traditional "liars' bench." To advertise this festival, I pay $100 to the local promotion council for advertising in its yearly brochure, and in the first year I called anyone who was recommended as a good tall-tale liar. I also visited several junior-high and fifth-grade classrooms to discuss tall tales. Once the word spread, the people came. Now the event sustains itself, and the proceeds go to help cover the expenses of the Tapestry of Talent Student Storytelling Festival in the spring.

Gail Neary Herman, Ph.D., of Swanton, Maryland, is a professional storyteller and educational consultant who performs throughout the United States and other countries. She has produced two audiotapes as well as a television program called The Storyteller *for Telemedia in Connecticut. The author of* Storytelling: A Triad in the Arts *(Creative Learning Press, 1986) and the co-author of* Kinetic Kaleidoscope: Exploring Movement and Energy in Visual Arts *(Zephyr Press, 1992), Herman leads workshops for teachers and students in mime, storytelling, and other topics.*

Although festival fund-raising might feel like begging, keep in mind that it's the children who benefit. Here's a list of fund-raising ideas. Start with these tips and the people you know, and network outward.

FESTIVAL FUND-RAISING

- Write a letter to the state superintendent of schools. I once received several hundred dollars from this source to run a state festival in West Virginia.
- Join a teachers' organization. Propose the idea of a regional or state festival. Ask for seed money for mailings, photocopying, and so on. I received several hundred dollars from such an organization—as well as plenty of helpers.
- Attend a regional PTA meeting and propose a regional or state festival. The local PTA might support you, or perhaps the local PTA president will give you information on whom to contact. Ask for seed money.
- Ask the state and local arts councils for support. Many are more than willing to help support the development of student festivals. Perhaps they will support your workshops for classes or interested groups of students.
- Speak to the state humanities council. Write a grant for a storytelling gathering if it involves people in such topics as preserving family and folklore stories, the history of storytelling, an understanding of the creative process, or the aesthetics of storytelling. I received grants in West Virginia and Maryland to develop and present workshops on the history of storytelling around

the world. I used some of the money to cover costs for the Tapestry of Talent Student Storytelling Festival. Another year I wrote a grant to support my giving workshops in schools and at a university to teachers. Some of those teachers became interested and brought students to tell stories at the festival. The funds paid for out-of-town storytellers to assist.

One year I ran a family-storytelling workshop in conjunction with a storytelling performance paid for by the humanities council and matching funds from local businesses. Another year I wrote a grant for the Stories for Global and Environmental Awareness Festival. The money I received from the grant, registration fees, and a local paper mill paid for storytellers John Porcino, Diane Edgecomb, and Michael Punzak to join me. They gave workshops on stories about global and environmental issues and did evening performances. When working with a state humanities council, you must be sure to present both sides of an issue and to address the humanities topics listed in the organization's request for proposals published each year.

- Ask civic organizations (American Association of University Women, Rotary Club, and so on) for money to help with your student festival. They are more apt to donate if you tell them exactly who will benefit—which school or which population (for example, those who cannot afford the $4 registration fee). Sometimes such organizations will ask you to speak at a luncheon or dinner. One year I spoke to an organization, and afterward someone handed me a check for $100! Never turn down an invitation to speak (or tell stories) to any and all such organizations. Ask them to cover your travel and photocopying or other costs ($25 to $50) associated with your talk. Then ask the leaders whether you may ask members to support the festival during your talk.

- Write 100 letters to those individuals in your region whom you think can most afford to give a $25 donation to the student festival. Of course, you will need to follow up with a thank-you letter. Rosalind Hinman did this recently in Connecticut and received $500.

- Speak to the public-relations person for a local business such as a large paper mill, bank, or coal company. I did this for a number of years and received several hundred dollars for festivals and for my school activities to help interested students learn stories.

- Band together with other storytellers and storyteller–teachers: when it comes to fund-raising, two heads are always better than one. Create a storytelling guild or organization. For a small fee the National Storytelling Association will send you information on how to begin such an organization (call 615-753-2171).

- If your state has a "special arts organization," it might support your working in the schools to develop special students' talents. I received such support for several years, and one year many of the students told stories at the Garrett County Tapestry of Talent Student Storytelling Festival.

- Call your governor's office to obtain phone numbers and addresses for the organizations listed above.

- Ask for free space from a school, college, university, or state park. I have asked seven colleges and universities, two public schools, and a state park for the free use of space for student storytelling festivals, and I have never been refused. If you're writing a grant, free space can often be used as in-kind funding to show community support for the project.

- Ask the school, college, or university if it can help with costs for photocopying and mailing. Some years this works; other times it doesn't.

- Ask a local McDonald's or other fast-food restaurant to help bear the cost of ice cream sundaes. Often a university food service will donate them or perhaps charge only $1 per sundae. If you have a local apple orchard, it might donate fruit, as ours did in Connecticut one year.

—Gail Neary Herman

13

RECOMMENDED
BOOKS FOR STORYTELLERS

THE ART OF STORYTELLING

Baker, Augusta, and Ellin Greene, *Storytelling: Art and Technique*, R.R. Bowker, 1977

Barton, Bob, *Tell Me Another*, Heinemann, 1986

Bauer, Caroline Feller, *New Handbook for Storytellers*, American Library Association, 1993

Breneman, Lucille N., and Bren Breneman, *Once Upon a Time: A Storytelling Handbook*, Nelson-Hall, 1983

Champlin, Connie, and Nancy Renfro, *Storytelling With Puppets*, American Library Association, 1985

Crosson, Vicky L., and Jay C. Stailey, *Spinning Stories: An Introduction to Storytelling Skills*, Texas State Library, 1988 (P.O. Box 12927, Austin, Texas 78711, 512-463-5448)

Farrell, Catharine, *Storytelling: A Guide for Teachers*, Scholastic Professional, 1993

Livo, Norma J., and Sandra A. Rietz, *Storytelling Activities*, Libraries Unlimited, 1987

—, *Storytelling: Process and Practice*, Libraries Unlimited, 1986

MacDonald, Margaret Read, *The Storyteller's Start-Up Book: Finding, Learning, Performing, and Using Folktales*, August House, 1993

—, *The Storyteller's Sourcebook: A Subject, Title, and Motif Index to Folklore Collections for Children*, Neal-Schuman/Gale Research, 1982

Maguire, Jack, *Creative Storytelling*, Yellow Moon Press, 1992

Ross, Ramon, *Storyteller*, Charles E. Merrill, 1980

Sawyer, Ruth, *The Way of the Storyteller*, Viking, 1962

Shedlock, Marie, *The Art of the Storyteller*, Dover, 1952

STORYTELLING IN THE CLASSROOM

Barton, Bob, *Stories in the Classroom: Storytelling, Reading Aloud, and Role Playing With Children*, Heinemann, 1990

Blatt, Gloria T., editor, *Once Upon a Folktale: Capturing the Folklore Process With Children*, Teachers College Press, 1993

Caduto, Michael J., and Joseph Bruchac, *Keepers of the Earth: Native American Stories and Environmental Activities for Children*, Fulcrum, 1988

Cooper, Pamela J., and Rives Collins, *Look What Happened to Frog: Storytelling in Education*, Gorsuch Scarisbrick, 1992

Cooper, Patsy, *When Stories Come to School*, Teachers & Writers Collaborative, 1993

Dailey, Sheila, *Storytelling: A Creative Teaching Strategy*, Storytime Productions, 1985 (1326 E. Broadway, Mount Pleasant, Mich. 48858)

De Vos, Gail, *Storytelling for Young Adults*, Libraries Unlimited, 1991

Denman, Gregory, *Sit Tight, and I'll Swing You a Tail . . . Using and Writing Stories With Young People*, Heinemann, 1991

Dubrovin, Vivian, *Storytelling for the Fun of It: A Handbook for Children*, Storycraft, 1994

Egan, Kieran, *Teaching as Story Telling*, University of Chicago Press, 1989

Farrell, Catharine, and Denise Nessel, *Word Weaving: A Teaching Sourcebook*, Word Weaving Inc., 1987 (P.O. Box 5646, San Francisco, Calif. 94101)

Griffin, Barbara Budge, *Students as Storytellers*, self-published, 1989 (P.O. Box 626, Medford, Ore. 97501-0042)

Hamilton, Martha, and Mitch Weiss, *Children Tell Stories: A Teaching Guide*, Richard C. Owen, 1990

Hedberg, Natalie L., and Carol E. Westby, *Analyzing Storytelling Skills: Theory to Practice*, Communication Skill Builders, 1993 (P.O. Box 42050, Tucson, Ariz. 85733)

Landor, Lynn, *Children's Own Stories: A Literature-Based Language Arts Program*, Zellerbach Family Fund, 1990 (San Francisco Study Center, P.O. Box 5646, San Francisco, Calif. 94101)

Rosen, Betty, *And None of It Was Nonsense: The Power of Storytelling in School*, Heinemann, 1988

Sierra, Judy, and Robert Kaminski, *Twice Upon a Time: Stories to Tell, Retell, Act Out, and Write About*, H.W. Wilson, 1989

Trousdale, Ann M., Sue A. Woestehoff, and Marni Schwartz, *Give a Listen: Stories of Storytelling in School*, National Council of Teachers of English, 1994

Watts, Irene, *Making Stories*, Heinemann, 1992

The Meaning and Value of Folk Literature

Bettelheim, Bruno, *The Uses of Enchantment: The Meaning and Importance of Fairy Tales*, Knopf, 1976

Bosma, Bette, *Fairy Tales, Fables, Legends, and Myths: Using Folk Literature in Your Classroom*, second edition, Teachers College Press, 1992

Cook, Elizabeth, *The Ordinary and the Fabulous*, Cambridge University Press, 1969

Harrell, John, *Origins and Early Traditions of Storytelling*, York House, 1983 (148 York Ave., Kensington, Calif. 94708)

Haughton, Rosemary, *Tales From Eternity*, Seabury, 1973

Lewis, C. S., "On Stories" and "Sometimes Fairy Stories Say Best What's to Be Said" from *Of Other Worlds*, Harcourt Brace Jovanovich, 1966

Luthi, Max, *Once Upon a Time: On the Nature of Fairy Tales*, Indiana University Press, 1976

Pellowski, Anne, *The World of Storytelling*, H.W. Wilson, 1990

Tolkien, J.R.R., "On Fairy Stories" from *The Tolkien Reader*, Ballantine, 1966

Researching Folk and Fairy Tales*

Aarne, Antti, and Stith Thompson, *The Types of the Folktale*, second revised edition, Folklore Fellows Communications, number 184, Academia Scientiarum Fennica, 1961

Ashliman, D. L., *A Guide to Folktales in the English Language: Based on the Aarne-Thompson Classification System*, Greenwood Press, 1987. The second most valuable book in a storyteller's library

Baughman, Ernest W., *Type and Motif-Index of the Folktales of England and North America*, Indiana University Folklore Series, number 20, Mouton & Company, 1966

Brunvand, Jan Harold, *The Study of American Folklore*, Norton, 1986

Clarkson, Atelia, and Gilbert B. Cross, *World Folktales*, Scribner's, 1980. Has an excellent introduction discussing story research.

Dundes, Alan, and Lowell Edmunds, *Oedipus: A Folklore Casebook*, Garland, 1984. All of Dundes's books include superb cross-cultural information.

Dundes, Alan, *Little Red Riding Hood: A Casebook*, University of Wisconsin Press, 1989

—, *Cinderella: A Casebook*, University of Wisconsin Press, 1988

—, *The Flood Myth*, University of California Press, 1988

* Compiled by Ruth Stotter. From *Storytelling Magazine*, spring 1993. Reprinted by permission.

Hearne, Betsy, *Beauties and Beasts*, Oryx Press, 1993

Lane, Marcia, *Picturing the Rose: A Way of Looking at Fairy Tales*, H.W. Wilson, 1994

Livo, Norma J., and Sandra A. Rietz, *Storytelling Folklore Sourcebook*, Libraries Unlimited, 1991

MacDonald, Margaret Read, *Tom Thumb*, Oryx Press, 1993

—, *The Storyteller's Sourcebook: A Subject, Title, and Motif Index to Folklore Collections for Children*, Neal-Schuman/Gale Research, 1982. The most valuable book in a storyteller's library

Schmidt, Gary D., and Donald R. Hettinga, editors, *Sitting at the Feet of the Past: Retelling the North American Folktale for Children*, Greenwood Press, 1992

Shannon, George, *A Knock at the Door*, Oryx Press, 1992

Sierra, Judy, *Cinderella*, Oryx Press, 1992

Smith, Ron, *Mythologies of the World: A Guide to Sources*, National Council of Teachers of English, 1994

Thompson, Stith, *The Folktale*, University of California Press, 1977

—, *Motif-Index of Folk-Literature*, revised edition, six volumes, Indiana University Press, 1955–58

Ausubel, Nathan, editor, *A Treasury of Jewish Folklore*, Crown, 1989

Chinen, Allan B., *In the Ever After: Fairy Tales and the Second Half of Life*, Chiron, 1989

Cole, Joanna, editor, *Best-Loved Folktales of the World*, Doubleday, 1983

Colwell, Eileen, *A Storyteller's Choice*, H.Z. Walck, 1963

The Complete Grimm's Fairy Tales, Pantheon, 1974

Courlander, Harold, and Wolf Leslau, *The Fire on the Mountain and Other Ethiopian Tales*, Holt, Rinehart & Winston, 1956

DeSpain, Pleasant, *Thirty-Three Multicultural Tales to Tell*, August House, 1993

Hamilton, Edith, *Mythology*, Little, Brown, 1942

Hamilton, Virginia, *The People Could Fly: American Black Folktales*, Knopf, 1985

Haviland, Virginia, editor, *North American Legends*, Collins, 1979

Jacobs, Joseph, *English Fairy Tales*, Penguin, 1970

Justice, Jennifer, editor, *The Ghost and I: Scary Stories for Participatory Telling*, Yellow Moon Press, 1992

STORY COLLECTIONS
(continued)

Lester, Julius, *Black Folktales*, Grove Press, 1969

MacDonald, Margaret Read, *Twenty Tellable Tales: Audience Participation Folktales for the Beginning Storyteller*, H.W. Wilson, 1986

Miller, Teresa, compiler, with assistance from Anne Pellowski, edited by Norma J. Livo, *Joining In: An Anthology of Audience Participation Stories and How to Tell Them*, Yellow Moon Press, 1988

Pellowski, Anne, *The Story Vine*, Macmillan, 1984

Phelps, Ethel Johnston, *The Maid of the North: Feminist Folktales From Around the World*, Holt, Rinehart & Winston, 1981

Schwartz, Alvin, *Scary Stories to Tell in the Dark*, Harper Collins, 1986

Shah, Idries, *World Tales*, Harcourt Brace Jovanovich, 1979

Shannon, George, *Stories to Solve: Folktales From Around the World*, Greenwillow Press, 1985

Singer, Isaac Bashevis, *When Schlemiel Went to Warsaw and Other Stories*, Farrar, Straus & Giroux, 1969

Wolkstein, Diane, *The Magic Orange Tree and Other Haitian Folk Tales*, Knopf, 1978

PERSONAL-EXPERIENCE STORIES

Akeret, Robert U., *Family Tales, Family Wisdom*, Morrow, 1991

Moore, Robin, *Awakening the Hidden Storyteller: How to Build a Storytelling Tradition in Your Family*, Shambhala, 1991

Pellowski, Anne, *The Family Storytelling Handbook*, Macmillan, 1987

Stone, Elizabeth, *Black Sheep and Kissing Cousins: How Our Family Stories Shape Us*, Times, 1988

Zeitlin, Steven J., Amy J. Kotkin, and Holly Cutting Baker, *A Celebration of American Family Folklore*, Pantheon, 1982

Bauer, Caroline Feller, *Celebrations: Read-Aloud Holiday and Theme Book Programs*, H.W. Wilson, 1985

Hunt, Gladys, *Honey for a Child's Heart*, Zondervan, 1969

Kimmel, Margaret M., and Elizabeth Segel, *For Reading Out Loud! A Guide to Sharing Books With Children*, Delacorte, 1983

Trelease, Jim, *Hey, Listen to This! Stories to Read Aloud*, Penguin, 1992

—, *The New Read-Aloud Handbook*, Penguin, 1989

Preschool and grades K–two
Allard, Harry, *Miss Nelson Is Missing!*, Houghton Mifflin, 1987
Demi, *The Empty Pot*, Henry Holt, 1990

Hoffman, Mary, *Amazing Grace*, Dial, 1991

Kasza, Keiko, *The Pigs' Picnic*, Putnam, 1992

McGovern, Ann, *Too Much Noise*, Houghton Mifflin, 1992

Grades three–five
Banks, Lynne R., *The Return of the Indian*, Scholastic, 1988

Chase, Richard, *Grandfather Tales*, Houghton Mifflin, 1990

Dahl, Roald, *James and the Giant Peach*, Puffin, 1988

Haviland, Virginia, *Favorite Fairy Tales Told Around the World*, Little, Brown, 1985

Naylor, Phyllis R., *Shiloh*, Dell, 1992

Grades six and up
Avi, *The True Confessions of Charlotte Doyle*, Avon, 1992

Hamilton, Virginia, *The People Could Fly: American Black Folktales*, Knopf, 1985

Peck, Robert N., *A Day No Pigs Would Die*, Dell, 1986

Staples, Suzanne F., *Shabanu: Daughter of the Wind*, Knopf, 1991

Taylor, Mildred D., *Roll of Thunder, Hear My Cry*, Puffin, 1991

*Compiled by Mary M. Harrison. From *Storytelling Magazine*, summer 1993. Reprinted by permission.

PARTICIPATORY STORYTELLING*

Alexander, Robert, *Improvisational Theatre for the Classroom*, edited by Wendy Haynes, Living Stage Theatre Company for the U.S. Department of Education, 1983

Barton, Bob, *Tell Me Another*, Heinemann, 1986

Bauer, Caroline Feller, *New Handbook for Storytellers*, American Library Association, 1993

Brody, Ed, Jay Goldspinner, Katie Green, Rona Leventhal, and John Porcino, editors, *Spinning Tales, Weaving Hope: Stories of Peace, Justice, and the Environment*, New Society, 1992

Butler, Francelia, *Sharing Literature With Children*, David McKay, 1977

Caduto, Michael J., and Joseph Bruchac, *Keepers of the Earth: Native American Stories and Environmental Activities for Children*, Fulcrum, 1988

Cooper, Pamela J., and Rives Collins, *Look What Happened to Frog: Storytelling in Education*, Gorsuch Scarisbrick, 1992

Egan, Kieran, *Teaching as Story Telling*, University of Chicago Press, 1989

Jaffe, Nina, and Steven Zeitlin, *While Standing on One Foot: Puzzle Stories and Wisdom Tales From the Jewish Tradition*, Henry Holt, 1993

Kinghorn, Harriet R., and Mary Helen Pelton, *Every Child a Storyteller: A Handbook of Ideas*, Teacher Ideas Press, 1991

Livo, Norma J., and Sandra A. Rietz, *Storytelling Folklore Sourcebook*, Libraries Unlimited, 1991

—, *Storytelling Activities*, Libraries Unlimited, 1987

—, *Storytelling: Process and Practice*, Libraries Unlimited, 1986

McCaslin, Nellie, *Creative Drama in the Classroom*, fourth edition, Longman, 1984

Miller, Teresa, compiler, with assistance from Anne Pellowski, edited by Norma J. Livo, *Joining In: An Anthology of Audience Participation Stories and How to Tell Them*, Yellow Moon Press, 1988

Paley, Vivian Gussin, *The Boy Who Would Be a Helicopter: The Uses of Storytelling in the Classroom*, Harvard University Press, 1990

Pellowski, Anne, *The Family Storytelling Handbook*, Macmillan, 1987

—, *The Story Vine*, Macmillan, 1987

Rosen, Betty, *And None of It Was Nonsense*, Heinemann, 1988

Schimmel, Nancy, *Just Enough to Make a Story: A Sourcebook for Storytelling*, third edition, Sisters' Choice Press, 1992

* Compiled by
Peninnah Schram

Vandergrift, Kay E., *Children's Literature: Theory, Research, and Teaching*, Libraries Unlimited, 1990

Way, Brian, *Development Through Drama*, Longman, 1967

PARTICIPATORY STORYTELLING
(continued)

Caduto, Michael J., and Joseph Bruchac, *Keepers of the Animals: Native American Stories and Wildlife Activities for Children*, Fulcrum, 1991

—, *Keepers of the Earth: Native American Stories and Environmental Activities for Children*, Fulcrum, 1988

Erdoes, Richard, and Alfonso Ortiz, *American Indian Myths and Legends*, Pantheon, 1984

Feldmann, Susan, editor, *The Storytelling Stone*, Laurel, 1991

Hinchman, Hannah, *A Life in Hand: Creating the Illuminated Journal*, Gibbs Smith, 1991

Lingelbach, Jenepher, editor, *Hands-On Nature: Information and Activities for Exploring the Environment With Children*, Vermont Institute of Natural Science, 1986

Mayo, Gretchen, *Earthmaker's Tales: North American Indian Stories About Earth Happenings*, Walker, 1989

—, *Star Tales: North American Indian Stories About the Stars*, Walker, 1987

Milford, Susan, *The Kids' Nature Book*, Williamson, 1989

ENVIRONMENTAL RESOURCES*

*Compiled by Pamela Bomboy. From the *Yarnspinner*, May-June 1993. Reprinted by permission.

Aardema, Verna, *Why Mosquitoes Buzz in People's Ears*, Dial, 1975

Bauman, Richard, *Story, Performance, and Event: Contextual Studies of Oral Narrative*, Cambridge University Press, 1986

Belanus, Betty, *Folklore in the Classroom: Workbook*, Indiana Historical Bureau, 1985

Bushnaq, Inea, editor, *Arab Folktales*, Pantheon, 1986

Caduto, Michael J., and Joseph Bruchac, *Keepers of the Earth: Native American Stories and Environmental Activities for Children*, Fulcrum, 1988

Carpenter, Frances, *Tales of a Korean Grandmother*, Doubleday, 1947

—, *Tales of a Chinese Grandmother*, Doubleday, Doran, 1937

MULTI-CULTURAL STORYTELLING*

*Compiled by Joan Leotta. From the *Yarnspinner*, August 1991. Reprinted by permission.

Clarkson, Atelia, and Gilbert B. Cross, *World Folktales*, Scribner's, 1980

Grigsby, J. Eugene, *Art and Ethnics: Background for Teaching Youth in a Pluralistic Society*, W.C. Brown, 1977

Kendall, Frances E., *Diversity in the Classroom: A Multicultural Approach to the Education of Young Children*, Teachers College Press, 1983

McDowell, Marsha, editor, *Folk Arts in Education: A Resource Handbook*, Michigan State University Museum, 1987

Ramsey, Patricia, *Teaching and Learning in a Diverse World: Multicultural Education for Young Children*, Teachers College Press, 1987

Simonson, Rick, and Scott Walker, *The Graywolf Annual Five*, Graywolf, 1988

Walker, Barbara, *The Dancing Palm Tree and Other Nigerian Folk Tales*, Texas Tech University Press, 1990

BOOKS ABOUT PEACE*

For kids

Davar, Ashok, *The Wheel of King Asoka*, Follett, 1977. True story of an Indian ruler who abandoned war for peace. Pillars inscribed with his philosophy still stand throughout India.

Druon, Maurice, *Tistou of the Green Thumbs*, Scribner's, 1958. Plants grow wherever Tistou places his hands. He places them on his father's armaments factory.

Durrell, Ann, and Marilyn Sachs, editors, *The Big Book for Peace*, Dutton, 1990

Exley, Richard, and Helen Exley, *My World/Peace: Thoughts and Illustrations From the Children of All Nations*, Passport, 1986. Writings from children around the world

Langton, Jane, *The Fragile Flag*, Harper & Row, 1984. A children's crusade to stop missile-making

MacDonald, Margaret Read, "Grandfather Bear Is Hungry" from *Look Back and See: Lively Tales for Gentle Tellers*, H.W. Wilson, 1991. Chipmunk's sharing calms an irate bear.

Scholes, Katherine, *Peace Begins With You*, Sierra Club/Little, Brown, 1990. A gentle discussion of the choices that bring about peace, in picture-book format

Silverstein, Shel, "Hug o' War" from *Where the Sidewalk Ends*, Harper & Row, 1974. A fun poem to tell or act out

* Compiled by Margaret Read MacDonald. From *Peace Tales: World Folktales to Talk About*, copyright 1992 by Margaret Read MacDonald. Reprinted by permission of Linnet Books, North Haven, Connecticut.

For adults who work with kids

Carlsson-Paige, Nancy, and Diane E. Levin, *Helping Young Children Understand Peace, War, and the Nuclear Threat*, National Association for the Education of Young Children, 1985

Drew, Naomi, *Learning the Skills of Peacemaking: An Activity Guide for Elementary-Age Children on Communicating, Cooperating, Resolving Conflict*, Jalmar, 1987 (145 Hitching Post Dr., Bldg. 2, Rolling Hills Estates, Calif. 90274)

Floating Eagle Feather, editor, *And the Earth Lived Happily Ever After*, Wages of Peace, 1987

Law, Norma, "Children and War," position paper for the Association for Childhood Education International, February 1973. A survey of research on children's attitudes toward war. Send 35 cents to the Association for Childhood Education International, 3615 Wisconsin Ave. N.W., Washington, D.C. 20016.

The Story Bag Newsletter—a compendium of reviews, short essays, and interviews—is published by Harlynne Geisler, 5361 Javier St., San Diego, Calif. 92117.

Storytelling Magazine, the premier national storytelling periodical, is published six times a year by the National Storytelling Association (NSA, formerly NAPPS), P.O. Box 309, Jonesborough, Tenn. 37659, 800-525-4514. NSA also publishes a bimonthly newsletter, *Inside Story*. Membership in NSA covers subscriptions to both.

Storytelling World is published twice a year by Dr. Flora Joy, East Tennessee State University, P.O. Box 70647, Johnson City, Tenn. 37614-0617.

Stories for Grades Three and Up

By Janice Del Negro

If you're looking for strong storytelling material, here's a list of top-notch tales, prepared by Janice Del Negro, youth-services consultant for the State Library of North Carolina.

For nearly 100 years children's services librarians have practiced and nurtured the art of storytelling. In addition to entertaining listeners, sharing the oral tradition, and promoting cross-cultural understanding, library storytelling has a mission—to promote literacy by connecting children with books. The following annotated listing provides suggestions for telling to children grades three through six and higher. All the tales were found in the children's room of a local public library. Although some are more complex than others, all the narratives embody strong plots, characters, and emotions. Those texts with accompanying introductions, notes, bibliographies, and glossaries are so indicated.

- "The Dauntless Girl." Young Mary fears nothing—including ghosts. Sent to the graveyard by her employer on a wager, Mary wins his bet—and herself a new place with the wealthy (and haunted) squire. Source: *British Folk Tales* by Kevin Crossley-Holland, Orchard, 1987. Pronunciation guide, sources, notes. Grades four through six.

- "The Chinese Red Riding Hood" by Isabelle Chang. A Chinese variant of "Little Red Riding Hood," this tale is similar to Ed Young's Caldecott Medal–winner *Lon Po Po* (Philomel, 1989). Three sisters left on their own outwit a hungry wolf who is disguised as their grandmother. Source: *Womenfolk and Fairy Tales* by Rosemary Minard, Houghton Mifflin, 1975. Introduction. Grades three through five.

- "The Three Sillies." A squire sets out to find three fools sillier than his intended and her parents. Needless to say, he finds them before journeying far—a woman with a cow on her roof, a man trying to leap into his trousers, and villagers rescuing the moon from a pond. Source: *English Fairy Tales* by Flora Annie Steel, Macmillan, 1962. Grades three through six.

- "Why the Chameleon Shakes His Head." A pourquoi story from the Bemba tribe of Northern Rhodesia that explains the relationship between Imbwa the dog and the hunter, man—and the chameleon's shock upon discovering the truth of it. Source: *The King's Drum and Other African Stories* by Harold Courlander, Harcourt, Brace & World, 1962. Notes and sources. Grades three through six.

- "Fiddivaw." A Danish tale (similar to the Grimms' "The Golden Goose") about a lazy young man seeking a life of ease. Following the advice of an old wise woman, he finds both his fortune and his love. Source: *More Danish Tales* by Mary Hatch, Harcourt, Brace, 1949. Grades four through six.

- "Molly Whuppie" by Walter De La Mare. The courageous Molly Whuppie recovers the king's stolen treasures from a not-too-bright giant and wins husbands and good fortune for herself and her two sisters. Source: *The Magic Umbrella and Other Stories for Telling* by Eileen Colwell, David McKay, 1976. Notes. Grades three through six.

It can be difficult to find stories simple enough for preschoolers through second-graders to retell. Here's a short bibliography of good choices.

STORIES FOR YOUNG CHILDREN TO RETELL

Baylor, Byrd, "Do You Want to Turn Into a Rabbit?" from *And It Is Still That Way: Legends Told by Arizona Indian Children*, Scribner's, 1976

Botkin, Ben, and Carl Withers, "How the Rabbit Lost His Tail" from *The Illustrated Book of American Folklore*, Grosset & Dunlap, 1958

Chorao, Kay, "The Hare and the Turtle" and "The Princess and the Pea" from *The Baby's Story Book*, Dutton, 1985

Ginsburg, Mirra, "Two Stubborn Goats" from *Three Rolls and One Doughnut: Fables From Russia*, Dial, 1970

Hamilton, Martha, and Mitch Weiss, "The Boy Who Turned Himself Into a Peanut," "The Dog and His Shadow," "The Frog and the Ox," "How the Rabbit Lost Its Tail," "The Sun and the Wind," and "The Tailor" from *Children Tell Stories: A Teaching Guide*, Richard C. Owen, 1990

Krauss, Ruth, *The Carrot Seed*, Harper & Row, 1989

Lester, Julius, "Why Dogs Hate Cats" from *The Knee-High Man and Other Tales*, Dial, 1972

Lobel, Arnold, "Clouds," "The Journey," "The Old Mouse," and "Very Tall Mouse and Very Short Mouse" from *Mouse Tales*, Harper & Row, 1972

Melser, June, and Joy Cowley, *One Cold Wet Night*, Shortland, 1980

Rojankovsky, Feodor, illustrator, "The Goose That Laid the Golden Eggs" from *The Tall Book of Nursery Tales*, Harper & Row, 1944

Stevens, Bryna, "The Fox and the Crow," "The Great and Little Fishes," "The Milkmaid," and "The Stag and His Reflection" from *Borrowed Feathers and Other Fables*, Random House, 1977

—Martha Hamilton and Mitch Weiss

- "The Magic Fiddle." After helping three strangers on the road, young Jack is rewarded with a magic fiddle. All who hear Jack's fiddle must dance until the music stops. The author's notes base the story in a Norwegian pantomime. Source: *More Once-Upon-a-Time Stories* by Rose Dobbs, Random House, 1961. Introduction. Grades three through six.

- "The Flea" by Ruth Sawyer. The king says any man who guesses his riddle can marry his daughter, the Infanta. A young shepherd—aided by an ant, a beetle, and a mouse—wins the day and the reward of his choice. An adaptation of a Spanish folk tale. Source: *Fools and Funny Fellows*, selected by Phyllis R. Fenner, Knopf, 1947. Grades four through six.

- "Wait Till Martin Comes" and "Milk Bottles." Two short, easy-to-learn tales of the supernatural. In "Wait Till Martin Comes" a traveler takes shelter in a feline-haunted house; in "Milk Bottles" the ghost of a young mother comes back to save her child. Source: *The Thing at the Foot of the Bed* by Maria Leach, World, 1959. Notes and bibliography. Grades three through six.

- "Payment in Kind." A Japanese trickster tale featuring Ikkyu the Wise. In this story reminiscent of the tale about paying for the smell of baking bread with the sound of jingling coins, Ikkyu outwits a larcenous innkeeper. Source: *The Possible Impossibles of Ikkyu the Wise* by I. G. Edmonds, Macrae Smith, 1971. Introduction, notes, and glossary. Grades five through six.

- "The Lad Who Went to the North Wind." After the North Wind steals his mother's meal, a young boy sets out to regain the stolen goods. An adventure and journey tale wherein the boy grows both wiser and richer. Source: *East o' the Sun and West o' the Moon* by Peter Christian Asbjørnsen, Candlewick, 1992. Grades three through four.

- "How Tammas MacIvar MacMurdo MacLennan Met His Match." The local strongman (who is something of a braggart) meets his match in the ghosts of three Scottish kings and their six sons. Source: *Ghosts Go Haunting* by Sorche Nic Leodhas, Holt, Rinehart & Winston, 1965. Glossary. Grades four through six.

- "To Your Good Health." A Russian shepherd refuses the foolish command of a pompous tsar—and wins the hand of the tsar's daughter. Source: *Favorite Fairy Tales Told in Russia* by Virginia Haviland, Little, Brown, 1961. Grades three through six.

- "Stan Bolovan." To feed his hundred children, Stan Bolovan volunteers to stop a dragon from stealing a shepherd's flock—and winds up in the dragon's house, hoodwinking the dragon's mother. From Romania. Source: *A Book of Dragons* by Ruth Manning-Sanders, Dutton, 1964. Grades three through six.

- "The Fairies." Also known as "Toads and Diamonds," this is Charles Perrault's tale of two sisters, their manners, and the fates that befall them. Source: *Complete Fairy Tales* by Charles Perrault, Dodd, Mead, 1961. Preface. Grades five through six.

- "The Candle of Death." A hero tale of Fleet-Footed Regan, the youngest of Finn's Fianna, and his destruction of the Ogress Grana and the candle of death. Source: *Thirteen Monsters* by Dorothy Spicer, Coward-McCann, 1964. Grades four through six.

- "Belenay of the Lake." A romantic, sorrowful tale about a water spirit won to wife by an earthly man and how through his error she must return to her watery home. Source: *A Bag of Moonshine* by Alan Garner, Delacorte, 1986. Grades five through six.

- "The Rose of Midwinter." On the banks of the Arno River in the city of Florence, a young man named Francesco releases an earthbound ghost with an embroidered, perfumed rose. Source: *Elves and Ellefolk* by Natalia Belting, Holt, Rinehart & Winston, 1961. Bibliography. Grades five through six.

From the Yarnspinner, *March 1991. Reprinted by permission.*

All the storytellers and educators whose original essays appear in this volume have books, tapes, or services for sale. If you'd like to learn more, here's the information you'll need.

TELLERS' PRODUCTS AND SERVICES

Sheila Dailey

1326 E. Broadway, Mount Pleasant, Mich. 48858

Books: *Putting the World in a Nutshell: The Art of the Formula Tale*, H.W. Wilson, 1994 • *Storytelling: A Creative Teaching Strategy*, Storytime Productions, 1985 (available from the author)

Audiotapes: *Stories of the Long Christmas*, self-published ($9.95 plus $1.50 postage and handling) • *Land of the Sky Blue Waters*, self-published ($9.95 plus $1.50 postage and handling)

Workshop: Storytelling: Pathway to Literacy

Gail de Vos

9850 91st Ave., Edmonton, Alberta, Canada T6E 2T6

Book: *Storytelling for Young Adults: Techniques and Treasury*, Libraries Unlimited, 1991

Workshops: Storytelling for Young Adults; Storytelling and the Contemporary Legend

Karen Golden

Golden Button Productions, 6152 W. Olympic Blvd. #9, Los Angeles, Calif. 90048, 213-933-4614

Audiotape: *Tales and Scales: Stories of Jewish Wisdom*, Golden Button Productions ($10 plus $2 postage and handling)

Residencies and workshops: History Alive; Everyone Has a History to Tell, to Write, to Share • Performances: A Walk Around the World in Stories and Shoes; Stories of Jewish Wisdom; Breathing Biographies

Martha Hamilton and Mitch Weiss

Beauty and the Beast Storytellers, P.O. Box 6624, Ithaca, N.Y. 14851-6624, 607-277-0016

Books: *Children Tell Stories: A Teaching Guide*, Richard C. Owen, 1990 (P.O. Box 585, Katonah, N.Y. 10536, 800-336-5588; $19.95 plus $3 postage and handling) • *Spinning Tales, Weaving Hope: Stories of Peace, Justice, and the Environment*, edited by Ed Brody, Jay Goldspinner, Katie Green, Rona Leventhal, and John Porcino (includes a story by Beauty and the Beast Storytellers), New Society, 1992 (may be ordered from Hamilton and Weiss; $22.95)

Audiotape: *Tales of Wonder, Magic, Mystery, and Humor From Around the World*, self-published, 1985 • Videotape: *Tell Me a Story*, Barr Entertainment, 1986 (tapes may be ordered from Hamilton and Weiss)

Workshops: Teaching Children to Tell Stories; How to Choose, Learn, and Tell a Story; Tandem Storytelling: How to Tell With a Partner; Why Every Teacher Should Be a Storyteller; How to Tell to Preschoolers, Middle-Schoolers, etc. • Residencies for schools and other organizations • Performances for all ages

Gail Neary Herman

Rt. 2, Box 967, Swanton, Md. 21561

Audiotape: *Stories and Songs of Creative Creatures*, with music by Dhruva and Elaine J. Wine, self-published, 1989 ($9.95 plus $2 postage and handling)

Books: *Kinetic Kaleidoscope: Exploring Movement and Energy in Visual Arts* by Gail N. Herman and Pat Hollingsworth, Zephyr Press, 1992 (P.O. Box 66006, Tucson, Ariz. 85128; $20) • *Storytelling: A Triad in the Arts*, Creative Learning Press, 1986 (P.O. Box 320, Mansfield Center, Conn. 06250; $8.95)

Workshops: Nurturing Kindness, Confidence, and Creativity Through Storytelling; Story Theater; Collecting and Telling Family Stories • Performances: Organic Storytelling: Stories That Change and Grow With Each New Audience (K through 6); Stories for Global and Environmental Awareness (K through 8); Folk Tales Around the World; Stories From Mischievous Martha's Journal

Joan Leotta

9728 Stipp St., Burke, Va. 22015, 703-455-4711

Booklets: *Telling Your Child's Birth Story*, self-published workbook ($7.50, including postage and handling; Virginia residents, add 4 percent tax) • *Adapting Aesop*, self-published workbook for teachers, grades 4 through 8 ($7.50, including postage and handling; Virginia residents, add 4 percent tax)

Workshops for children: Creative Dramatics; Storytelling • Workshops for adults: Storytelling for Teachers; Storytelling in the Workplace; Business Writing; Storytelling in the Multicultural Arena and in the ESL Classroom • School residencies: three days to two weeks on storytelling or storytelling and writing; can include performances for the school and the public • Performances: Storytelling and

Science, custom-tailored to the topic • Historical characters: Molly the Indentured Servant; The Whaler's Wife

Syd Lieberman

2522 Ashland, Evanston, Ill. 60201, 708-328-6281

Book: *The Wise Shoemaker of Studena*, Jewish Publication Society, 1994 (may be ordered from the author; $15.95 plus $1.50 postage and handling)

Audiotapes: *Intrepid Birdmen: The Fighter Pilots of World War I*, self-published, 1993 • *The Tell-Tale Heart and Other Terrifying Tales*, self-published, 1991 • *The Johnstown Flood of 1889*, self-published, 1989 • *Joseph the Tailor and Other Jewish Stories*, self-published, 1988 • *A Winner and Other Stories*, self-published, 1986 • *The Old Man and Other Stories*, self-published, 1985 (all tapes may be ordered from the author; $10 plus $1.50 postage and handling each)

Sarah Malone

505-832-4111

Workshop: The Therapeutic Uses of Storytelling • Storytelling performances are also available.

Hughes Moir

2816 Ridge Rd., Nederland, Colo. 80466, 303-258-0414

Book: *Collected Perspectives: Choosing and Using Books for the Classroom*, second edition, Christopher-Gordon Publishers, 1993 (480 Washington, Norwood, Mass. 02062, 617-762-5577)

Workshops: Techniques and Resources for Novice Storytellers; Coaching Experienced Storytellers; Storytelling in the Teaching of Social Studies and History; Storytelling in the Teaching of Reading and Language Arts; Children as Storytellers; Readers' Theater for Whole-Language Teachers • Performances: Storytelling for schools (K through 12), for family programs, and for teacher and librarian conferences

Tim Myers

Book: *Let's Call Him Lauwiliwilihumuhu-munukunukunukunukuapua'aoioi!*, Bess Press, 1993; a picture book about Hawaiian fish (P.O. Box 22388, Honolulu, Hawaii 96822)

Peninnah Schram

525 W. End Ave. #8C, New York, N.Y. 10024-3207, 212-787-0626 or 914-962-9387

Books: *Elijah the Prophet Study Guide/Instant Lesson*, Torah Aura Productions, 1994 • *Tales of Elijah the Prophet*, Jason Aronson, 1991 • *Eight Tales for Eight Nights: Stories for Chanukah* by Peninnah Schram and Steven M. Rosman, Jason Aronson, 1990 • *Jewish Stories One Generation Tells Another*, Jason Aronson, 1987 • *The Big Sukkah*, Kar-Ben Copies Inc., 1986

Performances and workshops are also available.

Jay Stailey

723 E. Shore Dr., Clear Lake Shores, Texas 77565, 713-334-1430

Book: *Spinning Stories: An Introduction to Storytelling Skills* by Jay Stailey and Vicky Crosson, Texas State Library, 1988 (P.O. Box 12927, Austin, Texas 78711, 512-463-5448)

Audiotapes: *Full Circle: Seasoned Stories*, self-published live recording, 1994 • *Sampler 1992* including Jay Stailey, Houston Storytellers Guild, 1992 • *Sampler of Tales* including Jay Stailey, Houston Storytellers Guild, 1989 • *Sittin' Together, Talking to Each Other . . . Sometimes Singin': Stories and Songs for Children*, self-published, 1991 • *Short Tales, Tall Tales, and Tales of Medium Stature*, self-published, 1989

Performances and workshops are also available.

Mark Wagler

602 Wingra St., Madison, Wis. 53715, 608-258-8833

Keynote speaker for educational conferences and districtwide inservices (teaching stories and narrative theory focused on specific curriculum components) • Instructor for university summer courses (storytelling for teachers, theory of narrative teaching, collecting and studying folk narratives, inquiry teaching, learning networks)

Videos: *Kid-to-Kid* (documentary video of Randall School community, with sections on history, kids' culture, and nature, plus excerpt on making the video; studio edits) and *Classroom Stories 94* (kids tell stories about what they learned this year; on-camera edits). Videos are about one-hour long; both were planned, taped, and edited by fourth- and fifth-grade kids with grownup help and are intended for global video exchange (both videos on one tape, $15)

Publications: *I Wonder: The Journal for Elementary School Scientists* and *It Figures! The Journal for Elementary School Mathematicians*: students write stories of their extended, original student inquiry (sample copy of each—'93 or '94 issues as available—$5)

Booklet: *Coaching Storytelling and Listening Performances: A Chapbook for Teachers* (working title), self-published essay, available January 1995 ($10)

Elaine Wynne, M.A., L.P.

Box 27314, Minneapolis, Minn. 55427-0314, 612-546-1662

Book: *Two Voices at Once*, an eclectic look at story-telling in psychotherapy

Audiotapes: *Running Scared and Flying High*, self-published, 1986 • *In the Beginning: Birth and Creation Stories* (forthcoming)

Video: Video letter exchange, Longfellow Elementary School (St. Paul, Minnesota) and Furzedown Primary School (London, England), co-produced with Larry Johnson, 1986; won grand prize, Tokyo Video Festival